Becoming an Academic:
International Perspectives

Universities into the 21st Century

Series Editors: Noel Entwistle and Roger King

Further titles are in preparation

Becoming an Academic: International Perspectives

Lynn McAlpine and Gerlese S. Åkerlind

palgrave
macmillan

First published 2010 by
PALGRAVE MACMILLAN

Palgrave Macmillan in the UK is an imprint of Macmillan Publishers Limited,
registered in England, company number 785998, of Houndmills, Basingstoke,
Hampshire RG21 6XS.

Palgrave Macmillan in the US is a division of St Martin's Press LLC,
175 Fifth Avenue, New York, NY 10010.

Palgrave Macmillan is the global academic imprint of the above companies
and has companies and representatives throughout the world.

Palgrave® and Macmillan® are registered trademarks in the United States,
the United Kingdom, Europe and other countries.

ISBN: 978-0-230-22791-0

This book is printed on paper suitable for recycling and made from fully
managed and sustained forest sources. Logging, pulping and manufacturing
processes are expected to conform to the environmental regulations of the
country of origin.

A catalogue record for this book is available from the British Library.

A catalog record for this book is available from the Library of Congress.

10 9 8 7 6 5 4 3 2 1
19 18 17 16 15 14 13 12 11 10

Printed and bound in Great Britain by
CPI Antony Rowe, Chippenham and Eastbourne

Contents

Preface

The origins of this book lie in the serendipity of the two co-editors having overlapping secondments to the Oxford Learning Institute in 2006/7, arriving in the UK context from two different continents – North America and Australia. Within the Institute, we were filling complementary roles – Lynn was focused on the developmental needs of doctoral students and postdoctoral researchers envisioning academic careers, and Gerlese was focused on the developmental needs of doctoral supervisors, including their ability to better support the personal and professional development of their students.

During this time, we had lively conversations about the nature of academic practice and preparation for academia, particularly in relation to early career academics and different national contexts. One area on which we strongly agreed was that academic practice was far more complex than teaching, research and service. This complexity meant that preparation for academic practice should involve much more than simply providing teaching experience and training to early career academics to complement the research training provided in their doctoral and postdoctoral experience. Another area that incited a mutual passion was our agreement on the key, but neglected, significance of individual purposes, meaning-making and identity in academic work, and the role such purposes can play in creating a sense of personal reward and integration of our work as academics – particularly needed in these times of challenge and fragmentation in academic work.

At about the same time, we received an invitation from Noel Entwistle to consider developing a book proposal for the Palgrave-Macmillan series on Universities into the 21st Century. Given our ongoing conversations about academic practice, preparing a book that addressed the complexity of that practice, and the key role played by academic identity and purpose, was an obvious response. The more we explored the idea, the more we saw that there was nothing already available that did what we hoped to do – provide a research-informed framework with heuristic value for considering preparation for academic careers.

With this idea in mind, we approached potential chapter authors, taking a collaborative approach to developing the final book proposal, so that the present book emerges very much from the ideas of all first authors of chapters: Ann Austin, David Mills and Sandra Acker as well as us. All authors committed to reading each of the chapters to exchange feedback and ensure integration across the book. Given the geographically dispersed locations of chapter authors, we took the opportunity of conferences to arrange face-to-face meetings. In April 2008, four of the authors met in Oxford after the CETL conference on academic practice. In December 2008, we met again at the UK Society in Higher Education Research conference in Liverpool to present a joint symposium around our preliminary chapters. We stayed on to collectively critique the draft chapters (with Sandra Acker joining us via Skype). These fruitful meetings (plus countless email exchanges) have resulted in what we believe to be a book which retains the particular voices and national contexts of the authors of each chapter while still intentionally linking across the chapters. We wholeheartedly thank Ann, David and Sandra who invested so much in creating the book you have before you.

We hope you find the book thought provoking, ideally insightful, but at the least, interesting.

Lynn McAlpine and Gerlese S. Åkerlind

Acknowledgements

We would like to thank the following individuals for the role they played in the development of the book. As mentioned in the Preface, the book would not have been written without the initial invitation from Noel Entwistle. We also appreciated his feedback on our proposal as it developed. The collaborative role played by each of the chapter authors was also vital to the book's development, as detailed in the Preface.

In addition, we are grateful to the early career academics, academic developers and administrators (named in the Commentaries section) who provided thoughtful responses to the ideas presented in Chapters 2 through 6. We also benefited from helpful feedback on Chapter 1 from Stephen Goss, Rod Pitcher and Beth Beckmann and on Chapter 7 from Anna Wilson, Maurice Nevile and Stephen Darwin.

Critical of course to the book as a whole was the willing participation of all the research participants whose experiences and perceptions provided the empirical basis for the interpretations and conclusions that form the essential messages of this book.

Last, we also thank Rocio Garavito and Francesca Salvi for their dedicated and careful editing and formatting of the text.

Notes on Contributors

Sandra Acker is Professor in the Department of Sociology and Equity Studies in Education, University of Toronto, in Canada. She has worked in the United States, Britain, and Canada as a sociologist of education, with interests in gender and education, teachers' work, and higher education. Her current research is focused on university tenure practices, women academics in leadership positions, and doctoral student experiences. She is the author of *Gendered Education* (1994) and *The Realities of Teachers' Work: Never a Dull Moment* (1999) and co-editor of *Whose University Is It, Anyway? Power and Privilege on Gendered Terrain* (2008).

Gerlese S. Åkerlind is Associate Professor and Director of the Centre for Educational Development and Academic Methods (CEDAM) at The Australian National University (ANU) in Australia. The Centre provides academic development support for academic staff at the ANU, and Gerlese convenes their Masters of Higher Education for academic staff. Her research and scholarship have primarily focused on the nature, and changing nature, of higher education and academic work. This includes investigations of the academic experience of teaching, research, academic freedom, academic development and career development for early-career academics. She is an honorary Research Associate of the Oxford Learning Institute, Oxford University, and a member of the Editorial Boards for the journals, *Educational Research Review, Learning and Teaching in Higher Education*, and *International Journal of Researcher Development*.

Cheryl Amundsen is Associate Professor in the Faculty of Education of Simon Fraser University in British Columbia, Canada. She is currently the Director of the Institute for the Study of Teaching and Learning in the Disciplines, and Coordinator of Graduate Programs in Educational Technology and Learning Design. She spent 10 years as a faculty member at McGill University where she was cross-appointed to the Centre for University Teaching and Learning and the Department of Educational Counselling and Psychology. Her career to date can be characterized by her continuing activity as a scholar and developer in higher education teaching and learning. Mostly recently this has been realized in research that investigates graduate supervision as an instance of teaching and learning. She would say she has completely embraced the notion of academic development (rather than development of teaching or other academic roles) as it suggests both the complexity of academic work and the integration of academic roles.

Ann E. Austin is Professor at Michigan State University in the US, where she has held the Mildred B. Erickson Chair in Higher, Adult, and Lifelong Education for the past three years. The students with whom she works are all at the doctoral and master's levels, each focusing on careers in higher education teaching or administration. Her research has focused for many years on faculty careers, roles, and professional development; the improvement of teaching and learning in higher education; reform in graduate education; and organizational change and transformation in higher education. She is also now directing a new university-wide Institute on Higher Education in the Global Context, and is also currently Co-Principal Investigator of the Center for the Integration of Research, Teaching, and Learning (CIRTL), a National Science Foundation-funded Center focused on improving doctoral education in science, technology, engineering, and mathematics to ensure greater attention to teaching development.

Eve Haque is Assistant Professor in the Department of Languages, Literatures and Linguistics at York University, Canada. Her areas of specialization include issues of language and critical race studies. In particular, she is interested in how issues of difference are organized and regulated through policies, laws and their implementation. Throughout her academic career, including her graduate student years, she has been interested in understanding how the conditions of knowledge production within the university serve to influence the process of graduate student training and graduate student experience overall. This interest finds its expression not only in research on issues of higher education but also in continued involvement in advocacy for improvements in graduate education.

Marian Jazvac-Martek is Postdoctoral Fellow at McGill University Canada who in her PhD dissertation examined the emerging academic identities of a group of Education doctoral students intensely over a two-year period. Currently, she is continuing to extend this work in collaboration with others on the research team, and relishes invitations to apply the findings in consultations on various interventions aimed at improving graduate education within her institution. While she seeks new ways to position herself as a becoming academic, she also enacts an academic teaching role as a faculty lecturer in the Department of Educational and Counselling Psychology in the Faculty of Education.

Lynn McAlpine is Professor of Higher Education Development at the University of Oxford in the UK where she is presently Director of the Centre for Excellence in Preparing for Academic Practice. Before that she was a Professor at McGill University in Canada where she was also Director of the Centre for University Teaching and Learning, and before that Director of the Office of First Nations and Inuit Education. While originally focusing on teaching in both her research and development work, in the past five years her interests have broadened to include all aspects of academic practice. She has received distinguished research awards from both the American Educational Research Association and the Canadian Society for Studies in Higher Education.

David Mills is a University lecturer in the Department of Education at Oxford University in the UK. After reading for a doctorate in Anthropology at the School of Oriental and African Studies, he held lectureships at Oxford (in Development Studies), Manchester (in Anthropology) and Birmingham (in Cultural Studies). Between 2000 and 2006 he also worked for C-SAP, the Centre for Sociology, Anthropology and Politics, part of the Higher Education Academy. He is the author of *Difficult Folk: A Political History of Social Anthropology* (Berghahn, 2008).

1 Academic Practice in a Changing International Landscape

Lynn McAlpine and Gerlese S. Åkerlind

▶ Why this book...and why now?

The international higher education landscape has been changing, and these changes are impacting on the perceived purposes of universities and academia, the work that academics do, the types of academic appointments available, and the support available for intending academics. In this context, it is timely to reconsider the nature of academic careers, and how developing academics prepare for their careers. In this book we ask: What does a career in academia mean nowadays? For instance,

- What do PhDs, post-docs and new academics think it means to have a 'career' in academia? Is 'career' a meaningful term?
- What are their perceptions of academic practice, and how do these perceptions relate to their intentions and hopes?
- What are the challenges they face in preparing for, participating in and influencing academic work?
- How do their perceptions relate to their sense of academic purpose and identity...their engagement in and contribution to an academic community?

Our aim in addressing these questions is to provide a research-informed perspective from which to develop personal, pedagogical and policy implications to better address the ways in which those who wish to pursue academic careers[1] develop and are supported in that development.

In considering early career development, we thought it important to start earlier than the first academic appointment. Therefore, this book explores the experiences of three early career roles: doctoral students;

postdoctoral researchers; and newly hired academics. A unique aspect of this book is the bringing together of these three roles as a progression supporting an academic career, thus positioning the development and preparation of doctoral students, postdoctoral researchers and newly hired academics as a combination of *cumulative formative experiences* – while acknowledging the individual and immensely varied nature of these experiences. We argue against treating these roles and experiences as discrete, disconnected periods. This stance is in contrast to much previous research, and many policies and practices that clearly differentiate these roles, often focusing on one in isolation from the others. Yet, experience of all three roles – and expectations of participating in them as part of a career trajectory – is increasingly common, not just in the sciences but also in the social sciences. We contend that more effective policies and practices for the development of future academics will emerge if we approach support for all three roles as a continuum.

Thus, this book is aimed at those interested in all three early stages of an academic career, both developing academics themselves wishing to take an active role in their own career development, and those who support them in their development. The latter include university administrators creating and implementing policies for doctoral students, postdoctoral researchers and new academics; supervisors and managers of early career academics; academic developers providing training and development for early career academics; academic mentors, heads of departments and supervisors supporting the development of research students and junior colleagues; and educational researchers investigating the nature of academic practice.

Academic practice in a shifting and complex landscape

The shifting higher education landscape affords challenges, as well as opportunities, to new (and more established) academics in developing their academic practices. Situating early career academics within the complexity of today's higher education practices and policies lays the groundwork for our examination in this book of how they experience, take up and sometimes question the challenges they are facing. Awareness of the potential as well as challenges of academic practice today is necessary in understanding how early career academics can best prepare for their careers, and more senior academics, policymakers and academic developers best support them.

Overall, we argue that acquiring knowledge about academic practice places early career academics in a better position to be able to respond to any unexpected opportunities and challenges that arise in their own experiences, and thus better able to manage their career development. We view developing academics as their own agents of learning and change. Individually and collectively, they have an important role to play in informing themselves and supporting each other in understanding how changes in higher education may influence their preparation needs and future career paths.

In the remainder of this chapter, we review some of the literature on the changing nature of academic work, and how these changes are being experienced by academics at all stages of their careers. In particular, we highlight the role played by:

- academics' own personal interpretations, meaning-making and experiences;
- the multiple contexts in which academics are operating; and
- the ways in which academic work has been changing over time.

We explore each of these points in more detail below (under slightly different headings). We end the chapter with a description of the rationale underlying the structure of the book, so that readers have a sense of the different ways in which they might use it.

▶ The importance of personal experience and individual interpretations of academic practice

What do we mean by 'academic practice', and how is it different from an academic career or academic work, for instance? The term 'practice' represents more than a job, appointment or title that academics hold; it is also more than the tasks, duties and responsibilities that academics engage in; and more than the skills or knowledge academics develop. 'Practice' incorporates the totality of individual (and collective) experiences – the ways in which we think, interact, enact and engage as academics in the work we do. The term 'practice' brings into play the underlying, sometimes implicit, purpose(s) that motivate us to be academics and through which it is possible to integrate an array of multifaceted duties, responsibilities, skills and knowledge into a coherent sense of academic identity. At the same time, individual purposes, identities and experience are positioned within a collective perspective, i.e. what is similar and different about varying academic practices. This perspective positions the notion of practice as simultaneously about the individual *and* the group. In other words, our academic practices are created socially, strongly influenced by the communities with which we identify and to which we feel a sense of belonging.

Of course, the notion of practice is not ours alone. There is a growing literature on the notion of social practices in professional settings (Schatzki *et al.*, 2001). Plus, the concept of 'professional practice', originally coined by Schön in 1983, is increasingly being used to highlight a view of professional expertise as reflective, integrative, experience-based and skilful, developing and changing over time. That is also our view of academic practice, and we would highlight the following four aspects of academics' experience of their practice.

Distinct individual histories, dispositions, and values

Our practice is not just what we do, but also who we are as individuals, what we think and what we value. In other words, an individual's day-to-day actions and related decision-making draw on distinct personal histories (based on gender, class, previous work experiences), professional characteristics and ethical frameworks. Further, these personal experiences and values are influenced by diverse disciplinary and institutional surroundings, but not in a uniform way; contextual influences are experienced differently depending on past and present histories. Thus, there is vast variation in how academic practice is perceived and conceived at an individual level.

Varied roles, motivations and intentions

Despite the traditional view that academic practice encompasses the three aspects of research, teaching and service (at least in North America and Australia; service is not as strongly emphasized in the UK), the reality is that many academics will hold different positions in their careers over time that may privilege one of these aspects over others. Further, different academics value these different aspects of what they do to different degrees. Some academics may choose to have principally administrative positions, others research, and others teaching. Such choices are partly driven by the labour market, by institutional decisions regarding staffing, and by personal choice – what one hopes to do, be, and contribute as an academic.

Tensions and allegiances in negotiating one's academic practice

In addition to the shifting expectations society has of academics, there are competing demands and different kinds of allegiances that one experiences in working with colleagues in departments, programmes, institutions and disciplinary organizations. For instance, there may be methodological disputes within a discipline so that individuals feel 'forced' to 'take sides'; there could be disagreements among colleagues as to how, or even whether, to respond to institutional policies; or there might be competing views within a programme as to how to prepare future academics. Thus, a critical element of developing academic practice lies in how an individual learns to navigate these tensions and competing pressures.

Cumulative development towards an academic career

Lastly, the daily experiences of academic practice can be situated in a long-term developmental view of an academic career, encompassing doctoral studies, postdoctoral work, being a newly appointed academic and a senior academic – with different development issues experienced throughout the journey. Development does not stop at one's first academic appointment or when one achieves tenure or permanency. So, regardless of an individual's present status, each is engaged in developing practice as an academic, in which the activities engaged in today influence the ongoing development of academic identity as well as present and future careers. Further, while some aspects of a career may be intentionally planned, others often emerge unexpectedly. For instance, the desire for an academic position immediately post-PhD may not be achievable, or there may be options that include moving in and out of academia. In other words, an academic career is not predictable. Yet, a sense of continuity which may not be apparent at the time can come later, through reflecting on and integrating different roles and positions in relation to personal goals, interests and values.

▶ Contexts that impact upon academic practice: tensions within disciplinary, institutional, national and international structures

While individuals create their own personal meaning and identity around academic practice, this practice is also situated within particular socio-geographical-historical contexts, that is, individual experience of academic work is situated within a series of nested contexts (McAlpine and Norton, 2006). Individuals are physically, socially and historically located in particular departmental and programme structures. These structures in turn are situated within disciplinary, institutional, national, and international contexts. In other words, both new and established academics are located within a departmental programme context with particular histories, expectations and practices. These disciplinary 'outposts' are themselves nested within an institutional context (e.g., faculties, a university), which are in turn nested within a societal and international context. Yet, boundaries between these contexts are permeable, with more immediate influence between close contexts and less immediate between contexts further apart.

Since the different contexts have different drivers and constraints, intersections between them may create tensions as well as support allegiances. For example, international and national priorities, such as competitiveness and accountability, lead to national policies (e.g., Funding Council reduction of the duration of doctoral fellowships/scholarships). These in turn influence institutional policies (e.g., an expectation that doctoral students, regardless of discipline, meet these time limits). These public drivers of the work environment can be experienced as a personal constraint among academics who feel, for instance, that consistent times to completion are inappropriate. Despite potential resistance, these more public policies perforce change the personal experience of the nature of inquiry and other research-related activities (Enders, 2007).

Or, given that academics are paid by institutions and thus bear some responsibility towards them, the university and the department may expect, even demand, that academics be available to teach a range of courses outside their area of expertise; or, that they comply with external expectations of teaching responsibility and accept that educational decisions are often made on an economic rather than a pedagogical basis. Such expectations can be perceived as an unwelcome constraint by some academics to their personal vocation, since their investment in research and research collaborations needs to be organized around institutional teaching demands (Schrodt et al., 2003). Further, they may feel more personal allegiance to their research community and an international network of colleagues than to the institution that provides their salary. Such tensions, which add to the complexity and variability of the experience of academic practice, are highlighted throughout the book to ensure that the reality of the academic workplace is evident.

▶ Changes over time in academic practices: impacts on early career academics

Also central to our view of academic practice is recognizing the shifting nature of academic work, acknowledging that academia is a variable and socially embedded concept. Notions of academic practice go back to universities' origins as teaching institutions in medieval Europe, and the introduction of the research university in Germany in the early 1800s – picked up quickly by the USA, but more slowly in other areas of the world (research PhDs were not introduced into the UK until 1917, for instance). However, changes to academia have increased apace over the last 50 years, with transformations in funding directives, doctoral and post-doctoral training reforms, and institutional competition for research resources. Such changes which we detail below highlight that the traditional expectation that those in the process of becoming academics can learn all they need from their supervisors/managers is no longer valid. Indeed, given the shifting environment, senior academics' past experiences may even be misleading in providing guidance on career development for early career academics.

The high emphasis placed on research productivity, and the substantial growth in student numbers and institutions of higher education experienced over the past 50 years were initially a product of the research focus inspired by the Second World War and a concern with equity and the social benefits of education. However, this expansion was followed by a widespread economic downturn in the 1970s and an associated increasing concern with the economic and vocational benefits of education – increasingly an issue today. Systems of higher education came under increasing economic pressures and constraints that continue today, and, in fact, have been exacerbated by the recent global economic crisis. Student participation has continued to rise, not just at undergraduate but also at postgraduate levels (especially since the 1990s); there has been a fall in staff to student ratios, a rise in the number of contract and casual staff employed as academics, increasingly uncertain employment prospects for postgraduate students and postdoctoral researchers, and pressures on university resources and research funding.

These changes have occurred within a context of ongoing exponential knowledge growth and technological advancements, facilitating the globalization of higher education, with international collaboration and competition increasing (Gingras, 2002; Marginson, 2000). And, these changes have been accompanied not just by the diversification of students but also of staff, and an increasing culture of accountability and audit of academic performance.

Not surprisingly, these changes have resulted in a shift in the sorts of activities considered appropriate for academics to do and for universities to fund and support. Universities are under increasing pressure to follow the agendas of various stakeholder groups, other than the traditional disciplinary and collegial stakeholders, including government, employers, professional bodies and student-clients (Marginson, 2007). Thus, changing public expectations of universities call academics to engage with and contribute different kinds of knowledge to society (Gibbons, 1999). And, universities and academics are expected to show increasing entrepreneurism in generating and attracting funding (Baruch and Hall, 2004). Overall, higher education is more frequently being referred to as an industry in a competitive market place. Such publicly-driven changes are broadly changing personal work practices and identities (e.g., Barnett, 2000; Kayrooz et al., 2007; Tight, 2000). In other words, wherever one looks in today's higher education world, global competitiveness and public expectations are fundamentally altering the personal contexts and practices of academic work.

How have these changes been experienced by academics?
Academics report that university governance is experienced as increasingly hierarchical and managerial; such governance conflicts with the desire of many for a more collegiate environment. At the same time, academics are commonly experiencing increasing work pressure and a sense of reduced control over their work; seemingly due to the expectation to maintain 'core' academic activities while also completing more and more 'non-core' activities that add to academic work. These additional pressures are seen as generated primarily by increasing demands for accountability and quality assurance, administration, searching for external funding, and marketing of teaching courses. Working conditions are frequently perceived as deteriorating, and many academics are experiencing increasing fragmentation of work time and energy due to the perceived intrusion of these 'non-core' activities into academic work (Kayrooz et al., 2007; Menzies and Newsome, 2007).

There is also widespread dissatisfaction among academics, with a perceived lack of institutional resources to support research and teaching. Financial support for research, in particular, is perceived as falling, and what is available, harder to obtain. There is a sense that salaries have not kept up with inflation, and there tends to be pessimism about future promotion and employment prospects. Associated with these changes has been a concomitant decline in the social status of universities, academics and university degrees. This change has meant that at the same time as the social value placed on universities and academics has declined the pressures and expectations placed on them have generally increased (Enders, 2007).

However, this somewhat gloomy picture is not a uniform experience. Some academics are thriving under the changing conditions, which present them with new opportunities for the development of their discipline, research, teaching and/or a valued exercise of a new range of skills (Baruch and Hall, 2004; Trowler, 1998). Furthermore, academics are still primarily motivated by the traditional values of intellectual scholarship and exploration of ideas, both for their own sake and for societal advancement. Although many are concerned by what may be perceived as relatively low salaries and job security, most are more strongly motivated by intrinsic interest in their work than by material rewards. The opportunity to pursue their own academic interests is typically still the most important factor in their reported level of job satisfaction.

What about developing academics? How are those early in their careers responding to the changing environment?

Austin (2002), in synthesizing several US studies, reports that new academics want to do good work, but are worried that expectations of them are not stated openly or explicitly. Further, they receive mixed messages – what they are told may not be what they see being modelled. In addition, many feel isolated – in contrast with the sense of community they had expected to find. As well, they are worried about the workload pressures and what that means in terms of quality of life – is it possible to give appropriate attention to both professional and personal responsibilities?

Becher and Trowler (2001), in their study of disciplinary cultures, note that academic careers are simultaneously influenced by personal preference, disciplinary difference and institutional imperatives, with contexts being powerful drivers as identity develops. For instance, acquiring a doctorate (contextual imperative) reduces the possible foci of research interest and, as a new academic there is the further necessity to decide on a research direction that can have results relatively quickly (as well as to teach). In addition, the mounting emphasis on publishing (as distinct from research), even pre-graduation, is a clear generational shift (Raddon, 2006).

Both doctoral students (Golde and Dore, 2001) and post-docs (Campbell et al., 2003) report that they do not feel well prepared for an academic career. In the USA, a report on a national survey of social science PhD graduates demonstrated the need for better career preparation and support for learning to manage careers (Nerad *et al.*, 2006). In Canada, a national study of postdoctoral fellows showed that 70 per cent of respondents felt that they had not received sufficient counselling for career planning (Helbing *et al.*, 1998). In Australia, a national survey of postdoctoral researchers showed widespread concern about long-term career prospects (Thompson *et al.*, 2001). Nevertheless, it appears that over a third of doctoral graduates are planning on taking up postdoctoral positions (Gluszynski and Peters, 2005). Even in the social sciences, where doctoral students have not traditionally engaged in postdoctoral work prior to academic appointment, there has been a 5 per cent growth in such staff in the UK over a five-year period (Mills *et al.*, 2006). In Australia, studies of postdoctoral staff report many negative effects related to their employment status, including job insecurity, and lack of career development and job opportunities (Åkerlind, 2005). In the UK, individuals in research posts report uncertain career prospects and a lack of clear career structures (e.g., Council for Science and Technology, 2007). Particularly striking are annual turnover rates among postdoctoral researchers, for instance, 35–50 per cent in the UK (Allen Collinson, 2004). And, even if individuals do find academic posts, those newly appointed often report frustration, high stress and isolation (Reybold, 2005; Schrodt *et al.*, 2003). Studies such as these suggest the need to better understand the experiences and related challenges for doctoral students, postdoctoral researchers and new academics of establishing themselves in the present environment.

Funding cuts and other changes have led to a tighter labour market and a growth in fixed-term and casual positions rather than permanent, tenured ones. Thus, the traditional expectation, at least in the humanities and social sciences, of finding a desired position almost immediately after PhD graduation is no longer valid. For instance, in the UK, a survey of PhD graduates' first employment destinations (UK Vitae, 2009) shows that newly graduated PhDs cannot expect to get academic positions right away. Only 23 per cent worked as research staff and 14 per cent as lecturers (called faculty in North America) in higher education institutions, though there was considerable disciplinary variation. (The remaining individuals could be found in teaching or research in other sectors, finance, business and IT, and public administration.). Nevertheless, over time, individuals who want academic posts may be successful. Thus, five years post-PhD in the US (Nerad *et al.*, 2006), about two-thirds of social science graduates report being in permanent academic positions, one-fifth in non-academic positions, and the remainder in academic-related positions. Overall, getting an academic position is not straightforward, may be preceded by several years of short-term work, and involve changes in one's institution and country. On the other hand, not all individuals doing doctorates continue to desire academic careers when they see close at hand the actual work expectations. Despite many academics enjoying academic work as a whole, there are aspects of an academic career that are not so attractive. Documented disincentives for both lecturer/faculty and postdoctoral research positions include: uncertainty and insecurity due to lack of clear career pathways; low salaries in comparison with other sectors; and competitive, pressured environments that impact quality of life. The disincentives associated with academic positions contrast with positive reports of non-academic professional positions, which are described as fulfilling and interesting. For instance, a study in the UK of first destination post-PhD positions (UK Grad, 2007) found that over 80 per cent of social science PhD graduates in non-academic positions reported they (a) had exactly the type of job they wanted; (b) perceived positive features, such as attractive salary level and other employment conditions; and (c) reported satisfaction ratings for promotion and job security very much higher than for those in academic positions.

In the USA, another study (Mason *et al.*, 2009) reported that from beginning to end of degree, more than 10 per cent of PhDs in research-intensive universities changed their desired career from posts in such universities to teaching-intensive universities, business and government because research-intensive universities were not seen as family friendly – students did not want the lifestyle of their supervisors. Additionally, after five years, those in academic posts reported being less satisfied than those in non-academic posts re work/life balance and work/family balance (Nerad *et al.*, 2006). It is clearly important to seek an academic career with one's eyes wide open!

▶ Rationale and structure of the book

Rationale: In this book we lay out the scope and complexity of academic practice today, attending particularly to national variation in higher education (while not overlooking institutional and disciplinary variation). While the chapter authors draw on studies of early career academics, they do not focus on the studies themselves, but rather the meanings and interpretations that the authors draw from them, and the implications of these for policy and practice.

Further, the chapters represent a range of countries – the UK, the USA, Canada and Australia – helpful in an increasingly international-ized workplace in which many academics will often experience work in countries other than the ones where they trained. Thus, the national contexts represented in each chapter are described within that chap-ter, so that this variation becomes visible, enabling a reader to read a single chapter as a stand-alone text. Further, each chapter is written in the local 'higher education discourse', to familiarize the reader with the ways in which what may appear similar across national systems is actually different, and what may appear different is similar. (Notes and other means, such as the glossary at the end of the book, are also used to clarify these differences.)

While we focus on English-speaking countries, the implications are relevant to other countries. For instance, there are changes in contin-ental Europe as a result of the Bologna Declaration that are aligning doctoral education with that of English-speaking countries; addition-ally, there are the same concerns regarding a lack of academic pos-itions post-PhD (Huisman *et al.*, 2002).

In this chapter and in most other chapters, there is reference to stud-ies that include all disciplines, as well as to inter-disciplinarity and the humanities and sciences disciplines. However, the bulk of the studies we focus on represent one broad cluster of disciplines: the social sci-ences. In this book we are already addressing variation in national contexts and academic roles; consequently, we felt that adding too much disciplinary variation to the mix would reduce the power and the usefulness of the analyses. Further, many of the concerns of early career academics are shared across disciplines, even though situated in different cultural practices. Indeed, many studies of early career academics do not distinguish along disciplinary lines.

Finally, each chapter addresses the implications of the studies for mentors of early career academics, supervisors/advisors of research students and post-docs, academic developers, policy-makers, as well as early career academics themselves. Rarely are such implications discipline-specific, and we believe that readers in the humanities and sciences will be able to draw on their own knowledge to modify the implications for disciplinary contexts other than the social sci-ences. Further, to ensure that the chapters represent early career academic experiences as well as generate useful implications, we have included in a separate section commentaries on each of the main chapters from early career academics, academic developers and senior administrators.

Structure: Following this chapter, there are five independently authored chapters addressing different national contexts, and different types of early career social science academics – PhD students, post-doctoral researchers and newly appointed academics. These chapters are followed by a concluding chapter and the Commentaries and Glossary of terms.

Chapter 2 by Ann Austin starts with the premise that the preparation of future academics is one of the major responsibilities for doctoral education. She presents findings from research conducted over the past fifteen years in the United States in a range of disciplines concerning the experiences of early career academics and doctoral students (referred to as aspiring 'faculty members' in line with North American terminology), and the implications of these experiences for career preparation for the 'professoriate' and support for early career 'faculty'.

Chapter 3 by Gerlese Åkerlind moves us to Australia and addresses a category of early career academics, postdoctoral researchers, that has been much overlooked in terms of both research and structured professional development opportunities – perhaps due to these potential academics being difficult to identify and track. This chapter is in two parts. The first highlights the substantial variation that exists in postdoctoral research positions and responsibilities, as well as the difficulties experienced in this not-quite-academic position. The second examines what post-docs can hope to gain from their experience in terms of their own growth and development as academic researchers.

The focus on the period post-PhD continues in Chapter 4. David Mills uses one discipline – social anthropology – to illustrate the changing shape of the social sciences in the UK, and the academic employment possibilities, pressures and dilemmas that result. Universities have long shaped, and been shaped by, the national and transnational economies in which they are located, and such shaping is even truer today. His analysis highlights how the 'big picture' trends point to the restructuring of the social sciences through its increasing involvement in the broader economy. He draws on interviews with early career academics to demonstrate how these pressures shape individual experiences of the academic workplace and the scholarly vocation, including difficulties finding the posts originally imagined, and decisions by some not to stay in academe.

In Chapter 5, we move to Canada. Sandra Acker and Eve Haque consider the question of whether continuity or disjuncture is to be expected between doctoral studies and new faculty work. After discussing relevant aspects of the Canadian post-secondary context, they reprise the concerns of early-career academics, gleaned from their own previous research and the literature. This context forms a prelude to the primary focus of this chapter, an analysis of academic career expectations based on interviews with doctoral students in advanced stages of doctoral study or those who had recently completed their degree. Few of their accounts revealed clear planning and understanding of the challenges of working as a faculty member. The chapter suggests that this finding may not be surprising, given important contextual features that work as impediments to long-term career planning.

Chapter 6 is also situated in Canada. Lynn McAlpine, Cheryl Amundsen and Marian Jazvac-Martek draw on excerpts from their longitudinal research to suggest that the experiences of doctoral students imagining academic careers and newly hired pre-tenure academics appear very similar. They suggest that it is possible to conceive one's developing academic identity as a trajectory through time, though not necessarily going where one had hoped or intended. While recognizing that the specifics of their argument will vary with context, they believe that the notion of an academic trajectory has resonance for both doctoral students and pre-tenure academics in a range of other institutional contexts. Thus, they end by describing how looking back and reflecting on these myriad and complex experiences of one's trajectory may facilitate a weaving together of apparently disparate experiences in a way that makes clearer one's future intentions and desired directions.

The final chapter, Chapter 7, pulls together the implications of the other chapters for different readers of the book. This chapter provides a framework for thinking about academic careers, one that integrates the implications in the chapters in a coherent fashion and enables a broader conceptualization of development for academic practice. In our analysis, we draw a distinction between the public and personal aspects of academic practice which we then use as an analytical tool for highlighting what is emphasized and what is downplayed in policy, research literature and academic preparation programmes. The importance of linking one's development as an academic into a continuum of experiences is one of the messages of this chapter. We position a developing academic career less in terms of the changing positions that individuals hold and more in terms of their growing sense of personal learning, purpose and identity. This situating includes how people feel about what they do as an academic and why they are doing it. It is in this way that a sense of personal coherence can be created out of the varying routes people take within academia and the often competing demands and pressures that they face as academics.

▶ Notes

1. While not all doctoral students or post-doctoral researchers wish to pursue a career in academia, this book is focused on those who do.
2. In using this term, we also include research staff (see Glossary).

▶ References

Åkerlind, G. (2005) 'Postdoctoral researchers: Roles, functions and career prospects', *Higher Education Research and Development*, 24: 21–40.

Allen Collinson, J. (2004) 'Occupational identity on the edge: Social science contract researchers in higher education', *Sociology*, 38(2): 313–29.

Austin, A. (2002) 'Creating a bridge to the future: Preparing new faculty to face changing expectations in a shifting context', *Review of Higher Education*, 26(2): 119–44.

Barnett, R. (2000) *Realizing the University in an Age of Super-complexity*. Buckingham: Society for Research into Higher Education and the Open University Press.

Baruch, Y. and Hall, D. (2004) 'The academic career: A model for future careers in other sectors?' *Journal of Vocational Behavior*, 64: 241–62.

Becher, T. and Trowler, P. (2001) *Academic Tribes and Territories*, 2nd edn. Buckingham: Open University Press.

Campbell, J., Crook, T., Damodaran, L. Kellett, B. and Valerio, R. (2003) *Supporting Research Staff: Making a Difference*. Sheffield: University of Sheffield/ HEFCE.

Council for Science and Technology (2007) *Pathways to the Future: The Early Careers of Researchers in the UK*. London: Council for Science and Technology.

Enders, J. (2007) 'The academic profession', in *International Handbook of Higher Education*, vol. 18, Amsterdam: Springer, pp. 5–21.

Gibbons, M. (1999) 'Science's new social contract with society', *Nature*, 402, C81: 11–17.

Gingras, Y. (2002) 'Les formes spécifiques de l'internationalité du champs sciéntifique', *Actes de la recherche en sciences sociales*, 141–5: 31–45.

Gluszynski, T. and Peters, V. (2005) *Survey of Earned Doctorates: A Profile of Doctoral Degree Recipients*. Ottawa, Canada: Statistics Canada.

Golde, C. and Dore, T. (2001) 'At cross-purposes: What the experiences of today's doctoral students reveal about doctoral education', Pew Charitable Trusts, available at: http://www.phd.survey.org (retrieved 3 December 2006).

Helbing, C., Verhoef, M. and Wellington, C. (1998) 'Finding identity and voice: A national survey of Canadian postdoctoral fellows', *Research Evaluation*, 7: 53–60.

Huisman, J., de Weert, E. and Bertelse, J. (2002) 'Academic careers from a European perspective: The declining desirability of the faculty position', *The Journal of Higher Education*, 73(1): 141–60.

Kayrooz, C., Åkerlind, G. and Tight, M. (eds) (2007) *Autonomy and Social Science Research: The View from United Kingdom and Australia Universities*, International Perspectives on Higher Education Research, vol. 4. Oxford: Elsevier JAI Press.

Marginson, S. (2000) 'Rethinking academic work in the global era', *Journal of Higher Education Policy and Management*, 22: 23–35.

Marginson, S. (2007) 'Freedom as control and the control of freedom: F. A. Hayek and the academic imagination', in C. Kayrooz, G. Åkerlind and M. Tight (eds) *Autonomy and Social Science Research: The View from United Kingdom and Australia Universities*, International Perspectives on Higher Education Research, vol. 4. Oxford: Elsevier JAI Press.

Mason, M., Goulden, M. and Frasch, K. (2009) 'Why graduate students reject the fast track: A study of thousands of doctoral students shows that they want balanced lives', *Academe Online*, January–February. Available at: http://www.aaup.org/AAUP/pubsres/academe/2009/JF/Feat/maso.htm (retrieved 2 February 2009).

McAlpine, L. and Norton, J. (2006) 'Reframing our approach to doctoral programs: A learning perspective', *Higher Education Research and Development*, 25(1): 3–17.

Menzies, H. and Newsome, J. (2007) 'No time to think', *Time and Society*, 16(1): 83–98.

Mills, D., Jepson, A., Coxon, T., Easterby-Smith, M., Hawkins, P. and Spencer, J. (2006) *Demographic Review of the Social Sciences*. Swindon: Economic and Social Research Council.

Nerad, M., Rudd, E., Morrison E. and Picciano, J. (2006) *Social Science PhDs – Five+ Years and Out: A National Survey of PhDs in Six Fields*. Seattle: Center for Innovation and Research in Graduate Education, University of Washington.

Raddon, A. (2006) 'Drawing the boundaries in academic work: Individual views and experiences of teaching, research and administration', paper presented at the Society for Research in Higher Education Annual Conference, Brighton, UK.

Reybold, L.E. (2005) 'Surrendering the dream: Early career conflict and faculty dissatisfaction thresholds', *Journal of Career Development*, 32(2): 107–21.

Schatzki, T., Cetina, K. and von Savigny, E. (2001) *The Practice Turn in Contemporary Theory*. London: Routledge.

Schön, D. (1983) *The Reflective Practitioner: How Professionals Think in Action*. New York: Basic Books.

Schrodt, P., Cawyer, C. and Sanders, R. (2003) 'An examination of academic mentoring behaviours and new faculty members' satisfaction with socialization and tenure and promotion processes', *Communication Education*, 52(1): 17–29.

Thompson, J., Pearson, M., Åkerlind, G., Hooper, J. and Mazur, N. (2001) *Postdoctoral Training and Employment Outcomes*, EIP report 01/10. Canberra: Higher Education Division, Department of Education Training and Youth Affairs.

Tight, M. (ed.) (2000) *Academic Work and Life: What It Is to Be an Academic, and How This Is Changing*. Oxford: Elsevier Science.

Trowler, P. (1998) *Academics Responding to Change*. Buckingham: SRHE and Open University Press.

UK GRAD (2007) *What Do PhDs Do?: First Destinations for PhD Graduates*. Cambridge: UK Grad Programme.

UK Vitae (2009) *What Do PhDs Do?: First Destinations for PhD Graduates*. Cambridge: UK Vitae Programme.

2 Expectations and Experiences of Aspiring and Early Career Academics

Ann E. Austin

> **Author perspective**

For the past twenty-five years or so, since the period of my own doctoral study, I have been involved in research on various aspects of the academic career. One of my mentors in graduate school invited me to join her in researching and writing about the 'academic workplace', a term only just emerging at the time. From this project, I found myself developing a particular interest in the experiences of early career faculty. This interest was partly fueled, I suspect, by an eagerness to understand my own experiences as I became a young faculty member, first, for a few years, at Oklahoma State University, and then, for several more, at Vanderbilt University. During those early years, I observed and experienced both the joys and the challenges of transitioning from being a doctoral student to becoming a faculty member. These experiences included discovering how much I loved both teaching and research; grappling with the multiple expectations confronting a faculty member each day; recognizing how different academic cultures affect how faculty go about their work; and welcoming three babies (two of whom were twins) and seeking my own sense of what 'balance' would mean in my life. As a young woman in the faculty career, I found that doctoral students (especially women) sought me out as a sounding board for reflecting on their own experiences in academe – which gave me more opportunity to examine the nature of this work.

As my career continued, my research agenda increasingly included a strong focus on faculty careers. In one funded study, I explored the experiences of early career faculty members at a number of universities who had participated in a year-long professional development experience focused on developing their expertise as teachers and as productive members of the academy. I also was one of the researchers for a study entitled 'Heeding New Voices', which concerned academic careers and work experiences and involved interviews with doctoral students and early career academics (Rice *et al.*, 2000). Than, about fifteen years ago, some of my research came to focus specifically on doctoral education as the socialization period for academic and scholarly careers. Informed by socialization theory, several colleagues and I conducted a four-year, funded, longitudinal study of key elements in the doctoral experiences of 79 aspiring faculty members in fields within the social sciences, humanities, sciences, and professional fields at two universities (as well as aspects of the graduate careers of a group of master's students at a third university). As the years continued, my research and writing concerned such topics as faculty morale, academic cultures, faculty career development, and diverse types of academic appointments. This line of work culminated in a recent co-authored book entitled *Rethinking Faculty Work: Higher Education's Strategic Imperative.*

In addition to what I have learned from my research, my own career as a faculty member – including the past twenty years teaching in a graduate program in Higher, Adult, and Lifelong Education at Michigan State University – has given me many opportunities to experience and observe academic life and to work with doctoral students. I use research findings to inform my own approach to working with doctoral students – and my own experiences help me assess the credibility of the research on doctoral education. The discussion presented in this chapter draws on my research on doctoral education and the early career faculty experience, and my knowledge of other such research studies in the United States; furthermore, my own experiences and observations as I work in academe create a filter through which I interpret research findings from my own and other colleagues' work.

▶ Focus and organization of this chapter

The preparation of future academics is one of the major responsibilities for doctoral education. This chapter presents findings from research conducted over the past fifteen years in the United States concerning the experiences of early career academics and doctoral students (whom I call *aspiring* faculty members). The chapter also highlights the implications of these experiences in regard to effective career preparation for the professoriate and support for early career faculty. I note here, at the start of this chapter, a comment on the term 'faculty', as it is used in the United States somewhat differently than in other countries. In the United States, academics with appointments in universities and colleges are called faculty members; the aggregate of departments in related areas is called a 'college', in which a group of academics collectively is called 'the faculty'.

I begin by explaining key features of doctoral education and the early career experience of academics in the United States. Some aspects of these stages of the academic experience in the United States differ from aspects of the parallel career stages in other countries. The chapter then addresses three questions that shed light on the question of appropriate preparation for academic careers in the social sciences. First, I consider which changes are occurring in faculty employment patterns and in the nature of academic work in the United States. The various employment contexts which doctoral graduates will enter are important to consider as decisions are made about career preparation. Second, I discuss findings from the research literature concerning the experiences of early career faculty, including concerns that many early career academics express about their work. Third, I examine the research literature on the doctoral experience, particularly for those pursuing the social sciences. What does the research reveal about the goals, concerns, and perceptions of students in regard to the preparation experience in U.S. doctoral education? The discussion of these three questions shows that the issues that concern early career faculty parallel key challenges that doctoral students report. Thus, helping doctoral students (aspiring faculty members) handle the challenges they face during their graduate education is likely to help them further as they continue into academic positions and grapple with similar concerns. I end the chapter with suggestions for various groups in regard to strengthening doctoral career preparation for academic work and supporting early career faculty members.

▶ Features of doctoral education and the academic career in the United States

American higher education includes a variety of institutional types. Doctoral education in the U.S. typically takes place in course-based programs in research-oriented universities (which heavily emphasize research as well as teaching and which include many fields of study). American higher education also includes comprehensive institutions (which may include some doctoral-granting programs but primarily emphasize master's and undergraduate degrees), liberal arts colleges (which offer only the four-year undergraduate baccalaureate degree), and community colleges (which offer two-year terminal degrees that lead to employment and two-year degrees that enable students to continue their education in other institutions that offer the baccalaureate degree). The components of doctoral programs usually involve a set of courses (some required, some electives), although the number of courses will vary by program; an examination either called a qualifying exam or a comprehensive exam (based on coursework and often based on an additional set of readings selected by the faculty advisor or guidance committee and the student, specifically chosen in relationship to the student's specialty); and a dissertation consisting of independent and original research and writing, completed by the student under the guidance of a faculty advisor (similar to a 'supervisor', in other countries). A student also has a dissertation committee, usually consisting of two or three faculty members in addition to the dissertation advisor; the committee approves the proposal for the dissertation study, offers suggestions, reads the finished draft, and conducts an oral defense in which the student responds to questions about the study. In some programs, students are called 'candidates' upon completion of the required amount of coursework and successful completion of the comprehensive or qualifying exam.

The details of the doctoral experience (and of each of these components of the doctoral program) vary across disciplinary fields. In fact, the specific disciplinary contexts in which scholars study and work frame many aspects of their experiences. Disciplinary cultures are strong and well established, influencing what work is done, how it is organized, publication patterns, interactions among students and faculty, and the criteria used to determine success (Becher, 1984, 1987; Clark, 1984, 1987; Kuh and Whitt, 1988). For example, doctoral students in the sciences are likely to have somewhat fewer courses required than students in the humanities. The structure and process of the qualifying or comprehensive exams vary by discipline. Students in the humanities and social sciences often take a year or more to construct reading lists in preparation for writing their exams, which consist of extensive research papers on questions specifically designed for each person's individual scholarly focus. Students in other fields may take an exam that is generic for a whole cohort and which is taken during the course of one day or over several days. The dissertation in most fields is a lengthy manuscript consisting of the presentation of a problem, a literature review, presentation of research data and findings, and extensive discussion and interpretation. In contrast, dissertations in mathematics may be very short, and, in some sciences, the dissertation may not be a long paper on one study, but, rather, three short pieces presenting research and written in journal-publishable style. (In the United States, this option is not very usual in fields other than the sciences, although there is discussion at some universities to offer this option more widely.)

Doctoral students in the U.S. often interact with a number of faculty members, particularly those who teach the courses they take. Each student, however, will have an advisor, with whom he or she interacts regularly for advice about course selection and, eventually, for guidance on the dissertation. Again, disciplinary contexts play a role in the nature and structure of the advisor/advisee relationship. In the sciences, doctoral students usually seek a place in the laboratory of a faculty member and develop a close relationship involving daily interactions, organized around the faculty member's research agenda. The student becomes part of a research team, led by the faculty member, and the quality of the student's experience is largely shaped by the working environment of the research team. The dissertation may evolve out of this work and is often a piece of the overall agenda being researched in the professor's lab. In the social sciences, a doctoral student may work as a member of a research team, or, just as often, may work independently, developing his or her own research avenue and checking in periodically (sometimes every few months) with the advisor. The degree of collaboration or competition a doctoral student may feel with other students also varies both by discipline and on the basis of the specific department.

Doctoral students in the U.S. may be full-time or part-time students, with the pattern varying by discipline. Students often serve as teaching assistants or research assistants. As mentioned earlier, doctoral students are paid for their work as teachers or researchers, working under the guidance of a faculty member. Such assistantships are one of the primary ways in which U.S. doctoral students fund their graduate study. In the social sciences, most departments have many undergraduate courses and require the services of teaching assistants to lead discussion sections and help with exam grading. In contrast, in the sciences, doctoral students often will serve as Teaching Assistants only in their first year, and will eagerly move to more prestigious positions as Research Assistants in subsequent years.

Understanding the academic career in the U.S. requires knowing how the tenure system works and understanding the titles used for academic staff. Some social science scholars will follow a doctoral experience with a post-doctoral research experience, but many enter academic work or other work immediately after the doctorate. Some individuals begin to teach while they are ABD (All But Dissertation) (i.e., they have completed all other requirements, usually including course work, comprehensive examinations, and the dissertation proposal defense). If they are teaching in four-year institutions (universities or four-year liberal arts colleges which grant undergraduate bachelor's degrees), those who teach without doctoral degrees are usually called 'instructors'. These positions usually do not have career trajectories. The typical entry faculty post that offers a career trajectory is called 'assistant professor'. In universities, a scholar usually holds such a post for three years, after which he or she, if evaluated as making adequate progress, is typically reappointed for three more years. During the sixth year, the individual is reviewed in a thorough process for consideration to receive tenure. If awarded, tenure protects the scholar's academic freedom and provides job security. The path to tenure may be somewhat shorter than six to seven years in smaller institutions that offer only undergraduate degrees or in community colleges that offer the two-year degree. The tenure process, (which pertains to academics in what are called 'tenure-track positions') is very significant in the career of an academic. If tenure is granted, it is accompanied by job security (which can be undermined only if the institution faces certain difficult financial conditions or if the faculty member violates certain points of integrity). If tenure is not granted, the individual must seek employment elsewhere. Thus, considerable importance is attached by the individual and the institution to the tenure decision. Peer review panels, as well as department chairs, deans, and institutional presidents, play a role in the decision. Once an academic receives tenure, he or she is promoted from the rank of 'assistant professor' to 'associate professor'. One can stay at that rank for the rest of the career or, after several years in which research and teaching contributions are evaluated highly, the faculty member can request to be reviewed for the rank of 'professor'.

Building on this description of key characteristics of doctoral education and the academic employment system in the United States, we now turn to consideration of how faculty work is changing. The changes we discuss here are important for developing an understanding of the issues that future faculty members must understand. A major change occurring in academic work in the United States involves a significant shift away from traditional tenure-track positions toward an increasing number of non-tenure-track, renewable fixed-term appointments. The tenure system, as described here, has been a dominant process for decades in many higher education institutions. However, over the past ten years or so, many higher education institutions have been hiring faculty members in what are called 'non-tenure-track positions'. A non-tenure-track position may be labeled 'lecturer' or may involve the same career progression from assistant to associate to full professor as is common with tenure-track positions. However, these positions do not offer the benefit of the secure employment or the protection of academic freedom that tenure provides. Those in a non-tenure-track appointment are usually reviewed and considered for reappointment every year or every three to five years. The increase in non-tenure-track appointments relates greatly to the interest of higher education institutions in retaining flexibility in their employment practices (Leslie, 2005; Gappa et al., 2007). A tenured faculty member cannot be easily released from employment. The institution is bound to the non-tenure-track faculty member only for the duration of the employment contract. New faculty entering academic appointments need to understand the nature of both tenure-track and non-tenure-track appointments, as their faculty careers may go in either direction.

Part-time positions are also becoming more numerous, with nearly half of all faculty members holding part-time positions in 2003 (this figures includes two-year community colleges). In fact, academics today hold many different types of positions and pursue a range of career tracks. In 1987, for full-time faculty members across institutional types (including research, comprehensive, private liberal arts, and public two-year institutions, briefly described above), 79 percent held tenure-track/tenured positions, with 21 percent in non-tenure track positions (or working at institutions with no tenure system). The comparable figures in 2003 had dropped to less than 70 percent in tenure-track/tenured positions and risen to 32 percent in non-tenure track/or no institutional tenure positions. The picture for full-time faculty social scientists follows the same pattern, although a greater proportion, as compared to faculty overall across fields, continues to hold tenure-track/tenured positions. In 1987, 89 percent of the social science faculty held tenure-track/tenured positions compared to 79 percent in 2003. Those social scientists in non-tenure-track/ no tenure positions shifted from 11 percent in 1987 to 21 percent in 2003. Clearly, a shift has occurred away from tenure track positions, a pattern true for social scientists, even if not as strongly as for those in other fields (U.S. Department of Education, National Center for Education Statistics, 1988, 2004).

At the same time that employment patterns are changing, so too is the nature of the work that academics do (Gappa et al., 2007).

Such changes, among others, involve new opportunities for faculty to engage in interdisciplinary work, new technologies that both aid and challenge faculty, an increasing diversity of students with new expectations of their faculty, and increasing pressures on academic staff in regard to accountability and entrepreneurialism.

▶ Key challenges in the work experience of early career academics

Having examined the context which new academics are entering and for which doctoral students should be prepared, I turn, in this section, to the research literature on the experiences of those in the early years of the faculty career, with focus on the areas of concern expressed by early career academics. On this topic, the studies focused on U.S. faculty typically do not separate out the experiences of social scientists as compared to their colleagues in other fields; however, social scientists have been included in the samples of a number of studies, so the research results are relevant to this chapter.

One major theme, throughout two decades of research on early career academics, concerns the reasons they enter the professoriate. Overall, new academics are excited by the intrinsic aspects of academic work – that is, the features of the work that are embedded in the work itself. To be more specific, they typically look forward to enjoying the autonomy and freedom to pursue their particular areas of interest, the flexibility to organize their work in ways they find most beneficial, the opportunity to continue learning, and the challenge of intellectual activity. As reported in one of the studies in which I was involved, *Heeding New Voices* (Rice *et al.*, 2000), new faculty members who were interviewed about their experiences often spoke with enthusiasm about the intrinsic elements of academic work: they enjoy 'the opportunity to stretch my mind', the 'cognitive stimulation', and 'the boundlessness in how I construct the work, [in which] I am my own boss and set my own agenda and hours – both intellectually and practically' (*ibid.*, p. 6). New academics also often express eagerness for the opportunity to serve society by contributing to the learning of the next generation. They look forward to helping novices discover the ideas that have excited them in their fields. In short, they are eager to engage in 'meaningful work' and they usually express passion for the career they have chosen to pursue (Austin, 2002b; Rice, 1996; Rice *et al.*, 2000). They are ready to work hard, want to have an impact on their fields, their institutions, and the broader community, and have a sense of idealism about what they can accomplish (Austin *et al.*, 2007; Boice, 1992; Rice *et al.*, 2000; Trower, 2005). This sense of idealism and motivation, however, runs up against concerns and frustrations that early career academics discover soon after they begin their careers. These concerns lead many to report feelings of anxiety and stress (Rice *et al.*, 2000).

Three themes, expressed as areas of concern, generally appear with regularity throughout the U.S.-based studies concerning full-time, tenure-track early career faculty (Austin and Rice, 1998; Olsen and Near, 1994; Rice *et al.*, 2000; Tierney and Bensimon, 1996; Ward and Wolf-Wendel, 2004). While the experiences of early career academics certainly include many more dimensions, I highlight these concerns as they suggest issues for which doctoral students considering academic work should be prepared.

Furthermore, these same three themes appear in the research on doctoral students, although the specific details of each theme play out in ways specific to the career stage. Overall, the themes that weave through the experiences of both early career academics and doctoral students (which also appear in the discussions in subsequent chapters) pertain to the following:

- clarity of expectations;
- workload and work/life balance;
- community and collegiality.

Lack of clear expectation
(the pressures of the tenure-track process)

Although new academics are enthusiastic, committed, and hard-working, as they progress in the career, they often express consider-able concern about how they will be evaluated and specifically, for those in tenure systems, the tenure process. One issue is the perceived lack of clarity about the expectations they are to fulfil. Early career faculty often report hearing one framing of expectations from colleagues who have just gone through the tenure process and another from well-established senior faculty. They also explain that expectations not only are unclear, but seem to change over time – especially if the department chairperson changes during a faculty member's pre-tenure period. In the words of one early career academic, 'Everything is so vague, ambiguous, and elusive; expectations are changing all the time' (quoted in Rice *et al.*, 2000, p. 10). In addition to concern about figuring out expectations, some new faculty members report that they perceive the expectations they face to be more extensive than the expectations faced by their senior colleagues. In some fields, where the publication of one book seemed to have been sufficient for a successful tenure bid a decade or so ago, faculty now have the sense that success in the tenure process requires more than one book.

Concerns about ambiguous or shifting expectations are coupled with worries about the nature of the feedback they are given. Early career faculty members often report that the feedback they receive is insufficient – and when they do receive it, the feedback may also be vague, imprecise, ambiguous, or, what some call, 'antiseptic' (Rice *et al.*, 2000, p. 11). In some fields, early career faculty are concerned that their senior colleagues, who evaluate them, may not have kept up with theoretical or methodological advances in the field, and, thus, may not have the knowledge to assess the work of the newer colleagues.

While some faculty say they value the way in which the tenure system emphasizes quality and protects academic freedom (Austin and Rice, 1998), many express great concern about the overall sense of pressure and anxiety that they feel in relation to the tenure process. Their comments are often poignant, suggesting that the system may be threatening the very sense of enthusiasm and energy that led them to academic careers. The sentiments of one participant in the *Heeding New Voices* study reflect the thoughts often expressed by many early career academics: 'I just want to get through this game, so I can get to the things I want to do' (Rice *et al.*, 2000, p. 12).

Concerns about workload and work/life balance

A second concern articulated by early career academics, including those in the social sciences, pertains to challenges related to time, managing multiple work responsibilities, and finding balance in relation to professional and personal responsibilities (Rice *et al.*, 2000). In studies of early career faculty, 'finding enough time to do my work' appears consistently as a major source of stress (Boice, 1992; Rice *et al.*, 2000, p. 17). Faculty members at every career stage are likely to experience multiple demands and high expectations. In fact, the research literature suggests that, overall, the time academics spend on work is increasing (Schuster and Finkelstein, 2006; U.S. Department of Education, 2004). While all faculty members are experiencing this trend, for early career academics, time concerns and the feeling of being pulled in too many directions loom large and can create skepticism about continuing in the career (Boice, 1992; Fink, 1984). One participant in the *Heeding New Voices* study explained: 'The main issue on everyone's mind is maintaining an equilibrium. Life before tenure is a juggling act that involves long hours and keeping all the balls in the air long enough to get through it' (Rice *et al.*, 2000, p. 17). While anyone who has experienced a long faculty career knows that the challenge of managing multiple responsibilities continues throughout the career, the point here is not to compare the experiences of early career faculty with that of their more senior faculty colleagues. Rather, the point is to emphasize that, from the point of view of early career faculty, the pressure of being pulled in many directions is a defining feature of work – and one that, for some early career faculty members, becomes a factor causing reconsideration of academic work as a career choice.

In a study of new faculty in geography, respondents indicated that time management was problematic in a way that had a negative effect on their performance (Solem and Foote, 2004). Time management issues pertaining to teaching responsibilities were most related to a negative impact on faculty performance. Teaching tends to be a source of stress for new academics, perhaps because new faculty members typically have minimal preparation for teaching (Menges, 1999). Additionally, in some departments, early career faculty members are given the large, lower-level courses, which are often believed to be more challenging to teach.

While in past decades academics tended to be males with spouses at home, today's faculty members, whether they be male or female, often are in dual-career situations, with partners who have their own professional responsibilities, requiring each person to contribute to domestic duties. Senior faculty members (especially those who had a spouse at home while the faculty member negotiated the early career years) sometimes do not understand the pressures on their early career colleagues to fit personal as well as professional responsibilities into their schedules. Women and men with the responsibilities of young families often find the time demands of the academic career especially demanding. It is noteworthy that, with the overall societal shift in recent decades toward greater involvement of men in handling family duties, studies of early career faculty show that both men and women are concerned about balancing family and professional responsibilities. However, given that women have the added physical role of bearing children (an event that may coincide with the start of an academic career), the research shows that the pressures of the early career can be especially demanding for them and that women academics especially feel the stress of balancing family responsibilities with professional duties (Ward and Wolf-Wendel, 2004). Other research findings also reveal troubling issues for women academics who are trying to manage the demands of the profession. Some women feel they must hide their personal responsibilities from their colleagues or decide to decline to take the leave time available to them after a family addition in order to appear to their colleagues to be highly committed to their work. In a well-cited study, Mason and Goulden (2004) found that only one-third of women who entered tenure-track positions before having children chose to have them subsequently. Additionally, in one university, they found that 38 percent of female faculty had fewer children than they desired. The evidence is strong that women especially find that the pressures of the early academic career can have a negative or constraining impact on their personal choices. The pressures of time and multiple demands undoubtedly also impact faculty members more advanced in their careers. However, this pressure is especially important to understand in the lives of young faculty members for two reasons. First, early career faculty members are still at a point where they can – and sometimes do – reconsider the career choice. Some find that academic work intrudes on the overall life and work situation that they wish to establish for themselves, and, thus, some choose to leave the academy. More senior academics have typically made the choice to develop their careers within academe, despite the pressures they experience. Second, the challenges of balancing work and personal responsibilities are especially poignant and pressing for young female faculty members. While older faculty members also experience pressures and conflicting demands, they are not also dealing with the specific issues that face individuals wishing to start a family (including the physical demands of pregnancy and childbirth, caring for young children, or reaching a decision not to start a family).

Concerns about community and collegiality

The third area of concern to new faculty members, according to our research, pertains to community and collegiality (Gappa *et al.*, 2007; Rice *et al.*, 2000). New academics report that they look forward to collaboration, stimulating interaction, and warm collegiality when they become part of the professorial ranks. Historically, a sense of the 'culture of collegiality' has been associated with work in academe (Rice *et al.*, 2000, p. 13). However, in contrast to this vision of a collegial environment, early career faculty often report that their early years involve competition, loneliness, and isolation. In one study, my colleagues and I asked interviewees to portray in visual form the key features of their early career experience. One of the most powerful and poignant images, drawn by one early career faculty member, showed a corridor in which each faculty office door had a sign: 'Gone Fishing', 'Out to Lunch', 'Do Not Disturb'. When asked what her office door would say if it were in this picture, the early career faculty member stated, ' "At Home"... I have so much to do and I get more done there'. Although this faculty member was acutely aware of the irony that she herself would choose to work away from the office, she also was concerned that her experience was characterized by loneliness rather than collegiality.

The time pressures mentioned contribute to this problem, as does the fact that computers enable faculty members to work from home or other locations, rather than be on campus, in close proximity to colleagues. Dual career households also are a factor; for example, an academic may live far from campus in order to accommodate a partner's drive to work, thus making spontaneous interactions with colleagues more difficult.

Having mentors might be a strategy to help early career academics feel more integrated into the community. However, new academics report that senior colleagues tend to be busy and unavailable, or, in some cases, that senior colleagues do not understand the newer directions of a field. Women and members of ethnic minorities especially report difficulties in finding mentors who understand their circumstances and the particular challenges they face, especially in departments with few other women or underrepresented faculty (Rice *et al.*, 2000).

Taken together, these concerns, which surface regularly in the research on early career academics, deserve attention from those who prepare social scientists for the academic career. Awareness of the typical challenges facing early career academics can alleviate surprises and enable future faculty to develop strategies for success.

▷ Salient features of doctoral preparation for social scientists

Having overviewed the changes occurring in the academic workplace and the most frequent concerns of early career academics, we turn now to highlight research findings concerning the nature of doctoral preparation for academia for social scientists in the United States. Again, my aim in this chapter is to examine both the employment context which new academics enter and the preparation they receive. A recent large-scale quantitative study by Nettles and Millett (2006), in which they define the social sciences, for purposes of their research, as economics, political science, psychology, and sociology, provides some useful data. There has been a 'modest growth' between 1980 and 2001 in the percentage of degrees awarded in the social sciences (a growth of about 20 percent) compared to the considerable growth in some fields such as mathematics and computer science (90 percent growth).

In terms of career plans, the Nettles and Millett study found that 55 percent of their social science doctoral student respondents 'expected to hold [higher education faculty positions] immediately after completing their doctorates', compared with about three-quarters of the humanities doctoral students and a little less than one-third of the doctoral students in engineering. About 7 percent of the social scientists 'expect to become researchers in the private sector' (Nettles and Millett, 2006, p. 101).

Nettles and Millett also gathered data about student productivity and research experiences. They found that just under half of the social science doctoral students they studied produced conference research papers or published articles, chapters, or books, fewer than their counterparts in engineering (66 percent of whom produced conference papers or published), in humanities (57 percent), and in the science and mathematics group (52 percent), but somewhat higher than those doctoral students in education (40 percent of whom produced conference papers or published). More specifically, 35 percent of the social science doctoral students in their sample had presented research papers, 22 percent had published a journal article, 13 percent had published a chapter, and 1 percent had published a book.

Overall, the social science respondents were confident in their decision to pursue a doctorate. Eleven percent of the sample had stopped out (in order to work or for financial or family reasons) and had returned to finish the degree. About 50 percent of doctoral students in social sciences completed the degree, compared to 75 percent in engineering, 72 percent in science and mathematics, and about 45 percent in the humanities (Nettles and Millett, 2006). Overall, in terms of expectations to be faculty members, research productivity in graduate school, and degree completion rates, the experiences of doctoral students in the social sciences tended to be 'in the middle' as compared to their science and humanities counterparts.

These data provide an overview of aspects of the doctoral experience for social science students. However, qualitative data provide a deeper sense of key aspects of the doctoral experience. Thus, we review the body of work, mainly conducted within the past dozen years, that identifies several common concerns or problems in doctoral education in the U.S. (Austin and McDaniels, 2006). Most of the studies have not focused specifically on social science doctoral programs, but they have included social scientists within their samples. In discussing qualitative data concerning the doctoral experience, I draw heavily on the results from a longitudinal four-year study that my colleagues Jody Nyquist, Don Wulff, Jo Sprague, and I conducted, along with a group of very involved doctoral research assistants. Participants came from a range of disciplines, including the social sciences (defined in that study to include history, psychology, and communication), the humanities (English and music), the sciences (chemistry, zoology, engineering, and mathematics), and several professional areas (including business, journalism, education, and food science). The study involved open-ended interviews with each participant twice each year for four years, beginning with their first year as doctoral students. The interviews provided the occasion for participants to discuss various aspects of their doctoral programs, their career interests and perceptions of faculty roles and responsibilities, their observations of faculty work and the faculty career, and their suggestions concerning how aspiring faculty members should be prepared.

Three key themes stand out in the research on the doctoral experience, and, overall, parallel the themes that characterize the experiences of early career faculty members:

- lack of clear expectations (and preparation);
- concerns about workload and work/life balance;
- concerns about community (and opportunities for reflection).

Lack of clear expectations
(lack of systematic preparation for an academic career)

Doctoral students learn much about faculty careers from observing and interacting with their own faculty members. They note which responsibilities are important and which receive less attention. They observe that administrators may articulate the importance of teaching as part of the institution's mission, but that decisions about promotion and tenure of faculty members often relate to research productivity. As they work as teaching assistants or in the laboratories, they are constantly processing information and striving to make sense of the academic career. As one doctoral student whom we interviewed explained, 'Every teacher I have is a teacher I can use in some way' (Austin, 2002b, p. 104). Messages are always being processed, even if they are not explicit. However, the doctoral students repeatedly mentioned that the messages they receive are often 'mixed messages'. That is, they may hear faculty members or deans say that all facets of faculty work are important, but they may also note that their faculty supervisors do not want them to carve out time from their research schedules to participate in seminars provided by the graduate school where they can learn about effective teaching. Furthermore, while students may serve as teaching assistants, they do not necessarily have systematic preparation for the many facets of teaching (Austin and McDaniels, 2006).

In contrast to some of the data from studies that include students from across disciplines, Walker *et al.* (2008) presented data specifically pertaining to doctoral students in history (which is sometimes considered a social science in the U.S.). They reported that more than 90 percent of the history doctoral students they studied self-reported 'high level[s] of proficiency in the ability to design and teach a course' (*ibid.*, p. 69). What is not addressed is whether these students felt prepared for the other aspects of their work as faculty members.

Given the mixed messages and the serendipitous nature of much doctoral student learning about the faculty career, an overall concern highlighted in the findings in a number of studies is that doctoral education typically does not offer systematic preparation for the professoriate (Austin, 2002a, 2002b; Golde and Dore, 2001; Nerad *et al.*, 2004; Nyquist *et al.*, 1999; Wulff *et al.*, 2004). In the longitudinal study that my colleagues and I conducted with doctoral students across two universities, we invited them periodically to draw images that characterized their experiences. Many of the drawings featured cliffs, sudden drop-offs, and roads with signs obscured. In explaining their drawings, interviewees explained that they found their paths through doctoral education to be challenging because of the lack of explicit direction and guidance, and, in some cases, the explicit barriers that they felt they were encountering.

Concerns about academic life
(especially workload and work/life balance)
Not only are doctoral students not prepared systematically for careers in academic. They also find that, while in graduate school, they develop

concerns about pursuing careers in academe. As we discussed earlier in regard to early career faculty, doctoral students who aspire to academic work are hoping to find 'meaningful' work in which they can connect their passions about their disciplines to a commitment to make a difference. However, as they progress through graduate study, some worry whether an academic career will actually enable them to find the meaningful life they are committed to living. They observe faculty members and wonder about the hectic pace of academic work and how to manage lives of balance. Their comments are often thoughtful, poignant, and sometimes hint at angst. One woman studying psychology whom we interviewed commented: 'I hope I'll be able to find what I'm looking for....I love the...research I'm doing...[but] sometimes when I observe the faculty in our department, they just seem too busy. I need more balance in my life....My husband and I both want to make sure we have time for our baby.' Another expressed similar concerns: 'For a while I thought maybe I'd like to work in a research university, if I could...but...I realized life is too short....I love teaching...I like research...but I need to choose a path that gives me time to have a life' (Austin, 2002b, p. 109).

These future faculty members speak of seeking 'meaningful work' that enables them to follow their passions and contribute to students and society. They want meaning and connection, as expressed by a doctoral student in the *Heeding New Voices* study: 'What I most want in a faculty career is a profession that makes me feel connected to my students, to my colleagues, to the larger community, and to myself' (Rice *et al.*, 2000, p. 16). Yet, they worry whether the pressures on faculty members are too daunting to make the career attractive (Austin, 2002a, 2002b; Austin and McDaniels, 2006; Golde and Dore, 2001; Nyquist *et al.*, 1999; Rice *et al.*, 2000; Wulff *et al.*, 2004). Some doctoral students are very explicit in their concern. When asked in the *Heeding New Voices* study about what they admired in faculty lives that they would like to emulate, many responded in this way: 'I don't want to have a life like theirs....They don't have a life' (Rice *et al.*, 2000, p. 19). While the studies do not single out social science doctoral students, there is no reason to think they differ from their counterparts in these concerns.

Concerns about community (and opportunities to reflect)

Learning can be deepened by opportunities to reflect, especially with the help of an interested advisor or guide. However, the studies of the doctoral experience in the U.S. indicate that doctoral students find that there is little opportunity for this kind of interaction (Anderson and Swazey, 1998; Austin, 2002b; Austin and McDaniels, 2006; Austin *et al.*, 2007). Students of color and minority students particularly experience less mentoring than other students (Taylor and Antony, 2001). In our longitudinal research study, we found that the doctoral student participants reported their enjoyment of the interviews. While it is not uncommon for participants in qualitative studies to note that they are enjoying their participation in the study, what was noteworthy in this study was that the doctoral student participants said they had no other place to step back and reflect with a trusted colleague or listener. Many reported relying on peers for information, but many shared a wish that their faculty advisors would play more of the role of trusted confidante. We found, in fact, that some participants stayed in touch beyond the study because they valued the interaction and the opportunity to engage in sense-making that the study interviews enabled.

While our research did not focus specifically on students in social sciences, Nettles and Millett's (2006) research adds some disciplinary perspective on the issue of student–faculty relationships. They reported that doctoral students in the social sciences and humanities have lower perceptions of and are less satisfied with the quality of their relationships with their program faculty than are students in engineering, science and mathematics, and education. They also rate the quality of their interactions with faculty around academic issues (including the availability of faculty to meet with them, and the quality of advising and feedback) quite low. In contrast, however, doctoral students in the social sciences report very positive interactions with their peers, including opportunities to be part of study groups, and to socialize and make friends. Overall, however, I believe the evidence is strong that doctoral students would value more opportunities to step back from their study and work, reflect on how their preparation is proceeding, and consider what kind of careers they wish to pursue.

▶ Implications for practice in doctoral education

The aim of this chapter has been to juxtapose the career context, the challenges experienced by early career academics holding faculty posts, and the areas of concern students express about the doctoral experience. If doctoral students are to be prepared for the variety of academic positions they may enter and the array of responsibilities they will encounter (such as teaching diverse students, using new technologies in their teaching and research, and engaging in entrepreneurial activity), they will need to be thoughtfully and thoroughly prepared. Yet, the research studies suggest that doctoral education typically does not take a systematic approach to preparing future academics for the full range of their responsibilities. Furthermore, students' observations of faculty life and the infrequency of opportunities for reflective conversations about faculty work may lead them to be uncertain about pursuing faculty work. Reviewing in one chapter the literature on the experiences of both early career academics and doctoral students highlights the similarity of issues that pervade the graduate preparation period and the early career stage: concerns about expectations and preparation, concerns about workload and balance, and concerns about the nature of the academic community and how it supports (or fails to support) professional growth and satisfaction.

Attention to these issues and concerns confronting aspiring and new faculty members is likely to help them succeed and find satisfaction in their work. The responsibility lies with administrators, faculty members, academic developers, scholarly associations, and aspiring and new faculty members themselves. Here I offer some suggestions for each of these audiences in order to help graduate students and new faculty members find satisfaction, meaning, and success in their work and career progress.

Recommendations for administrators
(department chairpersons, deans, and graduate deans)

Both doctoral students and new faculty members benefit from a *warm welcome and orientation to academe*. Department chairs, deans of academic units, and deans of graduate schools can ensure that newcomers – whether graduate students or new academic staff – know that the institution and their new colleagues are very pleased to have them join the community. Such a welcome immediately signals that the department and institution value a sense of community and intend to support the members of the community. In addition to expressing collegiality, administrators can ensure that new doctoral students and new faculty members have the information they need that will help them handle both personal and professional responsibilities. Such information includes highlighting the values and mission of the institution and department, and sharing perspectives on norms pertaining to work habits and collegial interaction within the unit. New graduate students and new academic staff also need to know what resources, policies, and programs are available to help them do their work and manage their personal lives. Resources might include professional development seminars or programs in which they can participate, and resources and policies pertaining to personal situations, such as health needs, child care, or family leaves. Newcomers also benefit from receiving information about the broader community and relevant activities and opportunities that might be pertinent to their situations. Providing such information is not only helpful to the new colleagues; it also symbolically conveys the message that institutional leaders recognize the multiple responsibilities that all academic staff must manage.

Department chairs and deans of academic units or graduate schools can also ensure that aspiring and new faculty members experience *ongoing advising and mentoring*, a suggestion offered also by Janet Bokemeier, an experienced department chair, in her commentary on this chapter. As graduate students and new faculty settle into their roles, experienced faculty members (or doctoral students' faculty advisors) can encourage newcomers to specify their professional goals and develop explicit plans for achieving these goals (one of the recommendations mentioned by Laura Border in her commentary on this chapter). Such plans might include systematically engaging in professional development opportunities, seeking out colleagues with similar interests, or arranging research plans to develop specific knowledge or expertise. Mentoring and advising should also include specific information about expectations. In the case of doctoral students, they need to know requirements, processes for exams and dissertation work, and standards of excellence. New academic staff should be informed about the details of the tenure and promotion process, including who will review them, the criteria used in the evaluation of their work, and the logistics of moving through the tenure process. On-going mentoring involves not only initial meetings but regular opportunities for the mentor and aspiring or early career academic to work with the mentor to assess progress, discuss feedback and critique, and make adjustments in professional development plans.

This kind of systematic on-going advising and mentoring addresses the concerns of doctoral students and new faculty members about unclear expectations and vague feedback. Mentoring may be carried out by individual administrators and experienced faculty members in one-on-one meetings with doctoral students or new academic staff. Additionally, individual mentoring can be supplemented with occasions for groups to assemble to discuss information of relevance to them all. At my own university, for example, the senior administrator responsible for faculty affairs arranges an annual half-day seminar for pre-tenure faculty members. The seminar, called 'Survive and Thrive', is attended annually by approximately 100 early career faculty members, and provides extensive information about the tenure and promotion process, as well as examples and testimonies about the process from faculty members who have successfully moved through this career stage and from a sample of department chairs and deans.

Administrators can also arrange occasions for doctoral students and early career academics to enjoy *informal interactions with each other, experienced faculty members, and administrative leaders.* Social occasions offer newcomers the chance to make new connections and to begin to develop their own network of colleagues and acquaintances. As doctoral students experience on-going, informal interactions with peers and faculty members, they come to feel part of a community of scholars, and gain deeper perspectives of what rewarding academic lives involve. New academics, too, benefit from occasions to meet and talk informally with colleagues. At my institution, senior university leaders host a reception one afternoon a month to which all faculty members from across the institution are invited for casual conversation. New faculty members can choose to attend on their own or experienced colleagues may invite them as a way to extend a hand of collegiality.

Recommendations for academic developers

Academic developers also play a key role in helping aspiring (doctoral students) and new faculty members learn about expectations, develop skills and abilities related to the various dimensions of their work, find ways to balance personal and professional responsibilities, and develop a sense of belonging. Laura Border, an academic developer who has provided a commentary on this chapter, offers several ways in which developers can support doctoral students and early career faculty. She suggests, for example, that academic developers can arrange seminars and workshops that offer *opportunities for collegial interaction* while simultaneously providing information that doctoral students and new academic staff need. For example, academic developers situated in the Graduate School at my university recognize that doctoral students typically do not have a wide array of knowledge about the full spectrum of institutional types in which they might pursue their careers. Thus, they offer professional development programs for graduate students at which leaders and faculty members from a range of higher education institutions discuss academic work in these various contexts. Some graduate programs in the United States are arranging for students to visit different higher education institutions and to talk with scholars in faculty positions at these institutions about the rewards and challenges of work in such situations. Some universities have also established internship programs with nearby institutions to enable doctoral students to explore what various career directions might be like. Doctoral students considering academic careers need opportunities to gain knowledge about their career choices and to think through how their own values, goals, and aspirations fit with the options available. Academic developers can provide needed information about the higher education landscape and the implications for career options as well as occasions for students to reflect on their own goals and preferences.

Aspiring and new faculty members staff also need *opportunities to talk with experienced academics* about all aspects of the scholarly career – certainly teaching and research, but also institutional governance and citizenship duties, advising, collegial interactions, and public service. Academic developers can convene workshops and resources to help new academics explore these aspects of their work, learn about institutional expectations, and reflect on their own preferences and choices. For example, some universities offer opportunities for new faculty members to participate in year-long monthly small-group seminars, organized as collegial discussions about faculty work.

Recommendations for scholarly associations

Scholarly associations also have the responsibility to *play a role in supporting aspiring and new academic staff*. In the United States, some associations are offering pre-conference workshops and seminars during conferences that focus on various elements of academic work. Topics include, for example, strategies for curriculum design, pedagogical delivery, innovative approaches to teaching in the discipline, and assessment strategies. Other topics might include grant writing, conducting scholarship on one's teaching and students' learning, integrating research and teaching, and engaging in outreach based on one's research. I hope that scholarly associations will initiate or expand such learning opportunities in the coming years, as they help address the concerns that aspiring and new academics have pertaining to understanding expectations, refining skills and abilities, managing personal and professional balance, and fostering collegiality.

Recommendations for graduate students and new faculty

Finally, I want to emphasize that aspiring and new faculty members can do much themselves to facilitate their own development and success and bring greater meaning and satisfaction into their professional experience. In her commentary, Melissa McDaniels, a recent doctoral graduate and early career scholar, emphasizes the importance of the notion of 'agency' – that is, the ability of doctoral students and early career faculty to take considerable responsibility for their own situations. I offer three suggestions relevant to this concept. First, doctoral students and early career academics need to be *proactive in seeking opportunities*. Aspiring and new faculty members need to take much responsibility for preparing themselves for their careers. They need to assess their strengths and capacities, and then make a priority to find faculty members and resources that can help address specific areas of weakness. Such personal assessment should occur on a regular basis, at least every six months.

Second, aspiring and new faculty should *be intentional in making connections*. I recommend finding a set of people to whom one can turn for advice, critique, and support. Relationships with a variety of colleagues enable these early career scholars to benefit from their diverse talents and perspectives. They can also do much to develop their sense of 'belonging' in academe by actively seeking opportunities to interact informally with faculty and student colleagues. Expressing interest in others' work can lead to the identification of reciprocal interests. Some doctoral students and early career faculty benefit from establishing small writing groups whose members hold each other accountable for producing work and encourage each other's progress. Some graduate students and new faculty members invite established faculty members to discuss lessons learned from their career paths. The possibilities are endless, but the point is specific. Aspiring and new faculty members can develop various strategies, on their own behalf, to diminish common concerns and enhance their likelihood of success, their sense of meaning, and their satisfaction in the academic career.

Third, aspiring and new faculty members *benefit from self-reflection*. They benefit from periodic occasions to consider their priorities and choices, their reasons for pursuing an academic career, the goals they want to achieve, and the paths they want to pursue. Such reflection requires designated time and often is aided by conversations with experienced faculty members. Self-reflection can be enhanced through the use of portfolios (another of the recommendations made by Laura Border). They are being used with increasing frequency in the United States to help students and faculty maintain records of their accomplishments and assess their strengths and weaknesses. Sharing one's portfolio with peers and invited faculty members can lead to conversations that enhance the strength of collegial relationships and highlight areas for further professional development.

Life as a faculty member is stimulating and meaningful. Yet, the challenges discussed in this chapter need to be addressed to ensure that new academics experience career progress and success. The responsibility to support aspiring and early career academics should be shared widely by administrators, academic developers, association leaders, and new academics themselves. With attention to these concerns, newcomers to the academy will be better able to fulfill expectations, balance work and life responsibilities, and find and create the kind of community that strengthens the quality and the meaning of academic work.

References

Anderson, M.S. and Swazey, J.P. (1998) 'Reflections on the graduate experience: An overview', in M. S. Anderson (ed.) *The Experience of Being in Graduate School: An Exploration, New Directions for Teaching and Learning, no. 101*. San Francisco: Jossey-Bass.

Austin, A.E. (2002a) 'Creating a bridge to the future: Preparing new faculty to face changing expectations in a shifting context', *Review of Higher Education* 26(2): 119–44.

Austin, A.E. (2002b) 'Preparing the next generation of faculty: Graduate school as socialization to the academic career', *Journal of Higher Education* 73(1): 94–122.

Austin, A.E. and McDaniels, M. (2006) 'Preparing the professoriate of the future: Graduate student socialization for faculty roles', in J.C. Smart (ed.) *Higher Education: Handbook of Theory and Research*, Vol. XXI. Dordrecht: Kluwer Academic Publishers.

Austin, A.E. and Rice, R.E. (1998) 'Making tenure viable: listening to early career faculty', *American Behavioral Scientist*, 41(5): 736–54.

Austin, A.E., Sorcinelli, M.D. and McDaniels, M. (2007) 'Understanding new faculty: Background, aspirations, challenges, and growth', in R. Perry and J. Smart (eds.) *The Scholarship of Teaching and Learning in Higher Education: An Evidence-based Perspective*. Dordrecht: Springer.

Becher, T. (1984) 'The cultural view', in B.R. Clark (ed.) *Perspectives on Higher Education: Eight Disciplinary and Comparative Views*. Berkeley and Los Angeles: University of California Press.

Becher, T. (1987) 'The disciplinary shaping of the profession', in B.R. Clark (ed.) *The Academic Profession: National, Disciplinary and Institutional Settings*. Berkeley and Los Angeles: University of California Press.

Boice, R. (1992) *The New Faculty Member: Supporting and Fostering Professional Development*. San Francisco: Jossey-Bass.

Clark, B.R. (1984) *The Higher Education System: Academic Organization in Cross-National Perspective*. Berkeley and Los Angeles: University of California Press.

Clark, B.R. (1987) *The Academic Life: Small Worlds, Different Worlds*. Princeton, NJ: The Carnegie Foundation for the Advancement of Teaching.

Fink, L.D. (1984) *The First Year of College Teaching, New Directions for Teaching and Learning, no. 17*. San Francisco: Jossey-Bass.

Gappa, J.M., Austin, A.E. and Trice, A.G. (2007) *Rethinking Faculty Work: Higher Education's Strategic Imperative*. San Francisco: Jossey-Bass.

Golde, C.M. and Dore, T.M. (2001) 'At cross-purposes: What the experiences of today's doctoral students reveal about doctoral education', Pew Charitable Trusts, available at: http://www.phd.survey.org.

Kuh, G.D. and Whitt, E.J. (1988) *The Invisible Tapestry: Culture in American Colleges and Universities*. ASHE-ERIC Higher Education Report no. 1. Washington, DC: Association for the Study of Higher Education.

Leslie, D. (2005) 'Faculty careers and flexible employment', paper presented at the annual meeting of the Association for the Study of Higher Education, Philadelphia, PA.

Mason, M.A. and Goulden, M. (2004) 'Do babies matter (Part II)? Closing the baby gap', *Academe*, 90(6): 10–15.

Menges, R.J. (1999) *Faculty in New Jobs*. San Francisco: Jossey-Bass.

Nerad, M., Aanerud, R. and Cerny, J. (2004) ' "So you want to become a professor!": Lessons from the PhDs-ten years later study', in D.H. Wulff and A.E. Austin, (eds.) *Paths to the Professoriate: Strategies for Enriching the Preparation of Future Faculty*. San Francisco: Jossey-Bass.

Nettles, M.T. and Millett, C.M. (2006) *Three Magic Letters: Getting to Ph.D.* Baltimore, MD: The Johns Hopkins University Press.

Nyquist, J.D., Manning, L., Wulff, D.H., Austin, A.E., Sprague, J., Fraser, P.K., Calcagno, C. and Woodford, B. (1999) 'On the road to becoming a professor: The graduate student experience', *Change*, 31(3): 18–27.

Olsen, D. and Near, J.P. (1994) 'Role conflict and faculty satisfaction', *Review of Higher Education*, 17(2): 179–95.

Rice, R.E. (1996) *Making a Place for the New American Scholar, New Pathways Inquiry, no. 1*. Washington, DC: American Association for Higher Education.

Rice, R.E., Sorcinelli, M.D. and Austin, A.E. (2000) *Heeding New Voices: Academic Careers for a New Generation, New Pathways Inquiry, no. 7*. Washington, DC: American Association for Higher Education.

Schuster, J. and Finkelstein, M. (2006) *The American Faculty*. Baltimore, MD: The Johns Hopkins University Press.

Solem, M.N. and Foote, K.E. (2004) 'Concerns, attitudes, and abilities of early career geography faculty', *Annals of the Association of American Geographers*, I(4): 889–912.

Taylor, E. and Antony, J.S. (2001) 'Stereotype threat reduction and wise schooling: Towards successful socialization of African American doctoral students in education', *Journal of Negro Education*, 69(3): 184–98.

Tierney, W.G. and Bensimon, E.M. (1996) *Promotion and Tenure: Community and Socialization in Academe*. Albany, NY: State University of New York Press.

Trower, C. (2005) 'How do junior faculty feel about your campus as a work place?' *Harvard Institutes for Higher Education: Alumni Bulletin*. Cambridge, MA: Harvard University Press.

U.S. Department of Education, National Center for Education Statistics (1988) *National Study of Postsecondary Faculty* (NSOPF: 88). Washington, DC: Author. http://nces.ed.gov/das.

U.S. Department of Education, National Center for Education Statistics (2004) *National Study of Postsecondary Faculty*. Washington, DC: Author. Available at: http://www.nces.ed.gov/das, retrieved 2 April 2006.

Walker, G.E., Golde, C.M., Jones, L., Bueschel, A.C. and Hutchings, P. (2008) *The Formation of Scholars: Rethinking Doctoral Education for the Twenty-First Century*. San Francisco: Jossey-Bass.

Ward, K. and Wolf-Wendel, L. (2004) 'Academic motherhood: Managing complex roles in research universities', *Review of Higher Education*, 27(2): 233–57.

Wulff, D.H., Austin, A.E., Nyquist, J.D., and Sprague, J. (2004) 'The development of graduate students as teaching scholars: A four-year longitudinal study', in D.H. Wulff and A.E. Austin (eds.) *Paths to the Professoriate: Strategies for Enriching the Preparation of Future Faculty*. San Francisco: Jossey-Bass.

3 Developing as a Researcher Post-PhD

Gerlese S. Åkerlind

▶ Author perspective

I started my academic career slowly and unintentionally, first as a Research Assistant and then as a non-academic 'Education Officer' in an education development centre (sometimes also called instructional or faculty development centres) at the Australian National University. This was a surprising outcome for someone whose studies had specialized in psychology, not education, but my early duties focused on designing student evaluation of teaching questionnaires, using the survey design skills I had developed as a student of psychology.

This situation continued for some 10 years, initially on rolling one-year appointments, but along the way I was accumulating academic experience and interests. I took on casual lecturing and tutoring positions outside the centre, while within the centre, the questionnaire-design I was engaged in involved clarifying with individual academics what their goals were as teachers. At the same time, I was analysing student questionnaire data that helped me to see the world from the students' perspective. As a consequence, I was developing unusual educational insights, knowledge and interests. Given the professional nature of my position, I was also supported by the centre in attending conferences on higher education research and development, and had access to the centre's library of books and journals. In effect, I was learning on the job, and my future research interests were developing.[1]

Then, in 1994, an academic position as an Associate Lecturer became available in the centre. Based on my teaching experience, familiarity with the educational literature and scholarly application of that literature to my own teaching practice as a sessional tutor/lecturer (work I had been documenting, evaluating and presenting at higher education conferences), I applied for the position and was successful, despite my lack of formal qualifications in education.

And so I became an academic, though it meant accepting a lower salary than for my non-academic position! At this point, research became a more consistent part of my life, and a couple of years later I decided to enrol in a part-time PhD (while continuing my full-time academic appointment). This was not for career reasons as such (although any chance of promotion to lecturer would be dependent upon having a doctorate), but because I felt intellectually isolated research-wise. I was the only person in Canberra researching in my particular area, which also meant that I was obliged to undertake my doctorate by distance in order to have supervisors with expertise in my area.

Being a doctoral student made me feel more comfortable about approaching researchers in the area outside my geographical region to form networks (an activity that was also completely justifiable as an Associate Lecturer, but my own personality meant that I was too shy and self-deprecating about being 'only' a Level A to do so). Being a doctoral student gave me a sense of legitimacy about approaching others that I didn't feel as an Associate Lecturer – a bit of a bizarre twist compared to those doctoral students who feel an academic appointment would give them a sense of legitimacy that they don't feel as a student. But as I discovered over time, a sense of legitimacy comes primarily from the inside, rather than the outside.

Undertaking a doctorate at this stage in my career was a very different experience to the earlier (uncompleted) doctorate that I had started in 1982. The first candidature had been motivated by a desire for the qualification (plus uncertainty about alternatives), with the research topic being of secondary concern. The second candidature was very much motivated by the topic, plus my desire to build a network of colleagues that would overcome my sense of isolation as a researcher; the qualification was a secondary consideration. So, I didn't undertake the doctorate to become an academic or a researcher. I was already an academic, albeit a lowly one. I was already a researcher, albeit a junior one. In fact, over time, my doctoral research came to feel like a subset of my larger research agenda, making completion of my thesis merely a milestone in my larger research plans. Unlike my first enrolment, this time the PhD was in no way an end in itself, and I recall starting work on my next journal article and future research plans the day after submitting my thesis – the actual submission feeling like no more than a step along the way.

Further academic appointments and promotions followed: Lecturer in 1998; Senior lecturer in 2004; Reader/Associate professor in 2009. In concert, my research productivity, professional service and leadership, and international reputation were growing. However, having spent most of my working life at one university, I yearned to experience other university cultures. Unfortunately, like many of us, my family commitments tied me to one place, so that taking up a long-term appointment elsewhere was not one of my options. However, in 2004, I was fortunate in obtaining a 6-month secondment (a secondment is when your existing university 'lends' you to another university) to Oxford University, to direct their Postgraduate Diploma in Learning and Teaching in Higher Education. This was to be the first of a series of secondments, accumulating to me spending 2–6 months working in Oxford every year from 2004–2008, while continuing my substantive appointment at the Australian National University when not in Oxford.

My research focus over the past decade has been on the nature of academic practice, as experienced by academics themselves: that is, why we as academics do what we do, what we are hoping to achieve, the meaning that teaching and research have for us, and how we go about growing and developing over time. I have had a particular focus on early career academics – that is postdoctoral researchers and those in their first academic appointment – as well as established academics.

One concern that I have found coming out of my research is the widespread lack of awareness that there is substantial variation in perceptions of academic work (including perceptions of teaching and research). Apart from an acknowledgement of disciplinary and career stage differences, there appears to be an implicit assumption (among academics, policy-makers and in much of the literature) that academics all have the same basic perception of what teaching and research involve and the same motivations for being an academic. This is definitely not the case. Furthermore, there is generally very little concern with the meaning or purpose that academic work holds for academics. Yet, this is what motivates us to do what we do, and what keeps us going when workload pressures are high or policy initiatives seem to reward other activities.

▶ Introduction

Since the 1990s, there has been rising concern internationally about the situation facing postdoctoral researchers, as the number of contract research positions has increased substantially without an equivalent increase in academic positions available. Although doctoral students are in a similar situation, unlike postdocs, their progress is more closely monitored and they are usually easy to identify as a group. In contrast, universities' ability to identify, and thus monitor, the progress of contract researchers in their institution is limited by the variable nature of these appointments.

Of the three categories of early career academics addressed in this book, postdoctoral researchers are the most neglected in terms of both investigative research and provision of structured professional development opportunities – perhaps partly because they are the most difficult to identify. As one of the small number of researchers in this area, I thought it important to focus this chapter on the nature of postdoctoral research positions, but at the same time I draw on my larger research into the development of early career academics more broadly. The particular studies that inform this chapter were undertaken during the early 2000s and include a questionnaire survey of over 1000 postdoctoral researchers in Australia (Thompson *et al.*, 2001), interviews with 22 postdoctoral researchers and 12 supervisors of postdocs[2] (Åkerlind, 2005, 2009), and interviews with 16 newly appointed academics and 12 established academics (Åkerlind 2008a, 2008b).

▶ Structure of the chapter

In this chapter, I adopt a two-part structure to explore key issues in postdoctoral researchers' preparation for academic careers. In part one, I start by mapping the postdoctoral research terrain, highlighting the substantial variability in types of contract research positions, duties performed by postdoctoral researchers, what postdocs hope to gain from these positions and how they see their future career. My aim is to highlight the substantial, often unacknowledged, variation in the nature of contract research positions, and in the intentions and expectations of contract researchers themselves. I see this emphasis as important in combating the default stereotypes of postdoctoral researchers (Åkerlind, 2009) that otherwise tend to dominate policy and practice in the area.

In part two, I move on to discuss similarly unacknowledged variation in what it means to develop as a researcher in academia. While this is particularly pertinent to research staff intending an academic career, it should be of relevance to all developing academics. In this section, I argue that researcher development can be thought of as having a 'how', 'what' and 'why' component, but that the why component is relatively neglected compared to the others. The how and what of researcher development are typically addressed through clarifying desired research skills, knowledge and outcomes, followed by identifying developmental activities that are most likely to provide the desired skills, knowledge and outcomes. In contrast, the why aspect is concerned with the underlying purpose of researcher development. A focus on the 'why' of researcher development provides an opportunity to consider developmental skills, knowledge and activities in terms of the larger purpose they are serving in developing academics' sense of themselves as researchers.

The postdoctoral research terrain

One of the most striking features of postdoctoral contract research positions is the variation in positions and responsibilities. They vary between and within countries, between and within institutions, and between and within disciplines. For instance, in Australia it is common for postdoctoral research positions to be academic positions, while in the UK it is more usual for them to be non-academic positions – though there is variation within both countries. While all countries have internal variation in whether postdoc positions are seen as representing the first step in an academic (or other) career, or as 'pre-career' training positions, in North America this is more commonly reflected in lack of full employee benefits and entitlements than in Australia or the UK (Association of American Universities, 1998; Helbeing et al., 1998; Ferber, 1999).

Consequently, a primary issue faced by studies of postdoctoral researchers is how to define the population, given the varied nature of contract research positions (Association of American Universities, 1998; Bazeley et al., 1996; Bryson, 1999; Helbeing et al., 1998; Thompson et al., 2001). As an example of the variability, my colleagues and I found the following range of position titles when surveying postdoctoral researchers in Australia: 'associate lecturer', 'postdoctoral fellow', 'postdoctoral research fellow', 'research associate', 'research officer', 'research fellow' and 'senior research associate'. This is even though all the positions were held by contract researchers with a PhD and on junior-level academic appointments. Such variation leads to inevitable complexities in providing career development support, especially as the variation is often not made explicit.

Our study also highlighted substantial variation within postdoc roles and responsibilities, even within the same disciplinary area, and not necessarily associated with any particular position title. These included:

- *being a completely independent researcher*, with one's own research funding (Fellowship) and full responsibility for the research design, analysis and write-up;

- *being a project manager*, with funding obtained by someone else (the chief/principal investigator) and the research goals determined by the project, but within those limits having complete independence and flexibility in decisions about research directions and the carrying out of the research;
- *being a research 'pair of hands'*, where the chief investigator and the project determines the nature of the research that is to be done, and the role of the postdoctoral researcher is simply to undertake the required experiments and analyses;
- *acting as a supervisor's aide*, where the postdoctoral researcher does whatever their supervisor (typically the chief investigator) asks of them, unrelated to any particular research project, including conference organisation, website design, student supervision, etc.

Although these role descriptions come from postdoctoral researchers themselves, the academics who supervise them confirm the same sort of variation (Åkerlind, 2005), distinguishing between those who are seen as assistants or trainees, and more independent postdocs who are seen as academic colleagues. Yet the distinction between these types of positions may not be obvious in a researcher's position title, salary or employment classification.

Furthermore, despite acknowledging this variation in roles with respect to any *specific* postdoc position, supervisors still tend to fall back on a stereotypical (one might even say romanticised) view of postdoctoral research when asked about the nature of postdoc positions *in general*, describing them in two primary ways:

- as a unique research opportunity – either a time to concentrate on research and writing in a way not possible at later stages of an academic career, and/or a time to follow research leads in a very open way, with fewer constraints than is possible later in one's career;
- as an opportunity to develop post-PhD – a time when budding academics set up their bona fides, develop research independence, create a name for themselves, develop the ability to gain research grants in their own right and show whether they have the ability to move into an academic career (Åkerlind, 2005, p. 34).

It seems that, although established academics acknowledge that there is substantial variation in the nature of postdoc positions (with consequent implications for the career development opportunities provided by those positions), they still tend to revert to stereotypical descriptions of these positions when thinking about them in a general way. This raises deep concerns about their ability to provide career advice as supervisors of postdoctoral researchers. Researchers on fellowships are not necessarily in a better position than grant-funded researchers, despite the higher status and independence of funded fellowships, as we found no difference in their predictions of long-term employment prospects (Thompson *et al.*, 2001).

Although social science research positions are on the increase (as described in Chapter 4), the majority of postdocs continue to be in science and technology fields. This means that not only has most of the (limited) research into postdoc career outcomes been focused on postdoctoral researchers in the sciences, but that the default image of a postdoctoral researcher is of a young, male scientist. In contrast, most postdocs in the social sciences are women, and they are much more likely to be in their late thirties or early forties than science postdocs, with associated issues of family and child care (described in further detail in Chapter 4). As one of the postdocs I interviewed stated:

As a woman in particular, I suppose, as someone who's got a career and family balancing acts to maintain, it's difficult to have a career because I select myself out of the race quite often for all sorts of reasons ... Because I am working half-time, because I choose to have children and look after them, have maternity leave and have babies. Life goes on. Life is more than a job and I have to put on quite strict limits to what I can do, what I'm capable of doing, in terms of I can't work 15 hours a day because I've got two small children to consider and a partner, and in the end those things are more important to me.

(Female postdoc, Community Environment)

In addition, we found social science postdocs more likely than those in the sciences to describe their research as independent rather than collaborative (though less likely than in humanities disciplines), with the associated issue of isolation. However, unlike the humanities, social science postdocs were just as likely as in the sciences to describe their research as supervised (Thompson *et al.*, 2001), putting emphasis back on the role of the chief/principal investigator in providing mentoring support – a role we have found to be a varied and unreliable one (Åkerlind, 2005).

Career development for postdoctoral researchers

What role do postdocs themselves see contract research positions playing in their careers? And what type of careers do they aspire to? While just over half of the social science researchers we surveyed desired an academic teaching and research position, 40 per cent wanted to remain as researchers (typically in universities). In my interviews with postdoctoral researchers, it was common for them to refer to academic positions as 'teaching' positions, in contrast to their current 'research' positions (in Australia, the default proportion of time devoted to research in academic positions is 30 per cent, with the remainder of an academic's time spent on teaching, administration and service). This raises the issue of why people who have embraced 6–10 years of primarily research activities (a 3–4 year PhD – the standard full-time allowance in Australia and the UK – followed by 1–3 postdoctoral positions) should be expected to look forward to reducing their research activity to 30 per cent of their time. While there are acknowledgements of the problems this can create in terms of the skill *preparation* process for academic careers, there is little acknowledgement of the problems is also creates as a *selection* process for people moving into academic teaching and research careers.

This teaching-and-research versus research-only separation in career aspirations is in accord with what postdocs themselves say about their desired career. In interviews with postdoctoral researchers, I found three ways in which they described their contract positions as contributing to their career (Åkerlind, 2005):

- as a stepping-stone or interim position towards a permanent teaching and research position;
- as being their career, with ongoing contract research positions the nature of their career;
- as a non-career opportunity to engage in research, with a focus on its intrinsic value to them, with career implications of lesser significance.

A stepping stone – Contract researchers who regarded their position as being an interim one, sitting between their PhD and a permanent academic post, referred to their postdoc period as a time of growth, development and learning. This represents the traditional view of the postdoctoral period as a time for broadening the skills developed during doctoral study and developing greater independence as a researcher:

> As a student, you are still learning, so you look to other people
> to help you with that. [As a postdoc] I think probably all the same
> things, just not as much, or perhaps not in as much depth, like
> an apprentice to that [an academic appointment]. It's like an
> in-between stage.
>
> (Female postdoc, Community Environment)

Most of these researchers felt confident of getting another postdoc
position after their current one, if necessary, however few felt confident of making the shift to a permanent academic position. Also, some
of these researchers, in their second or later appointment, felt that
they had already gained as much research independence and breadth
of skills as could be expected during the postdoc period and so they
no longer felt engaged in further development, but were simply marking time. They and their supervisors were also concerned that if they
hadn't made the shift to an academic position by their third contract,
it would become increasingly difficult to do so.

Being their career – Some postdoctoral researchers envisaged getting ongoing contract research positions for the rest of their working
lives, even though they knew there was no guarantee of doing so. In
the UK and Europe, these hopes are supported by the recent introduction of a European Charter for Researchers and Code of Conduct
for the Recruitment of Researchers (European Commission, 2005),
designed to provide more sustainable career prospects for researchers.
In Australia, the possibility of ongoing contract research positions is
really only possible in particular fields, such as medicine or agriculture,
due to the types of funding sources available.

Unlike other contract researchers, who commonly associated a new
research position with a change in location, these postdocs seemed
to expect that, as long as they could keep getting grants, they could
stay in their current institutional or geographical location. So, in this
regard, they experienced a greater sense of stability than many other
contract researchers, despite the shared insecurity about ongoing funding or employment. Not surprisingly, a primary aspect of their work as a
researcher was to write applications for grants to continue funding their
research. In this, their view contrasts with that of other postdocs that
ongoing contract research positions were simply not available.

A non-career opportunity – Other researchers viewed their positions primarily as an opportunity to engage in full-time research,

with career implications of lesser concern to them. In the interview sample, these postdocs were all in funded research fellowship positions of some sort, in contrast to less independent grant-funded or institution-funded positions. However, these researchers expressed uniformly strong pessimism about the chances of finding another such position after their current fellowship. They had chosen to take up a research fellowship because of their commitment to research, not because they thought the fellowship would provide any career benefits:

> It means a chance to focus on some of my own research. And it means a job, because I'm not likely to have a career after it...I don't see what comes next. Theoretically, they [postdoc positions] are for you to lead into academia or an academic appointment somewhere, but I don't see how at this point.
>
> (Female postdoc, Community Environment)

Sadly, given their pessimism about obtaining future research positions, these postdocs typically had difficulty identifying any other employment options that they would find acceptable.

> On the one hand, I can say it wasn't a choice. I had to apply for a [Fellowship] because it was the only hope I had left to stay in academia. There was no other choice available to me that I could see.
>
> (Female postdoc, Community Environment, quoted above)

▷ The how, what and why of researcher development: developmental activities, outcomes and intentions

Having outlined common variation in research staff roles, purposes and career goals, I now turn to a consideration of variation in approaches to development as a researcher. While this is of particular relevance to research staff, it is an important issue for all early career academics. Consequently, I draw on a range of academic views and research perspectives in considering this issue.

Development as a researcher (and as an academic) can be viewed from different perspectives. In this section, I group these perspectives into three categories that I call the 'how', 'what' and 'why' of researcher development. The how of development focuses on the developmental *activities* available to researchers, what they *do* in order to develop. The what of development focuses on the *behaviours and outcomes* of researchers, and what an established researcher does that is different to a novice researcher. In contrast, the why of development focuses on the *intentions or goals* underlying individuals' development. Each category is illustrated in further detail below, with a particular emphasis on the why of development. I argue that while this is the least visible aspect of researcher development, it underpins the other two aspects.

The how of researcher development – activities and support

Developmental activities available to postdocs typically consist of both formal and informal support, plus 'on-the-job' learning. Formal programs of support for contract researchers are more common in the UK than Australia or North America, and have been illustrated in detail elsewhere (eg Gough, 2009). Informal support is common from mentors and peers but is highly variable in nature. During my interviews with chief investigators and other supervisors of postdocs (Åkerlind, 2005), I asked them to describe how they supported their postdoctoral researchers in preparing for academic careers. They mentioned the following activities:

- providing their postdocs with opportunities to develop additional skills – e.g. through undergraduate teaching, supervision of research students, grant writing, and attendance at skill development courses and academic conferences;
- enhancing postdocs' research productivity and profile – e.g. by encouraging them to speak at conferences and putting them as first author on publications;
- providing direct support for finding another position – e.g. by bringing new positions or grants to their postdocs' attention, or by mentioning their postdocs to people with jobs available; and
- general advice, support and networking.

However, the support provided was typically ad hoc and unstructured, and entirely up to the good will and mentoring skills of each individual supervisor. In addition, there are factors that may prevent postdocs from taking advantage of some of these opportunities for informal support, including uncertainty about the responsibilities of supervisors with respect to contract researchers. This lack of clarity inhibited some researchers from approaching their supervisors for discussions of either career or research issues. A number added that as PhD students they had felt less inhibited than as postdocs because the role and responsibilities of supervisors had been clearer.

> I have also begun to and will continue to seek lots of help and other people to talk to. Part of the [funded Fellowship] process is that the Fellow has to be supported in the research environment, in other words, through collegiality and supervision and networks and those sorts of things. Well, when I first started, I was officially in one place and physically at another in terms of the departments on campus. So I had to sort that out on my own, and that really sent home the message to me that you are on your own. The advice was, we'll cross the t's and dot the i's, but there is no talk of real engagement with what I am doing or interested in. It was just, oh, well, you are a [funded Fellow]. You've got to have money; bring money. There is no talk of what are your aspirations as an individual or how can we help you, or what do you need from us. It's all, you're good for our books ... I actively sought a mentor. I thought, I'm not going to get through this on my own, I really need some help. So I spoke to a colleague ... But I strongly feel that I don't know whether I have a right to ask for any [advice] because I don't have, I am not a student any more. Students have a right to that sort of mentoring and negotiate it with whoever it is. But I didn't want to take up any of his time because I am not a student.
>
> (Female postdoc, Community Environment)

In addition to support from others, there are also many opportunities for experiential or on-the job opportunities for development, but once again these may be highly variable between positions, and are not well documented. Given the widespread emphasis on postdoctoral positions as research-only positions, postdocs in our Australian study reported engaging in a surprising amount of non-research activity, in particular: research student supervision (52 per cent of postdocs), lecturing (39 per cent), tutoring (25 per cent) and conference organisation (26 per cent – Thompson et al., 2001). Less commonly (5–8 per cent), reported:

- Committee work
- Reviewing/editing
- Examining
- University administration

- Presenting at conferences/seminars
- Preparing grant applications
- Staff or group supervision
- Consultancies.

In our survey, only 13 per cent of contract researchers did not report engaging in additional duties, and just over 50 per cent estimated that such additional duties took up more than 20 per cent of their time.

> Beyond that [research and publication] obviously I have a professional role on the board of a journal. That takes time, going to meetings in Sydney, refereeing papers for journals. I am an office holder in the local branch of the History Society and therefore have all these professional functions there. I organized a conference last year and am involved in another one now. I also have a departmental role. I have done some teaching. I have taught and supervised at Honours[3] level. I have done a little postgraduate supervision. I have obviously given guest lectures and tutorials from time to time. I am co-organizer of our own seminar series in this department. I see the postdoc as primarily a research role; that is basically what I am being paid to do. But I think that it is important to play other roles within the department and the profession, and also community roles as well of course … I also see the postdoc as a kind of professional training. It is important to keep one's hand in as a teacher, as someone who organizes seminars and conferences, and that applies to those other community roles and professional, too … because that is part of what training as an academic is about.
>
> (Female postdoc, History)

This indicates that contract researchers may commonly receive a higher degree of experience in a breadth of academic related duties than is usually recognized. Unfortunately, opportunities for such experience are typically available in an ad hoc rather than systematic way, with substantial variation in opportunities between research positions. (I should also note here that what some supervisors regard as a developmental opportunity for postdocs, some postdocs regard as unpaid exploitation.)

The what of researcher development – behaviours and outcomes
What distinguishes a less developed from more developed researcher in terms of actions and achievements? How does what one does as a

Table 3.1 A model for the development of research expertise (from Rowley and McCulloch, 1999, p.108)

Stage/role	Apprentice	Member	Expert	Leader
Networking activity	Entering the fray	Establishing national networks	Being part of natural (sic) networks	Building and strengthening networks and international reputation
Scope of research activity	Single project, e.g. PhD	Two or three core projects with participation in one or two others	Leading large funded research projects	Participation in multinational research collaborations
Dissemination	First articles, First conference presentations	Regular contributor to a focused set of conferences and journals; Occasional reviewing and refereeing	Possibly higher quality publications; Editorial board membership; Regular refereeing	Editor of journal, monograph series, etc; Invited contributor, keynote speaker; Contributions in both academic and business/ professional arenas
Involvement with academic community	Becoming acquainted	Collaborative work; Supervision of PhD students	Valued as an experienced researcher; Attendance at international conferences; Growing network of contacts; PhD external examination	Guru, with whom others wish to be associated; Expenses-paid invitations to international conferences; Regular contact with researchers in several countries

researcher change as one develops? This perspective on researcher development may be illustrated through Rowley and McCulloch's (1999) succinct model of how what one does as a researcher changes as one becomes more established (see Table 3.1).

Rowley and McCulloch see the 'Apprenticeship' stage as typical of 'research students and junior members of academic staff'; this would include postdocs and those in their first academic appointment. The 'Member' stage is seen as typical of 'most academic staff and research fellows'. The 'Expert' stage is seen as representative of those whose research contribution has been recognized through an Associate Professorship (sometimes also called Readership in the UK and Australia) or Professorship. The 'Leader' stage is reserved for the academic crème de la crème, those 'whose reputation permeates beyond their own national and possibly disciplinary community'.

Rowley and McCulloch write from a UK context, which is also largely relevant to the Australian context. While I would argue that few academics in Australia could expect a professorship without meeting most of the 'leader' criteria, as well as the 'expert' criteria, the overall progression rings true. However, in Australia and the UK, Associate Professorships and Professorships are achieved by only a minority of academics (approx 20 per cent and 10 per cent, respectively) during their careers, so the implication of Table 3.1 is that the majority of academics will only achieve 'Member' level in their research activities.[4]

The why of researcher development – goals and intentions

In contrast to the externally observable behaviour and activity focus of the preceding perspectives, the why of development takes a more internal and intentions-focused perspective. This may be illustrated through the outcomes of interviews I conducted with newly-appointed as well as established academics (Åkerlind, 2008b), investigating the meaning that their development as a researcher holds for them, what growing and developing feels like, and what they were trying to achieve through the developmental activities they engaged in. I found four primary aspects to academics' sense of development as researchers, in terms of an increase in their:

- confidence
- recognition
- productivity
- sophistication.

In brief, you could say that academics envisage or experience development as an increasing sense of knowing what they are doing as a researcher (confidence), having others become aware of what they are doing as they establish themselves in a community of researchers (recognition), an increase in the amount and efficiency of research that they do (productivity), and that in addition to doing more research they also do better research (sophistication). I elaborate on each of these below.

Becoming confident as a researcher – Academics who described their development as researchers in a way that I have categorized as 'increasing confidence' described the development of an internal sense of confidence and competence, a sense that they know what they're doing and that they are on the right track. This might involve acquiring the skills required to do research successfully, such as learning how best to choose a research topic, to give conference papers and write-up research, but it might also involve becoming clear as to what research direction to follow for the future. For instance,

> I'm less naive and more self-confident, as far as being able to resist the fashions that come and go in the research field. If you're young, a student or an undergraduate, your teachers will say, look at this theory, this is the latest theory … When I was writing my PhD, my supervisor said to me, you have to look at this approach … I did all of those things suggested for my research and tried to make use of them. Now I would never allow myself to be swayed by current trends in fashion. I am much more, I think, self-confident as far as determining what approach I'm going to take doing research.
>
> (Male academic, Community Forestry)

> There are so many ways in which I think I could take my research, and I haven't actually worked out which way is the best way of doing it at the moment. I mean, I am at a point now where I am quite undecided about the best way of growing in research because I haven't decided what I want to grow to be … I haven't decided whether I want to try and develop a very strong specialization and work towards getting a book contract or whether I really want to do more articles … you know, which I think is going to be beneficial to my long-term goals.
>
> (Female academic, Law)

A developing sense of confidence that you are on the right track with your research was commonly associated with one or more successful experiences. For example:

> Yeah, growth, I suppose, really comes, primarily it comes out of succeeding.
>   I was very lucky, because my first conference was a success, so that made a tremendous difference to my morale really.

The unfortunate corollary is that unsuccessful experiences can rob one of confidence,

> I think I've gone backwards actually. When I came down here, I knew what I wanted to do, I was very keen ... and then I realized after a while that this thing had sort of been done, and I had to find something else. This [new topic] is a topic that someone else suggested to me, and I haven't really got into it yet. So, I think maybe my research skills have gone back a bit.
>
> (Male academic, Economics)

Becoming recognized as a researcher – While developing an *internal* sense of confidence and competence as a researcher is essential, most academics also desire *external* recognition of their competence by others in their field. This is where becoming part of a research community is particularly important. Academics who described their development as researchers in a way that I have categorized as 'becoming recognized' described coming to feel recognized as a member of a community, building a reputation in the community, and having their ideas picked up and used by others. For instance,

> I think one of those things I've done is that I haven't been bashful about trying to make contact with established people in my area of study around the world. That's a really good thing to do, and to follow that up. Because that is also part of rethinking yourself as a colleague of theirs [vs a student].
>
> (Female academic, Women's Studies)

> I had to learn to give papers at conferences and go public with ideas, and I didn't enjoy that...The only way in which I have met people is through a particular conference...I really do need that kind of support from these people who are in contact with me now

> to make me feel like someone…because I haven't and didn't have a public face.
>
> (Female academic, Classics)

This focus on external recognition may extend from the desire to be recognized as a colleague, equal to others in the research community, to the desire to be recognized as a leader and become famous in the field. Such external recognition is seen as being achieved through the passage of time and accumulation of experience as a researcher in the field, as well as by producing a certain quality of work:

> Part of it is just people. I mean, it is just having more of your research out there and people responding to it, and responding to it positively. So, therefore I need to get to know people, and do enough research to be able to send myself to international conferences where people see my face again and again. If you want to say that you are established in a certain area, first you have to do that for quite a long time for people to recognize you, and also you have to do a significant quality work to say that you are a pioneer.
>
> (Male acedemic, Engineering)

Becoming more productive as a researcher – Many academics experience a quantitative element to being a researcher. Academics who described their development as researchers in a way that I have categorized as 'increasing productivity' described achieving more publications, more conference presentations, more funding, larger research projects, more PhD students, etc.

> So, I try to think quantitatively…you start thinking, 'Well, in the next year I must publish an article. I don't know which article, but at least one. And I must give one or two papers somewhere, and possibly go to a conference, and start a new project.'
>
> (Female academic, History)

As an aside, I feel it is important to note, for the benefit of early career researchers, that increasing productivity is not necessarily an issue of quantity versus quality, but quantity *and* quality. That is, a large quantity of high-quality work is obviously worth more to one's reputation than a low quantity of high-quality work, but questions of whether more publications of lower quality are worth more or less than fewer publications of a higher quality can lead early career academics in the wrong direction. Journal editors will always push for a paper that is the best it can be. At the same time, this should not be confused with perfectionism. For instance,

> Now, I think that it is important, very, very important to maintain rigour, but the problem with rigour is that you become excessively concerned about the quality of your work and it is very hard sometimes to produce things…Research has to be rigorous, but you also have to curtail a natural tendency to hold your work back, and try to produce within a relatively respectable timeframe.
>
> (Female academic, Law)

From the perspective of the academics I interviewed, quantitative increases in productivity could involve the *simple accumulation* of research activity over time and/or an *increase in the rate* of productivity through improved efficiency and the beneficial impact of one area of activity on another. Sadly, issues of quantity of research output are often associated with a sense of performance anxiety and workload pressure, whether one is on a short-term contract or tenured appointment.

> Academics have to work extremely hard. The more senior they are, the harder they seem to work. It doesn't get easier for people, it just gets to the point where they have got to work harder and more efficiently…You do learn how to use time better, and perhaps to focus a bit more, but that's just because you are more experienced.
>
> (Female academic, History)

> [When I think of developing, I think of] generally horribly pragmatic things, promotions and all that sort of thing … That is something that really bothers me because you have to kind of do all that stuff just for success. It's that kind of management ethos where it seems that you have to measure what you're doing to aid your quality. So, I try to think quantitatively. It's that whole kind of ethos, which does affect the way that you perceive what you're doing … These are short-term goals where, on the one hand, you have something to show what you are doing which looks good on your annual report, but also on the other hand, sometimes there are good spin-offs from those things too, and you might

actually get something out of it ... That is the positive side of it, but the danger I think is that one gets overtaken, not by growth, but by outcomes [things you can put on your CV], because one knows that is what people look for, that's how they form their judgements.

(Female academic, History, quoted above)

Becoming more sophisticated as a researcher – For some academics, developing as a researcher involves not just doing more of the same (even if faster and faster), but also doing things differently, in a qualitatively better way. Interestingly, not all of the academics I interviewed experienced or expected to experience such growth in sophistication. Many academics felt that their development as researchers had stopped at the completion of their PhD, postdoc or first academic appointment. Only some academics felt the potential for ongoing development as researchers throughout their career. This group, who described their development in a way that I have categorized as 'increasing sophistication', described developing greater sophistication of thinking, becoming more theoretically aware, increasing breadth of knowledge, greater depth of understanding, increasing awareness of wider perspectives, being better able to resolve issues and having an overall enhanced capacity to do research. To illustrate:

Personally, I feel that I have become more sophisticated at the sort of research that I am doing ... that your growth enhances your functioning ... Personal growth makes you much more skilful in research. It therefore enables you to perhaps identify research issues more saliently, that is, identify the important research issues. It might help you to pursue that research more effectively ... In those ways you become enhanced as a researcher, it enhances your capacity to do that.

(Male academic, Archaeology)

But improving work in a qualitative sense is hard to measure and hard to pin down...in terms of that kind of improvement of sophistication of thinking, I would say, 'Yes, I've improved during my career.'... Simplistically, it means being theoretically aware, being reflective about what you're doing, trying to think about the assumptions you are making in your research and writing, trying to be aware of that, as well as actually producing something ... So, I'll be thinking, 'What are the assumptions that I'm making?'

(Female academic, History)

What is the route to greater sophistication as a researcher?

Keeping up with the literature, revising what you're doing, searching, looking around you at what other people are doing. I ask colleagues what they think of what I'm doing. I publish and have colleagues confirm if they think what I'm doing is worthwhile, or whatever, get their impressions ... To continue growing, I have to continue to research in that area and to continue evaluating what I am doing, and seeking evaluation from others of what I'm doing.

(Female academic, Languages)

Becoming more sophisticated in my science. Becoming a better archaeologist, more capable of comprehending archaeological material. It involves acquiring material that is more powerful, whether that's becoming better at statistics or reading, and pursuing some additional explanatory models, whatever that might represent... It's fairly clear to me that I am circulating amongst a series of issues which for me are very important. So I keep coming back to them. But I think that in most instances I keep coming back at a more sophisticated level. I don't think it's a directional thing. I'm not going anywhere except acquiring extra skills in what I do.

(Male academic, Archaeology)

Contrasting the how, what and why

Each of these perspectives on development (how, what and why) opens up different ways of thinking about development as researchers. But I would argue that a focus on the how and what without an accompanying focus on the why can take the purpose out of development, making it task-focused rather than meaning-focused. Furthermore, a focus on activities alone can hide the fact that the same developmental activity can be understood in very different ways, and seen as appropriate to very different goals. For instance, with all four of the 'why' categories of developmental intentions that I described above, academics talked about attending conferences as one way of achieving their developmental goals. However, their intentions in undertaking that activity, and their awareness of possible developmental outcomes from the activity, varied substantially depending on *why* they were doing it, i.e. on their developmental intentions.

For example, for those focused on developing confidence as a researcher, conference attendance was engaged in as a route to that developing confidence, where giving a successful conference paper was seen as a way to improve one's confidence. In contrast, for those focused on developing recognition as a researcher, the primary aim of conference attendance was to network with other researchers, in order to become known and recognized by others in the field. For those focused on increasing research productivity, the purpose of conference attendance was more about completing another paper, finding potential research collaborators and potential funding opportunities. For those developing increasing sophistication as a researcher, conference attendance was seen more as an opportunity to discuss and receive feedback from others on their research and research area, in order to improve their knowledge and understanding of the area. (This may be contrasted with those focused on increasing research confidence, where the aim of conference feedback on their research is more for affirmation from others than for developing their thinking and understanding.) Of course, academics can have multiple goals in attending a conference, we're not necessarily restricted to one purpose. But postdocs being advised to attend a particular conference by their supervisor or mentor, can't assume that they both have the same underlying purpose in mind.

Similarly, a focus on researcher behaviours and outcomes can hide different academic purposes underlying those behaviours and outcomes. For instance, Brew (2001) has shown that highly successful academics (those performing at Rowley and McCulloch's expert stage) can have quite different overall intentions underlying the research they do and their reasons for being a researcher. According to Brew, and in line with my own research (Åkerlind, 2008a), academics' focus in conducting research can vary from seeing research as a personal voyage of discovery that informs the life issues being faced by the researcher to thinking about their research more in terms of the funding, prestige and recognition that it accrues for them. Alternatively, research can be experienced more in terms of a problem-solving activity or a process of discovery.

► Implications

For more than any other category of early career academic, the position of contract researchers is an uncertain and variable one. They may be on academic or non-academic appointments, they may be strongly supervised or largely independent, regarded by others as academic trainees or as colleagues, engaged solely in research activities or in a broad range of academic work. They also experience less structured sources of mentoring and development than either doctoral students or newly appointed academics. At the same time, in common with other types of early career academics, what development support is available focuses more on the how and what of development as a researcher than on the why.

What this downplaying of the why fails to acknowledge is that the same research behaviours, outcomes and developmental activities may be undertaken for very different reasons. Variation between academics in their developmental intentions and their reasons for conducting research is something that is rarely discussed or acknowledged. Yet, academics are not all the same, our work has different meaning and purpose for us as individuals. Ignoring this is like trying to take purpose and meaning out of academic work, a dangerous approach when it is the meaning our work has for us that intrinsically motivates so many academics. Counting on extrinsic motivations alone is likely to encourage the growing sense of fragmentation and demoralization that has been so consistently reported in recent studies of academics (see Chapter 1).

For early career academics reading this book, my hope is that you will now more actively consider your developmental goals and opportunities in terms of your underlying purpose and intentions as a researcher. Hopefully, taking the opportunity this chapter provides to reflect on what you are trying to achieve as a researcher will facilitate decision-making about your developmental priorities (especially when you are faced with conflicting pressures and high workloads) and encourage you to search for integration and synergy across the developmental activities that you engage in.

Given that variation in purpose is so frequently implicit, I would also encourage you to talk to your colleagues about their approaches to development, asking not just what they do, but why they are doing it (i.e., what they hope to gain from it). For instance, try asking your colleagues what they focus on when they go to conferences and you may be surprised by the variation in response. Gaining a sense of what those around you are trying to achieve personally with their research will have many insights to offer you as you plan your own career and developmental activities.

For policy-makers, academic developers and academic mentors reading this book, my hope is to expand your sense of the range of issues that need to be considered when encouraging early career academics' development as researchers. I would suggest that the developmental activities that you support *not* be considered in isolation from developmental purposes. Adding opportunities for those you mentor or have responsibility for to actively reflect on their developmental goals and to be exposed to the varying goals of others would be valuable.

One thing that is clear from my research is that not all researchers experience all of the aspects of development that I have outlined. Even senior academics may experience development solely in terms of increasing confidence and recognition, without a sense of ongoing development in productivity and sophistication. This means that some academics also experience their development as complete at an early point in their careers – some time between their PhD and first academic position. At the point that they feel confident and recognised enough, no further development is experienced or envisaged. In contrast, others see an endless potential for ongoing development in their sophistication as a researcher.

This implies that simple experience as a researcher does not guarantee maximizing one's development as a researcher. That depends more upon how each individual experiences research, why they are interested in research and why they want to be a researcher. One of the hidden aspects of academic careers and preparation for academia is individual variation in reasons for being a researcher and conducting research, and associated variation in what we are trying to achieve through our research. Making this hidden aspect of academic work more explicit when preparing future academics can only be beneficial.

Notes

1. Australia has five levels of academic appointment, Levels A-E, with the following titles: Associate Lecturer – Level A; Lecturer – Level B; Senior lecturer – Level C; Associate Professor or Reader – Level D; Professor – Level E. It is not uncommon to refer to academics by their classification level rather than their classification title, i.e. to say 'I'm a Level D' rather than 'I'm an Associate Professor'.
2. In Australia, all contract researchers have a formal supervisor in a line management role. In the case of researchers appointed on funded grants, this would be the chief investigator on the grant proposal; in the case of researchers on funded Fellowships, an academic would be assigned as supervisor.

3. Honours is a distinctive part of Australian higher education. It refers to an optional additional component of a bachelor's degree, typically involving an additional, separate year of study in a particular discipline, with a smallish research project and associated thesis/dissertation as well as coursework. While this is officially still part of one's undergraduate work, the most common practice in Australia is for students to graduate with a three-year Bachelor's degree rather than a four-year degree with Honours. Until recently, an honours year was the most common route to subsequent doctoral study, but with the post-war massification of higher education, it has also become a way of distinguishing oneself from other graduates in the general job market. This contrasts with the UK, where a small research project is commonly integrated into the undergraduate degree, and an honours versus pass degree is based on the quality of undergraduate work, not enrolment in a separate program.

4. Given the different definitions of Associate Professor and Professor in the UK/Australia vs North America, my best translation of Table 3.1 to the North American academic classification system is that the apprenticeship stage would be relevant to research students, postdocs and assistant professors; the member stage to associate professors; and the expert and leader stages to professors.

▶ References

Åkerlind, G.S. (2005) 'Postdoctoral researchers: Roles, functions and career prospects', *Higher Education Research and Development*, 24: 21–40.

Åkerlind, G.S. (2008a) 'An academic perspective on research and being a researcher: An integration of the literature', *Studies in Higher Education*, 33: 17–32.

Åkerlind, G.S. (2008b) 'Growing and developing as a university researcher', *Higher Education*, 55: 241–54.

Åkerlind, G.S. (2009) 'Postdoctoral research positions as preparation for an academic career', *International Journal for Researcher Development*, 1(1): 84–96.

Association of American Universities (1998) *Report and Recommendations: Committee on Postdoctoral Education*. Washington, DC: Association of American Universities.

Bazeley, P., Kemp, L., Stevens, K., Asmar, C., Grbich, C., Marsh, H., and Bhathal, R. (1996) *Waiting in the Wings: A Study of Early Career*

Academic Researchers in Australia, ARC commissioned report no. 50. Canberra: Australian Government Publishing Service.

Brew, A. (2001) 'Conceptions of research: A phenomenographic study', *Studies in Higher Education*, 26: 271–85.

Bryson, C. (1999) 'Contract research: The failure to address the real issues', *Higher Education Review*, 31: 29–49.

European Commission (2005) *The European Charter for Researchers and the Code of Conduct for the Recruitment of Researchers*. EUR 21620, available at: www.europa.eu.int/eracareers/europeancharter.

Ferber, D. (1999) 'Getting to the front of the bus', *Science*, 285: 1514–17.

Gough, M. (2009) 'Evaluating the impact of newer researcher training and development: Which direction forward?', report of a joint seminar, *International Journal for Researcher Development*, 1(2): 57–67.

Helbeing, C., Verhoef, M. and Wellington, C. (1998) 'Finding identity and voice: A national survey of Canadian postdoctoral fellows', *Research Evaluation*, 7(1): 53–60.

Rowley, J. and McCulloch, A. (1999) 'Developing research capacity: moving on', *Scottish Journal of Adult and Continuing Education*, 5: 106–16.

Thompson, J., Pearson, M., Åkerlind, G., Hooper, J. and Mazur, N. (2001) *Postdoctoral Training and Employment Outcomes*, EIP report 01/10. Canberra: Higher Education Division, Department of Education Training and Youth Affairs.

4 Employment Patterns In and Beyond One's Discipline

David Mills

▶ Author perspective

I have long felt a slight unease with my anthropological relations. Why did my colleagues take their disciplinary affiliation so seriously? How could a community of scholars committed to understanding 'identity' claims remain so defensive about their own sense of belonging? The question troubled me, but no-one had a straight answer. After reading for a PhD in Social Anthropology at the School of Oriental and African Studies, carrying out fieldwork in Uganda, I began to get restless. I was determined to make sense of the deeply-held intellectual identifications I had encountered as a postgraduate, and the antagonistic attitudes existing between cognate social sciences. Like many a questing teenager, I decided to go travelling.

En route I have held lectureships (professorships in North America) in four different disciplines (Development Studies, Anthropology, Cultural Studies and now Education), and I am unlikely to return 'home'. Perhaps I am guilty of disciplinary tourism. But perhaps all academics should occasionally apply for an intellectual travel permit, and recognize that. I look forward to the social sciences becoming increasingly permeable, retaining their differences yet strengthened by their shared engagements with 'society'.

A less visible aspect of my academic identity is that I am intrigued by – and committed to – the process of university reform. While universities depend on the idealism, some of their inhabitants care too much. In one of his last books, Bourdieu captures this problem in his description 'of the tendency of the scholarship boy towards awe-struck hyper-identification with the educational system' (2004, p. 91). Rather than try to resist, as he puts it, the 'effects of academic thinking', I have constantly, and perhaps foolishly, tried to shape that system of thinking. My 'hyper-identification' has led me to repeatedly get involved in what many have come to call educational development. However, I dislike the terminology and its evolutionist

71

connotations, and try not to use it. It is another affiliation in a world too full of affiliations.

Like many a new lecturer, I took my first teaching post intensely seriously, and at the expense of my publications. I went on to a second post in Manchester, and then to a research fellowship. But I couldn't ignore teaching: it opened up too many intellectual questions. I found myself moonlighting for a national network of anthropologists interested in teaching, writing their policy briefings, and co-organizing their final conference. When the network turned into a nationally-funded 'Subject Centre' in 2000, I was offered a half-time lectureship at the University of Birmingham's Department of Cultural Studies and Sociology combined with a role as an academic coordinator at C-SAP (Centre for Sociology, Anthropology and Politics), part of the UK's Higher Education Academy network.[1] When the department was 'restructured' (read closed down) after its research output was rated poorly in the national research assessment exercise, I found myself dependent on a series of short-term grants on projects led by others. I then experienced the underside of the social sciences' renaissance – a period characterized by insecurity, fragmentation, and a shortage of intellectual autonomy. The flexibility suits some, but the lack of status and recognition is less appealing. Things weren't looking good.

And then things changed again. Oxford received national funding for a 'centre of excellence' in the preparation for academic practice. I successfully applied for a University lectureship in Pedagogy and the Social Sciences that was partly created to support developmental work within the Social Sciences with doctoral students. So I continue to wear two very different institutional hats at the same time – and try not to drop either.

Introduction

> Just everyone bangs on about publications all the time and they're right, if you want to get a job you need to do it but I don't want to have just a functional experience. I'm not a utilitarian character where my goal in life is to be Mr. Fantastic Professor. My goal is to have a rounded life. I enjoy teaching and I like the students and I have to sacrifice that goal I guess.
>
> (Howard, Teaching fellow at an elite UK university, cited in Mills, 2005)

> The proto-body of an academic is male, unattached, and 100 per cent committed to work.
>
> (Nanda, Anthropology Lecturer, 2005)

This chapter makes no apologies for using the case of one small and seemingly marginal discipline – anthropology – to illustrate the changing shape of the social sciences in the UK, and the academic employment possibilities and pressures that result. Complementing Chapter 2's focus on the US, my analysis seeks to show how 'big picture' statistical trends are made meaningful in UK universities and for individual academics in their working lives, professional commitments and scholarly vocations.

I draw on two different sets of research projects in my analysis. One is a demographic review of the social sciences (Mills *et al.*, 2006), that revealed an increasing movement of research and lecturing staff[2] between disciplines and specialisms, along with growing numbers of contract research staff in the social sciences, many employed in interdisciplinary environments. This picture is then echoed in a more focused study of a population of 700 previous students who completed their doctorates in UK anthropology departments between the early 1990s and 2003 (Spencer *et al.*, 2005).[3] Tracking down the email contacts of 600 of these (using both personal networks and the omnipresent Google), more than 300 responded and completed on-line questionnaires. We then interviewed 40 of these respondents, representing a diversity of training institutions and subsequent career paths, both within and outside universities.[4] They were a cosmopolitan group, with less than half being UK nationals, almost 60 per cent female, and an average age on completion of 34. Only a minority had followed a 'classic' career path of pursuing a doctorate immediately after an undergraduate degree. Many brought with them extensive work and policy experience, particularly in health and development.

Our demographic data on these anthropological careers highlighted the increasing number of researchers involved in non-academic consultancy, policy and applied research. This was a relatively new trend for the UK discipline. Universities have long shaped, and been shaped by, the national and transnational economies in which they are located. Today postgraduate qualifications and high-level research analytical skills are increasingly in demand beyond the university. One-third of our cohort who went into non-academic employment found work as independent research consultants. Employment opportunities in interdisciplinary and applied research environments are also promoting academic migrations across, as well as out of, the social sciences. This diversity of research opportunities mirrors the increasing 'flexibilization' of research labour in the social sciences more generally. Universities are competing to maximize research income from a range of national and international funding sources, whether corporations, private and public sources – all driving what one could call the new 'research economy'.

In this chapter, I use these findings to reflect on the relationship between one's disciplinary and institutional location as a doctoral student and one's subsequent academic career trajectory. I focus particularly on the stratification that exists within and between disciplines. The findings open up questions about academic hierarchies, the implications of the new research economy for universities' dependence on contract research staff, and personal experiences of moving into new fields and areas of expertise.

The changing political economy of academic life becomes meaningful through individual accounts and experiences. Weber's 1918 lecture on the 'scientific vocation' still has resonances for many. Drawing on the 40 interviews we conducted (Spencer et al., 2005) with early career academics both within and beyond anthropology, I focus on how academics reconcile (or fail to reconcile) their sense of purpose and vocation with the lived experiences of academic practice. I particularly focus on the silences around hierarchy, security and gender within universities. Why is it so hard for young academics to discuss and confront the implications of this new research economy? Knitting together the statistical evidence from the demographic review and the biographical 'evidence' from the interviews, I suggest that part of the reason is the continued dominance of an academic vocation that embraces scholastic detachment and disembodiment. This has profound consequences for academics with caring and domestic responsibilities.

▶ The changing landscape of the social sciences in the UK

What do we know about the changing shape of the social sciences? In demographic terms, social research in the UK seems to be in good health. The social sciences as a recognized set of disciplinary fields are relatively new, gaining institutional legitimacy after the Second World War. Their growth coincided with the expansion of the university sector. UK universities jostle over reputational league tables, but the status hierarchy is still largely determined by age. Oxford and Cambridge head the elite so-called 'Russell Group' of 20 'old' universities, named after the London square where this lobby group first met in 1994. Of these 20, only one (Warwick) was founded in the last half-century. Warwick, like a significant group of universities established in the

1950s and 1960s, was the beneficiary of unprecedented public funding and a growing demand for higher education. A final group of universities, the so-called 'post-92' universities, resulted from the renaming of the polytechnics (more vocationally focused tertiary institutions) in 1992 to create a unitary higher education sector. Fields such as Education and Business are particularly developed within the newer institutions, and their size and growing identification with the social sciences have boosted the field as a whole. Along with the growing numbers of academic posts, there has been a near doubling in the number of PhD students over the past decade (Commission on the Social Sciences, 2003).

Today, the precise size of the social sciences remains moot. Figures vary from 25,000 to 40,000 staff, depending on if one includes Law, and how one classifies Geography and Psychology, fields that bridge the social and natural sciences. Numbers are related to the overall funding of the sector. Deep cuts that occurred in the 1980s under Margaret Thatcher's government were replaced by a steady growth in research funding during the 1990s. The global financial crisis of 2008 and 2009 does not augur well for public sector finances, and funding shortfalls (not to mention a decline in the population of 18-year-olds) are once again likely to lead to job losses.

The history of the 1980s is worth recounting, for it helps explain the contemporary policy field. Ministerial antipathy to the social sciences led to major cuts in research funding for doctoral students, and an attempt to close down the Government's funding body – the Social Science Research Council – in 1982. Given a last-minute reprieve (and renamed the ESRC – the Economic and Social Research Council), the years that followed led to an efficiency drive as the ESRC sought to justify its mandate. There was much talk (if less evidence) of the supposedly 'poor' submission rates and completion times among social science students in comparison to the natural sciences. The ESRC introduced sanctions against underperforming departments, forcing institutions to be more rigorous in their monitoring and support of students, and increasing the influence of the ESRC over the social sciences as a whole. During the 1990s, the ESRC went one step further, setting a precedent among the research councils by requiring departments to provide students with 'rigorous' research training, leading to what some saw as a 'national curriculum' in research methods. It also sought to restrict its funding to departments with a 'critical mass' of students, reinforcing existing hierarchies between old and new universities.

There has been a steady convergence in disciplinary form and function as the social sciences have competed with each other for a share of the ESRC research funding pot (Mills, 2008). Despite this convergence, the social sciences are a highly diverse set of fields. While anthropology remains a determinedly minority interest (only 300 full-time equivalent (FTE) staff are employed in UK anthropology departments), many social science fields have more than 1000 faculty. Multidisciplinary fields such as Business and Education have over 5000 academic staff involved in teaching and/or research (Mills *et al.*, 2006).

One consequence of this expansion is that social scientists are getting academic jobs. Evidence suggests that between 60–65 per cent of doctoral students in the UK social sciences finds initial employment within higher education, whether in the UK or internationally (UK Grad, 2007; Spencer *et al.*, 2005). This is higher than in the natural sciences, where around 40–45 per cent go on to initial academic employment.

But look a little closer. This impressive figure requires several caveats. Up to half of these staff are on fixed-term contracts of all kinds, the majority of which are short-term research posts. A little context is needed here. While the hurdles placed around 'tenure' in the UK tend to be relatively minor in comparison with North America, there is a tripartite employment divide: staff holding 'permanent' lectureships, those holding lectureships funded on a fixed-term basis (between 9 months and three years), and those employed on 'research-only' contracts (again, for periods of up to three years). There are very few 'permanent' research-only positions in the social sciences.

The expansion of social sciences has come with strings attached. In order to maximize its share of the government research funding pot, the ESRC has been very responsive to the political agenda of creating a knowledge-based economy driven by university-based innovation. Increasingly, the social sciences have become pivotal to this future. The growth of interdisciplinary research agendas and centres has been partly driven by the increasing government interest in 'evidence-based' policy and in funding applied and 'user-oriented' research (Gibbons *et al.*, 1994). These centres and funding initiatives have created opportunities for a whole new research workforce.

This responsiveness and willingness to address pressing policy questions have a social cost – a growing reliance on research staff as a reserve pool of academic labour (Gibb, 2004; Mills *et al.*, 2006). In the elite universities, temporary and fixed-term contract research staff in the natural and medical sciences outnumber permanent academic staff by 2 to 1. European Union employment legislation has sought to limit the use of fixed-term contracts, and there has been a shift to the use of 'open' contracts[5] in the natural sciences. Meanwhile the social sciences are increasing their use of such contracts – they now make up 40 per cent of all academic staff in the UK social sciences. This is a new development, and unlike the working environment in laboratory-based fields, these staff are often isolated, working alone under a single principal investigator on a specific, externally-funded contract or consultancy. One could argue that this flexible labour force allows individual academics to respond quickly to research opportunities, and offers opportunities for new researchers and graduates. On the other hand, it results in very short-term research contracts (three-month posts are not unheard of), and no continuity of employment. Sociologists have shown how such staff have to work doubly hard at 'staying in the game' by creating networking career opportunities and publishing, often in their own time (Bryson, 2004; Bryson and Blackwell, 2006; Collinson, 2003). A related development is the 'outsourcing' of teaching responsibilities onto overloaded 'teaching fellows' and fixed-term part-time staff whose contracts provide no time for their own research.

This is not just a challenge for the research-intensive universities. Recent national statistical data indicate that 43 per cent of all staff in UK universities are on fixed-term teaching or research contracts (HESA, 2008). More than two-thirds of new academic staff start on fixed-term contracts, and nearly 80 per cent of research staff are on fixed-term contracts (though this figure is falling markedly). These posts offer a seeming foothold on a precarious academic ladder, and so are welcomed by many. The benefits this workforce brings for established staff make it hard for union activists to challenge this casualization of academic labour. Strikes and disputes over the employment rights of graduate teaching assistants have a long history in American higher education (Nelson, 1997; Nelson and Watt, 2004), but there is little history of staff activism within the UK. This could potentially change if the employment of doctoral students as Graduate Teaching Assistants becomes more widespread.

There are other demographic shifts at work. Many social science fields in the UK are employing increasing proportions of international staff, such that the academic labour market in fields such as economics is now global. In anthropology, more than half of all academic staff under 40 are non-UK-nationals. This has led some to worry about the sustainability of the UK's 'research base'. Others applaud this diversity, measuring academia's vitality by this flow of ideas and people across national boundaries.

▶ Anthropology in the research economy

How are these changes affecting a small and relatively research-intensive field such as anthropology? The field has its own particular institutional history. The first departments of Anthropology were established at the beginning of the twentieth century in the elite so-called 'golden triangle' of Oxford, London and Cambridge, and departments in these institutions continue to train the most students. Unlike the US where some institutions try to maintain a training that links four different fields (cultural anthropology, biological anthropology, linguistics, and archaeology), in the UK, the discipline is dominated by 'social' anthropologists. Only two or three departments have significant numbers of biological anthropologists. Nationally, there are around 20 departments, nearly all in the 'old' universities that traditionally made up the research 'elite'. As a result, its undergraduate students tend to be disproportionately white and middle-class. But the discipline has benefited from a growth in student numbers, particularly in the lucrative market for international students, by offering intensive and well-regarded one-year Masters courses. This has also led to growing numbers of doctoral students, many of whom are also non-UK nationals. As Figure 4.1 shows, the number of doctoral completions each year rose from around 50 in the 1990s to almost 100 by 2002 (Spencer *et al.*, 2005).

As in the other social sciences, a few institutions – particularly the London School of Economics (LSE), and Cambridge – train the

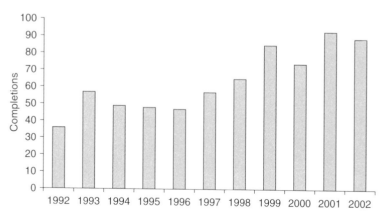

Figure 4.1 Completions/year from UK anthropology departments

majority of students. Disciplinary expansion has brought some institutional diversification, with other metropolitan and 'Russell Group' universities also producing increasing numbers of doctorates. As with the staff, doctoral students are an increasingly diverse group, with less than half holding UK nationality, and almost two-thirds being female, a proportion that has changed markedly over the past 20 years.

Evidence suggests that almost two-thirds of all those who complete doctorates in anthropology initially go into academic employment – roughly 60 out of the 100. But if between 10 and 15 permanent anthropology lectureships are advertised each year in the UK, less than one quarter of these is guaranteed a continuing career in the field (and this doesn't allow for the way in which increasingly US-trained anthropologists are successfully applying for UK posts). What happens to the rest? A snapshot (see Figure 4.2) of our participants' career biographies reveals that the employment 'cake' can be roughly divided into four (Spencer *et al.*, 2005).

One quarter find fixed-term employment as researchers and/or teachers within anthropology departments, while another quarter is on similarly vulnerable contracts in other social science fields. The final quarter obtain permanent posts in other social science departments, such as in Religion, Sociology and Development Studies. Predictably this division is gendered – men are disproportionately more likely to gain permanent posts in social anthropology (they made up 43 per cent of the sample, but obtained 57 per cent of such posts, making them almost twice as likely to get such posts), while women are more likely to be found in posts outside the field, especially in fixed-term posts.

This complexity and diversity of career paths are matched in other disciplines. An intriguing statistical exercise can be carried out using data on staff numbers from the UK HESA (Higher Education Statistics Agency), comparing social science academics' fields of training with

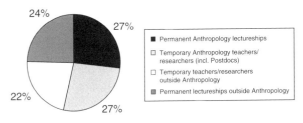

24% 27%

22% 27%

- ■ Permanent Anthropology lectureships
- □ Temporary Anthropology teachers/ researchers (incl. Postdocs)
- □ Temporary teachers/researchers outside Anthropology
- ■ Permanent lectureships outside Anthropology

Figure 4.2 Employment status of sample of anthropologists in UK universities

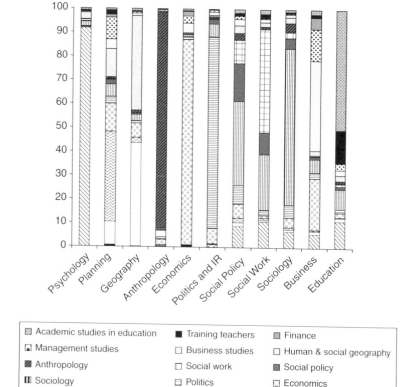

Figure 4.3 Migration patterns within the social sciences: field of academic training (Joint Academic Coding System) by fields of current employment (RAE Unit of assessment) (HESA 2004/5)

their current field of employment. Figure 4.3 reveals this heterogeneity. Comparing across columns allows one to compare individuals' field of academic training with their field of current employment. This reveals certain patterns.

Substantial numbers of doctoral graduates in the social sciences find employment outside their home discipline, though this is truer of some disciplines than others. The graph shows the relative 'disciplinary purity' of the different social sciences, by revealing what proportion of staff employed in a field have been trained in that field. Departments of Psychology, Economics, Politics and Anthropology maintain the strongest degree of 'purity', employ the highest proportion of their own graduates, and the smallest numbers of those trained outside the discipline (less than 10 per cent in the case of Psychology, up to 15 per cent in Economics). It is perhaps no surprise that these are also among the social sciences with the highest status, the most research active staff, and the strongest sense of research autonomy.

At the same time, irrespective of disciplinary purity, some fields (such as Psychology and Economics) train substantial numbers of staff subsequently employed in other fields. For instance, Economists are well represented in Planning, Geography, Politics, Social Policy and Business Studies. Similarly, those with training in Psychology are also able to sell their skills in Social Work, Sociology, Education, Business Studies, Social Policy and even Sociology. One could call fields such as Psychology and Economics 'exporter' disciplines (Mills *et al.*, 2006). Meanwhile, some fields could be regarded as 'importer' disciplines, with relatively little disciplinary purity. Note, for instance, the diversity of backgrounds of those staff employed in Planning, Social Work, Business Studies and Education. Only one-third of staff working in Business did their highest degree in that subject. The figure also significantly underestimates the huge diversity of staff backgrounds within Education, for it does not include those whose highest degrees were outside the social sciences.

While this is a simplified 'snapshot' of a complex and dynamic set of employment trends, it nonetheless reveals the job openings for those trained in the 'older' disciplines within the newer multidisciplinary, applied and policy fields that have expanded with commercial and public sector research funding. The pattern also offers a statistical insight into the informal pecking order that exists between different disciplinary research cultures.

This statistical picture chimes with our interview evidence from anthropology that many students find post-doctoral employment in interdisciplinary settings or in other fields. But is this testament to the discipline's adaptability, the relative academic capital offered by an anthropology doctorate, or simply to the survival strategies of individuals within it? And what of those who are unable to move department, city or discipline, or reluctant to accept the new disciplinary identities available to them?

In the next section, I bring life to these statistical measures, exploring each quarter of the employment cake of Figure 4.2 in turn. In doing so, I draw on interviews from those of our original group of 40 (Spencer *et al.*, 2005) who had chosen to remain in academia, and were now junior academic staff in a range of institutions, positions and environments. Analysing these conversations, personal compromises, ideological contradictions, and gender inequities became increasingly visible. The first section focuses on the experiences of staff now developing careers in the disciplinary 'core' – namely those who held permanent positions in the elite departments. A second section focuses on that quarter of the employment cake who are creating homes in new fields and interdisciplinary areas, offering new perspectives on disciplinary identity. The final section of the chapter explores the experience of that third group (who make up the other half of the employment cake) who by choice or situation are edged out to the margins of their discipline or institution, working on short-term contracts with little or no teaching and research autonomy. This group is particularly vulnerable, and presents significant human resource and educational development challenges.

▷ Nurturing the disciplinary core: permanent anthropology lecturers

Arguably, every discipline has its institutional centres and its peripheries. British social anthropology traces its methodological roots to a research seminar at the London School of Economics (LSE) in the 1920s: a brilliant young Polish émigré named Bronislaw Malinowski championed his vision of in-depth, long-term participant-observation as key to successful anthropological fieldwork. This experience of spending a year in a research field-site remains a key aspect of disciplinary identity.

In the UK, the LSE remains the discipline's flagship, training more than one-third of academics employed in UK anthropology departments. Cambridge is in the number two spot, and many of its non-UK students obtain jobs across the world, in an increasingly global academic labour market. Anthropology postgraduates are a cosmopolitan bunch. Less than half of all anthropology doctoral students are UK nationals, and the proportions at LSE, Cambridge and Oxford are much smaller still.

The LSE's status and influence ensure that the department continues to reproduce the discipline, while resisting the ESRC policy blandishments that over the past decade have encouraged speed, efficiency and utility in the doctoral training process. As a result, LSE students continue the 'classic' anthropological tradition of spending an average of 18 months on fieldwork, a full six months longer than other departments (Spencer, pers. comm.). Its students embody both the field knowledge and the disciplinary cultural capital that can be drawn upon to develop a successful disciplinary career (Spencer, 2000).

So what sort of academic training and doctoral experience is offered in these institutions, and how does it differ from that available elsewhere? Some take the opportunities for granted, and are given the support to juggle the different expectations of work and life. Michaela, a young female scholar holding a Cambridge 'postdoc' (a funded research fellowship), described how her academic family background made an academic career the norm. Asked why she chose to do a PhD, her response was simple:

> I've never applied for a non-academic job. Academia comes with my upbringing. Both my parents are researchers, and have doctorates. I didn't see any other model in my nearby environment. They have been very supportive.

She was unusual in having conducted doctoral research while having young children, based in her home town in Southern Europe. She insisted it made no difference, in a way that hinted less at insouciance than surprise:

> Having children, also...no, I don't think it has really influenced my life as a student...It didn't really make a difference in my case because my PhD was on religious culture and so I didn't have the children with me during fieldwork.

She went on to have two further children, while holding a research fellowship in France, and now holds a permanent post in a German university. Building an academic career often depends on a willingness to be mobile and to take a succession of short-term appointments, but this respondent made light of the implications for her domestic and caring responsibilities.

A rather different, if strangely parallel, account of the recipe for success came from Moira, a more senior LSE-trained anthropologist now working at another major UK anthropology department. Rather than downplaying the consequences of having a family, she was ruthlessly explicit about her career strategizing:

> If you want an academic career, you have to start on year one with your PhD with publication strategies and everything...It is quite easy to become marginal, if anthropologists as academics aren't playing by the new institutional rules (of) collaboration and inter-disciplinarity.

Moira went on to describe her total commitment to the field, while also acknowledging 'the whole obsessiveness of anthropology':

> One or two kids is manageable, but it is not possible to have more, given the self-absorbing nature of this vocation. You can't do this thing for 5 days a week, and not do it at weekends…You should also look at how many women in academic professions have kids. That's the key question – caring responsibilities of all sorts – academics who are permanent academics just care for themselves.

Aware of the rather cynical vision she is presenting, Moira wittily mocked her own extreme sense of vocation: 'in a sense what allows me to do anthropology is the take-away around the corner'. What she is less explicit about are the many small acts of disciplinary inclusion, endorsement and affirmation that may have accompanied her training and doctoral experience, and helped her develop in confidence, acts that less assertive women (and those training elsewhere) may not have received.

Other female respondents were more open about developing one's academic capital and confidence. Agnieszka described her research training at Oxford as 'ambiguous in terms of confidence, with lots of support…but also an intimidating experience, particularly in research seminars, which are very hierarchical, you feel you have to earn your entitlement to speak'.

Increasingly, anthropologists are competing in an international labour market. The dominant trend has been for US anthropologists to take posts in UK institutions, but occasionally the direction is reversed. Matthias, a UK-trained Eastern European anthropologist who obtained a tenure-track job in a top US department, was very perceptive about what had worked for him:

> It depends on [shaping] the dominant trend. Hegemony in academia is achieved through networking, creating trends and space to pursue your own ideas.

He went on to acknowledge the importance of creating a doctoral training environment that had 'a balance between intellectual ethos and careerism', and that worked at 'creating awareness and motivation'.

Among those just starting out on their academic careers, stories of the need for mobility, flexibility and adaptability were common. Petr, a Scandinavian anthropologist, described how, after three years as a contract researcher, he and his wife were prepared to go to wherever the first job came up:

> In fact, I applied I think three times altogether for a job back home and didn't get one. If I had, we would have gone there. But, as I say, all over Britain I was applying to Anthropology, Sociology, anything that I thought I might fit into.

It may have been a coincidence, but respondents not trained at Cambridge and LSE were more likely to acknowledge that, as students, they had found the academic career structure confusing. As David, a British post-doctoral fellow put it; 'It seemed very shrouded in mystery how you got from one thing to another.' He went on to note that his current three-year post gave him some breathing space, and was a 'useful time to train yourself in applying for funds' even if it was 'hard to do much more than getting other applications in'. David felt that he was building the capacity to 'pick up information and communicate it more effectively', while also 'trying to think of something that would make me employable in other branches of the discipline and in area studies'. He admitted to looking for 'new areas becoming sexy', because 'if you can teach these core courses, you are more likely to be able to get a permanent post'. Nonetheless, there was still some way to go for him: 'I felt very neurotic most of the year. But hopefully I'll be more employable after three years.'

▶ Disciplinary emigrations: permanent lecturers outside anthropology

In our qualitative research with those who completed doctorates over the 1990s (Spencer *et al*., 2005), we sought out a representative sample of participants who had left anthropology for employment in cognate disciplines or multidisciplinary fields, and asked them about their work and sense of academic identity. Esme was very frank about making a pragmatic decision at the end of the PhD to rebrand herself, as the jobs available in anthropology were so competitive:

> Well, I suppose I've redefined myself. I call myself a medical soci-ologist now rather than a social anthropologist. I work in the Medical School but I basically do social science research.

Esme went on to admit that this new environment came with 'an enor-mous pressure to do things, which are policy relevant, [that] may, in some direct and obvious way, inform people's healthcare', and made her 'very applied and practical', which made her research profile, and publishing in academic journals, much more difficult.

Juliet, an Oxford-trained anthropologist, described negotiating a Janus-faced identity on obtaining a permanent post in a Geography department:

> If they have a very different approach, you need some legitimation for the way you work – as soon as I arrived, they made it clear that they didn't want me to be an anthropologist. I worked so hard to make myself clear to them that I am barely understandable to anthropologists.

She too experienced a sense of disorientation, noting that 'I've had a number of papers reviewed where they really haven't understood what I was on about'. This gradually led, Juliet felt, to a situation where 'you start to doubt your anthropological credentials'. She acknowledged the personal benefits and costs:

> It is very rewarding to work across the boundaries, and to make explicit and to rethink your basic assumptions. But it is one-sided . . . people expect you to behave like them.

She also observed 'a definite favour towards people who've published in one field over those who have published widely' when it came to university promotion decisions.

Not everyone survives such uncertainties. Several of the women in our sample left permanent academic posts. Barbara had a post in a multidisciplinary research environment, but found that collaborating in research teams with doctors and other scientists left her uncertain about her own research interests and disciplinary identity: 'We used to talk about whether we were losing it – are we forgetting how to be anthropologists?'

Working in an environment that prioritized applied research conducted to tight policy deadlines made life particularly hard for her:

> The multi-tasking was overwhelming – my work was my life. How do people do it? You are expected to be as aggressive in your teaching as with your research. Most of us over-estimate our abilities to multi-task.

We detected a sense of nostalgia and loss among those who no longer worked in anthropology departments, and many found it difficult to come to terms with very different working conditions and epistemological outlooks. The discipline's strong collectivism makes this particularly pronounced. But anthropology is not unique. One does not have to look far in academia to find similar struggles over affiliation and belonging and identity.

▶ Surviving on the disciplinary margins: temporary teacher/researcher positions

Away from the disciplinary core are those whose research profile is less highly rated or in demand. We interviewed a number of individuals who characterized their postdoctoral experience as a matter of surviving on short-term teaching and research contracts.

In the past two decades many UK universities have sought to boost their reputations and rankings within the controversial six-yearly Research Assessment Exercise. These exercises began in 1986, and amount to a massive system-wide peer-review exercise paid for by the government's funding council, where nominated disciplinary representatives spend up to six months confidentially reviewing and rating the work of their colleagues. At stake is not just status within the research 'league table', but also the proportion of government funding available to departments for research and training activities, and so it is in the interests of universities to get the best possible rankings. The results can be divisive, especially if some staff are not 'submitted' to the exercise on the grounds of having poor quality research profiles, and instead expected to do more teaching.

In order to free up research time for established staff, some institutions have introduced one-year teaching fellowship posts, with a heavy set of teaching responsibilities, and no time allocated for research or for writing up publications. Yet as long as teaching is undervalued within institutions, such posts remain marginalized and low status. With good teaching evaluations, a good teacher can end up having such a post renewed for a number of years. While any job is appealing for those whose doctoral grants have long since run out, one has a steadily decreasing chance of gaining a permanent lectureship, and no guarantee that teaching appointments will be made secure.

Jason, who had held such a post for three years, bemoaned the career trap he had created for himself, and how he now no longer gets considered for permanent academic posts because he was not seen as having published enough high quality articles:

> What does it do to one's sense of identity? I was interested in teaching fellowships. I get on well with various people – I carry on, but get a feeling that there is a degree of resentment. They were saying I'd been given a chance.

Jason admitted that his own 'naivety' was partly to blame: 'Because we began as older people, we did what we did because we wanted to do it, rather than because it was an ideal career path.'

His views about age were reflected in the statistics. From our survey, we found that of the 20 respondents now teaching in anthropology departments on temporary contracts, nearly half had completed their doctorate after the age of 35, suggesting that these older students were disproportionately likely to end up holding temporary teaching posts.

If teaching-only posts reflected an age hierarchy, fixed-term research contracts were strongly gendered. Women were particularly over-represented (71 per cent of those employed) in academic posts outside anthropology departments. One female researcher, Zoe, felt that there were 'structural things that make women go after research jobs. It is not just necessarily that they want it all.' She described the consequences of seeing 'women in the department sidelined' or the 'men getting the permanent lectureships', and felt that 'these are strong messages that dent the post grad/doc self-esteem' and 'create a self-perpetuating picture of inequality'.

Sometimes insecurity is felt in very small ways. In one department, the hierarchy is made evident in the pigeonholes. Permanent staff have their own pigeonholes on one side of the corridor. Meanwhile, fixed-term contract researchers have to make do with pigeonholes labelled by the title of the project, rather than by the individual staff names. In a myriad of ways, from who gets invited to attend meetings to who one speaks to at coffee, symbolic hierarchies make themselves felt. Short-term posts are still seen as somewhat anomalous: a grey zone of semi-citizenship in the republic of letters, for whom permanent tenured staff feel limited degrees of solidarity. In an academy where one is measured by one's ability to publish, collegiality and the free exchange of ideas are eroded. This is important to all academics, not just for those suffering from job insecurity and underpayment.

▷ Gender and the academic vocation

In this final section, I explore how both gender and family commitments constantly recurred in our research. One could argue that academia's origins in medieval monastic communities of learning are still visible in an unworldly self-image and even an implicitly anti-family outlook. At its best, this sense of self-sacrifice and cloistered disregard for worldly things are a source of intellectual autonomy and disciplinary strength. It may also explain the single-minded (one might even say overwrought) commitment to academic work articulated by many of our respondents. But it may also explain why people with families to look after find the routines and pressures of academic life so difficult.

Half of our interviews were conducted with women. Some were prepared to question this expectation, and to call the academy to account, as Serena, a junior lecturer in an elite department, noted:

> Yes, it is a vocation, but that doesn't mean that there aren't other things in my life. When I compare myself to my male contemporaries, who are male and unattached, and put in more hours…they are the ones who are going to get the top jobs, and ultimately I don't want to sacrifice my family life for a career…it is never so simple.

She felt that women 'do end up having to compromise – we've been taught we can have it all…but we can't'. This was, she averred, a difficult thing to say, when 'societal individualism made structural explanations unwelcome'. One woman pointed out that all the young male academics in her department had 'full-time' wives to look after the children. Another noted that 'women are brought up to see things outside of work as just as important as work, and that men who adopt a (similarly) holistic approach to life suffer from the same thing'.

One of our respondents pointed to the difficulty of getting universities to take these issues seriously. She described a meeting on gender issues in her institution, at which a Dean meeting several junior female colleagues couldn't see why the negotiating strategies employed by male academics (such as threatening to leave to go to another university in order to secure a promotion) were a gender issue, or that women were far less able to bargain in this way to secure pay rises because of their domestic commitments.

We were particularly struck by the way that several women, forced to constantly compromise their family commitments, had left full permanent lectureships. This was unusual – we knew of no similar cases involving men. Terezinha confessed that it was 'gruesome that I gave up a permanent job – it was one of the toughest decisions I've ever made'. While she felt she had achieved 'a great deal professionally', and had the 'competitiveness to establish herself as a woman and an academic', she had worked hours that were 'probably illegal by international labour laws…[but] one of the difficulties is that we love our jobs'. Her commitment led more and more students to flock to her courses, and also to shoulder heavy administrative responsibilities. Terezinha also pointed to the lack of awareness of life outside the department:

> The time for meetings is always set at impossible hours – departmental meetings at 4.30, and so they could go on for hours…with agendas of 30 points. Among the permanent members of staff in anthropology in my department – there were two women and ten men – of the ten, some didn't have children, and those who did had women who were looking after them.

Several respondents pointed to the culture of late-afternoon departmental seminars – nearly all anthropology seminars, like most seminars in universities, they are held at this time. The seminar timetable and ritual are often sacrosanct, with intellectual debate continuing in a nearby hostelry. This nexus of alcohol and intellectual sociability may suit some, but not those who have families to care for and other lives to lead.

Terezinha acknowledged that the pressures on her were made worse by the end of her marriage:

> At the time I was in no position to laugh at – I had no support to turn to at home…and there is still an expectation that children won't disturb the career of a male…I realized that something was wrong when my daughter was the first to arrive at school, and the last one to leave every day – it is not right.

What did she feel she could do in response? 'The only way to fight these issues is to take them up with Heads of Departments and administrators – but that's a big job – I don't want to be on a warpath with colleagues – I have better things to do.' But she did have her own theory about the reason that some men (and some women) downplayed the importance of a 'family-friendly' workplace: 'there is a cosmological greatness in intellectual achievement that is so averse to reproduction'.

Of course, these women found themselves in extreme positions, and we also spoke to men who were committed to their families and to sharing household responsibilities. But none articulated a direct tension in their working lives.

To what extent are these tensions peculiar to anthropology, a field that has historically rewarded the solitary iconoclast and the lonely fieldworker? Certainly, there is a disciplinary dimension at work, and one could argue that there is something fundamentally self-alienating in the ethnographic method (long periods of fieldwork, often conducted alone) that makes it hard to switch off from 'being an anthropologist' in order to nurture the rest of one's life. Indeed, some anthropologists would even question the 'work/life' dichotomy, and argue that an anthropological sensibility is core to their being. But it is not just anthropology. There are also historical and structural forces at work, as shown in the voluminous literature on gender inequalities in higher education. Despite institutional reforms, the pressures to be continually 'productive' in research terms, despite the implications for one's caring and family responsibilities, remain, and indeed have become more acute. These pressures reflect the contemporary expectations made of academics (and indeed of professionals more generally), both men and women, inside the research economy.

▶ Implications

The stories I tell are selective. They differ by institution, by individual, and at different points over the academic life course. But these are not just accounts of life in one small social science discipline. They also reflect the changing nature of the contemporary academic workplace and the expectations it places on academics' own bodies and relationships. While practising academics implicitly 'know' much of this, it remains hard to write about or convey fully. My aim has been to bring this embodied knowledge to the 'front' of the stage, to reflect on the contradictions that structure academic practice, and to help early career academics prepare for some of the challenges ahead.

What might this focus on academic hierarchy contribute to a broader sociological understanding of higher education? Bourdieu's monumental work *Homo Academicus* rightly remains a seminal analysis of the rival fields of social and institutional power structuring academic life (Bourdieu, 1984). Yet much of his writing can be critiqued for having a very antagonistic vision of social relations (see also Bourdieu and Passeron, 1977). Academia for Bourdieu is a field of power, a zero-sum game of competition for social status and institutional control. There is little space in it for reciprocity, affect, care and empathy, all of which could be seen as core aspects of academic practice. His lack of attention to the relationality of academic life explains why his determination to lay bare the scientific field doesn't quite work. It doesn't grapple with the academic idealism of many, the willingness to work long hours, and the way in which academics rely on other social relationships in order to pursue their vocation. And it also doesn't explore the way in which our own unworldly vocationalism allows us to ignore the very worldly practices that sustain such power games.

What are the implications of this account for developers, for administrators, and for academics themselves? How best can each respond to the challenge of helping those torn between the (over)powerful influence of a scholarly vocation and the reality of their working lives? An open, frank and honest discussion of the pros and cons of academic life would seem to be important, especially one that does not shy away from discussing the absurdities and excesses that an overwrought scholasticism can induce in people. This account has to grapple with the *realpolitik* of academic life, and to present doctoral students with an accurate picture of the changing employment market and the limited potential career opportunities. Scholarly associations have a particularly important information and dissemination role to play, but given their investment in promoting particular disciplinary identities and worldviews, this is not a responsibility that many take seriously.

Developers and academic careers advisors have an additional responsibility of helping academic staff prepare for futures in a diversity of disciplinary and research environments, and they are best placed to anticipate the expectations that disciplinary migrations might create. Finally, there are also implications for the *academic community* itself. There are many ways to make university life more inclusive, supportive and family-friendly, from better scheduling of seminars all the way to a proper recognition of the core contribution that research staff make to departmental and disciplinary research cultures.

Academic idealism is a strange thing. The utopian potential of a free republic of letters, for all its flaws and fractures, motivates many, and lies behind what can become an intense academic vocationalism. It is an idealism that many anthropologists would be highly sceptical of in a field context, and yet as our respondents demonstrate, it is an abstraction that structures feelings, relationships and working lives. If academic idealism plays a powerful role, this chapter has illustrated the 'unmentionables' that accompany this ideal, and the risk of seeing this ideal as separate from difficult political questions about defending a space for academic work. It is particularly hard to turn such ideals into pragmatic political demands – is the priority the defence of permanent contracts, the conditions of temporary staff, or the very space for critical thinking itself? The message for *young scholars* then is to take seriously these aspects of academic practice, and find spaces in which to talk about the everyday challenges and issues that academic communities collectively face.

Max Weber's powerful essay 'Science as a vocation' (Weber 2004 [1919]) begins with a frank admission that 'it is extremely hazardous for a young scholar without funds to expose himself [*sic*] to the conditions of the academic career'. He goes on to note that 'I know of hardly any career on earth where chance plays such a role.' His discussion of the scientific vocation rarely returns to the contradiction that this idealism presents. The danger is that the unworldly academic ideal becomes an ideology that disguises the mundane and sometimes exploitative demands of academic work. The contradiction has not gone away.

Notes

1. The Higher Education Academy (www.heacademy.ac.uk) is a UK-wide initiative to raise the professional status of higher education teaching through individual, disciplinary and institutional accreditation and reward schemes. It has created a set of national professional standards for higher education teaching.
2. 'Lecturer' is the generic title for academics in the UK, like 'professor' in North America. It implies academics engaged in both teaching and research (as opposed to research-only academics).
3. This research was funded by the ESRC, and conducted collectively, with Anne Jepson as project researcher and Professor Jonathan Spencer as principal investigator.
4. Semi-structured interviews were conducted at an individual's place of work, and also on the phone where necessary.
5. This refers to an open-ended appointment with no specified end date; it is often contrasted with fixed-term contracts. An open-ended contract can only cease if the need for the role ceases.

▶ References

Abbott, A. (2001) *Chaos of Disciplines*. Chicago: University of Chicago Press.

Bryson, C. (2004) 'What about the workers? The expansion of higher education and the transformation of academic work', *Industrial Relations Journal*, 35(1): 38–57.

Bryson, C. and Blackwell, R. (2006) 'Managing temporary workers in higher education: still at the margin?' *Personnel Review*, 35(2): 207–24.

Bourdieu, P. (1984) *Homo Academicus*. Stanford, CA: Stanford University Press.

Bourdieu, P. (2004) *Science of Science and Reflexivity*. London: Polity.

Bourdieu, P. and Passeron, J.-C. (1977) *Reproduction in Education, Society and Culture*. London: Sage.

Collinson, J. (2003) 'Working at a marginal "career": The case of UK social science contract researchers', *The Sociological Review*, 51(3): 405–22.

Commission on the Social Sciences (2003) 'Great Expectations: The Social Sciences in Britain', available at: http://www.acss.org.uk/docs/GtExpectations.pdf, accessed April 16, 2010.

Gibb, R. (2004) 'Seminar culture(s), rites of passage and the unmentionable in contemporary British social anthropology', in D. Mills and M. Harris (eds) *Teaching Rites and Wrongs: Universities and the Making of Anthropologists*. Birmingham: Sociology, Anthropology and Politics (C-SAP) and the Higher Education Academy Network.

Gibbons, M., Limoges, C., Nowotny, H., Schwartzman, S., Scott, P. and Trow, M. (1994) *The New Production of Knowledge: The Dynamics of Science and Research In Contemporary Societies*. London: Sage.

Higher Education Statistics Agency (2008) *Students in Higher Education Institutions*. Cheltenham: HESA.

Mills, D. (2005) 'Juggling acts: Teaching and the disciplinary vocation', in D. Carter and M. Lord (eds) *Engagements with Learning and Teaching in Higher Education*. Birmingham: Sociology, Anthropology and Politics (C-SAP) and The Higher Education Academy Network.

Mills, D. (2008) 'Compare, contrast, converge: A biography of the Demographic Review of the UK Social Sciences (2006)', *Twenty-First Century Society*, 3(3): 263–78.

Mills, D. and Harris, M. (eds) (2004) *Teaching Rites and Wrongs: Universities and the Making of Anthropologists*. Birmingham: Sociology, Anthropology and Politics (C-SAP) and The Higher Education Academy Network.

Mills, D., Jepson, A., Coxon, T., Easterbury-Smith, M., Hawkins, P. and Spencer, J. (2006) *Demographic Review of the UK Social Sciences*. Swindon: Economic and Social Research Council.

Mills, D., Jepson, A. *et al.* (2006) *Demographic Review of the UK Social Sciences*. Swindon: Economic and Social Research Council.

Nelson, C. (ed.) (1997) *Will Teach for Food: Academic Labour in Crisis*. New York: Routledge.

Nelson, C. and Watt, S. (2004) *Office Hours: Activism and Change in the Academy*. New York: Routledge.

Spencer, J. (2000) 'British social anthropology: A retrospective', *Annual Review of Anthropology*, 29: 1–24.

Spencer, J., Jepson., A. and Mills, D., (2005) *Career Paths and Training Needs of Social Anthropology Research Students: Final Report to the ESRC*. Edinburgh: University of Edinburgh.

UK Grad (2007) *What Do PhDs Do? Trends, a Commentary on 2004–2006 Survey of PhD Graduates*. Available at www.vitae.ac.uk.

Weber, M. (2004 [1919]) *The Vocation Lectures: 'Science as a Vocation'; 'Politics as a Vocation'*. Indianapolis: Hackett Publishers.

5 Doctoral Students and a Future in Academe?

Sandra Acker and Eve Haque

▶ **Author perspectives**

Sandra's story

I have spent much of my adult life studying or working in universities and doing research on higher education. My own long-ago graduate studies at the University of Chicago in the late 1960s focused on the sociology of education. For my dissertation I did a survey of graduate students' aspirations for academic careers, with a particular emphasis on what we then called 'sex differences', at a time when actual women academics were amazingly scarce. Much of my subsequent work has been on gender issues, often in combination with higher education topics and with themes like 'career' and 'workplace culture' that spoke to my own experience as well as my intellectual concerns.

My career took an unexpected turn when I married and followed my husband across the Atlantic to England, where I secured a precarious temporary position in a sociology department for a year, thankfully followed by a more secure post in a School of Education. At the University of Bristol I taught courses on sociology of education and inequality, mostly to teachers who aimed for qualifications beyond initial certification, including master's and doctoral degrees. In retrospect, the 1970s were halcyon days in universities (before the memories of my co-author – see below), to be followed by the era of Thatcherism which (as described in Chapter 4 by David Mills) was characterized by hostility towards social scientists and intellectuals in general, resulting in cutbacks and closures and eventually followed by a plethora of accountability mechanisms starting in the late 1980s. Around the same time, I had the opportunity to direct my first funded research project, a study of doctoral students and supervisors that built on my own previous doctoral work but was qualitative rather than quantitative.

That study was interrupted by another migration across the Atlantic, this time to Canada to the Ontario Institute for Studies in Education (now part of the University of Toronto), where I was able to teach more specialized courses such as Teachers' Work, Women and the Educational System, and Women and Higher Education and develop several research projects on aspects of academic life (described briefly later in an endnote to our chapter). I remained interested in the lives of graduate students and so accepted an invitation to write a chapter on dissertation advising for Eric Margolis's edited book, *The Hidden Curriculum in Higher Education*, that brought together the results of the study I had done in England with some small-scale work in Canada (Acker, 2001). I was particularly intrigued by the transition that I had observed during my career from the days of the normative young, white male student to the diversity (gender and beyond) evident in more recent times. In my current project, a study of tenure practices in Ontario (with Michelle Webber and Elizabeth Smyth), I see a similar tension where the population (in this case, early career academics) has become more diverse but the process (the tenure review and other evaluative mechanisms) is still shaped in many ways by traditional understandings of academic life.

I have also written about the experience of being a department chair (head of department) in a recent collection (Acker, 2008) and taken up related issues around gender and university administration (management) in several conference papers. The project that forms the basis of our chapter started out as a piece of action research intended to inform decisions made in the department during the time I was chair in 1999–2002. I was fortunate to connect with Eve, then a graduate student research assistant, and together we designed the small-scale study that eventually produced the set of interviews with doctoral students that we draw upon here.

Eve's story

My interest in issues of higher education began when I re-entered post-secondary education as a mature graduate student pursuing a master's degree in the mid-1990s. At that time, with a big swing to the right in Ontario politics, major neo-liberal reforms were being introduced into post-secondary education in the province which meant cutbacks in student funding, escalation of tuition fees and introduction of other forms of restructuring supposedly in the service of efficiency. As I began to question how I was supposed to survive as a graduate student – survival entailing the basics like rent and food – and took on more paid jobs as a result – I became increasingly curious about the policy changes which were challenging our daily lives as students and this concern in turn led to my increasing involvement in campus issues at my university. The process was gradual, but the more I learned and saw, the more involved I became and the more my awareness increased of how student labour (jobs on and off campus) was intertwined with academic progress. After I finished my master's degree – now with a sizable government-held (and interest-generating) student loan debt – I taught for a few years and then entered a PhD program with a competitive government scholarship secured (or so I thought) to pay my way. However, a year into my PhD program, I was informed that I would not be able to apply to renew my scholarship because the student loan arm of the same provincial government was in disagreement with me about my earnings between my MA and PhD programs. Since there was no mechanism for appeal, I had to take a year off to go abroad and earn money so I could continue with my graduate education.

I returned to my PhD program a year later, this time determined to learn more about higher education policy both at the university and provincial levels. At this time, students in our education departments were launching a huge effort to obtain the same minimum levels of graduate student funding that were being awarded to students in other faculties and departments at the same university. This was a struggle of several years and my involvement was on many fronts, while simultaneously working through doctoral requirements and writing my dissertation. I became active in the student research and teaching assistants' unions; I became involved with different student groups working on these issues; I attended meetings, rallies and protests around student funding and tuition escalation; and I served on various university committees and participated in governance structures. It is during this time that the possibility for carrying out this research project with Sandra (who was our departmental chair in this critical period) emerged, and I saw an excellent opportunity to capture and understand the impact of these policies in the day-to-day lived realities of graduate students. What we found from our in-depth interviews was proof of the link between the material conditions of graduate education and the academic experience and learning process for graduate students of diverse backgrounds.

Now, having finished my PhD and secured a tenure track position, I realize that these experiences are not just in my past; rather, they inform how I currently tackle the treacherous terrain of tenure track academic life and make clear in what ways I have been adequately prepared and, in other ways, arrived grossly unequipped. The familiar inequities and challenges are now somehow magnified and yet also strange, as at the same time many of my student-life academic priorities and concerns have been turned around as I have become a faculty member. In all this, the relentless neo-liberalizing march of the university system remains a constant weight; fourteen years after beginning my graduate student career it is hard to imagine academic life within any other context.

▶ Introduction to the issues

Are doctoral students best thought of as faculty-in-waiting? While they are often contemplating academic careers, it could be misleading to think of them as merely undergoing a period of apprenticeship before moving on to the 'real thing'. There are not enough academic jobs to go around, and there are other possible objectives. More than half of doctoral graduates in Canada find work outside the academy (McAlpine and Norton, 2006, p. 11). Not all doctoral students will complete their studies. In the social sciences in Canada, those who finish will require an average of more than six years for the task (Gluszynski and Peters, 2005, p. 25), which is comparable to the US data (see Chapter 2). They will spend a long time working their way through a set of requirements prior to beginning the main thrust of the degree, the dissertation. Most will design their own individual project rather than work in a team headed by a professor. Whether a future as an academic is planned or accidental, desired or rejected, these students undergo lengthy immersion in the departmental, disciplinary and institutional cultures of academe.

If doctoral students are to be oriented to a career in academe, then increasing the component of their work devoted to professional development seems a logical consequence. In the United States, as part of widespread concern about outcomes of graduate study (Brooks and Heiland, 2007), there have been innovations in professional development for students, supported by various foundations and organizations (Walker *et al.*, 2008). However, if the demands of the typical graduate school are such that the future is murky or seems a long way off, then such efforts might not be successful. An earlier publication on doctoral students by one of us (Acker, 2001) used the metaphor of the iceberg to suggest that students may only know a portion of the information they need to succeed at their studies – the visible part of the iceberg. The original subtitle for the current chapter was 'From the Iceberg to the Shore'. While institutions provide ever more information on the formal process, now through websites as well as paper publications, there is still much tacit knowledge that eludes many students about navigating the doctoral waters, let alone how to reach, and survive, 'on the shore' – i.e. in a faculty role that holds the possibility of permanence.

This chapter addresses the question of whether continuity or disjuncture is to be expected between doctoral studies and the work of new faculty (called academic staff in some countries). After a discussion of relevant aspects of the Canadian post-secondary context, we turn to a brief reprise of the concerns of early-career academics, gleaned from our own previous research and the literature. This discussion forms a prelude to the primary focus of this chapter, an analysis of academic career expectations based on interviews with doctoral students. After describing the particular circumstances under which the interviews took place, we explore aspects of the data related to the anticipation of academic careers. Although the students interviewed were in advanced stages of doctoral study or had recently completed their degrees, few of their accounts revealed clear planning and understanding of the challenges of working as a faculty member. We then argue that this scenario is not surprising, given important contextual features that work as impediments to long-term career planning. In the conclusion, we consider the extent to which preparation of doctoral students for future faculty roles can be improved.

▶ The Canadian post-secondary context

McAlpine and Norton (2006; see also Chapter 6) develop a model of 'multiple, nested contexts' with which to consider doctoral study. Local relationships (e.g. student and supervisor) take place in a departmental/disciplinary context, nested within an institutional context, itself within a societal and global context. In this section, we describe some salient aspects of the Canadian post-secondary scene in general, noting particularly the paucity of funding for social sciences. We concur with David Mills in Chapter 4 that the political and economic context of funding for the social sciences plays an important part in shaping the opportunity structures for doctoral students and new academics.

Canada is unusual due to its lack of a national department of education (Leyton-Brown, 2008). At any point in time, the post-secondary scene is 'negotiated through three significantly autonomous institutions: universities, provincial governments and the federal government' (Williams, 2008, p. 249; see also Shanahan and Jones, 2007). The federal government's influence in post-secondary education is significant but indirect, mostly through provision of scholarships and research grants and money transferred to the provinces. Particular national initiatives like the Canada Research Chair program[1] provide additional funding through competitive bidding. Our doctoral interviews were conducted in the academic year 2001–2002. In 2001, there were approximately 3660 new doctoral graduates and over 27,000 enrolled doctoral students in Canada (Williams, 2008, p. 264).[2] Fifteen universities trained almost 80 per cent of all doctoral candidates; half of the students studied in Montreal, Toronto or Vancouver, making Canadian doctoral education 'an urban phenomenon' (ibid., p. 264).

Williams describes how federal government support for post-secondary education was reduced from 1980 to 1997, both through limits and conditions placed on transfers to the provinces and through research policies. From 1995 to 1998, for example, funding to all research councils was cut. Re-investment has largely been through targeted funds in areas considered to be in the national interest. Initiatives in the late 1990s and early 2000s typically favoured science and medicine, leading to increasing distress about underfunding in humanities and social sciences. 'It was not until 2003 that that the government provided direct support for graduate education [through scholarships] in a way that addressed some of these concerns' (ibid., p. 259). Nevertheless, the social sciences and humanities are still considerably less well funded than the sciences and medicine.

While many aspects of Canadian academe parallel those in the United States, there are some important differences. American commentaries often identify a discontinuity between graduate school education and academic careers, given the elite and research-oriented nature of institutions that train doctoral students compared to the teaching-focused colleges (described by Ann Austin in Chapter 2) where many will work (Austin, 2002; Golde and Dore, 2001). Although there are differences among institutions, Canadian universities do not show the dramatic variations of type and status found in the United States (Shanahan and Jones, 2007) and most universities are public, including all doctoral-granting ones (Leyton-Brown, 2008, p. 112). Consequently, while the destinations of doctoral graduates may not be as research-intensive as their training grounds, they will not be wholly different in other respects.

▶ Concerns of early-career academics

The early years of an academic career are generally thought of as a stressful time, a point also noted by other authors in this volume. There is much to learn. Many newly hired academics in Canada will be told that they need to engage in some combination of research, teaching and service to the institution. Yet each of these categories can be divided into many parts, often including unfamiliar activities. For example, in a useful guide, McCormick and Barnes write:

> The challenges encountered by new faculty include learning the culture of the new academic institution, understanding the processes and policies for academic performance review, establishing meaningful and constructive mentoring relationships, creating a sustainable research agenda as well as fostering the writing attitudes and strategies that promote turning research projects into publications.
>
> (2008, p. 5)

They then go on to detail aspects of each one of these areas. Even what might seem a minor learning activity – communicating by e-mail – contains pitfalls and needs careful thought (ibid., p. 7).

Similarly, Solem, Foote and Monk provide a list of professional responsibilities:

> Preparing and leading a complete course as primary instructor; working effectively with colleagues; dealing with nuts-and-bolts issues of writing and publishing such as responding effectively to peer reviews and editors' comments; finding and then managing grant funding; managing time effectively; confronting ethical issues in research and teaching; balancing work, family, and personal interests and responsibilities; creating a professional development plan; and many other issues.
>
> (2009, p. vii)

With all that to do, the early years can be a 'sink or swim' experience (ibid., p. vii). Moreover, in recent years global trends towards surveillance, audit and performativity in academic cultures have raised the standards new academics are expected to strive for (Archer, 2008).

Our own previous research confirms that there are significant challenges for today's new faculty in Canada.[3] Here is an example from an interview with an early-career academic in the mid-1990s in a Canadian university:

> I'm a pretty strong person and I'm quite athletic. But I would say that this level of stress and fatigue really wears on me. And my health is pretty good but I think emotionally it wears you down and … it's aging me actually … I think current, untenured academic life is quite stressful and draining and demanding. And that

it fills all of your waking hours. It would fill every minute of my
week if I didn't walk from it.

(Helen, assistant professor)

Junior faculty remarked on the pervasiveness of evaluation. For
example, in a different university:

In a way, during the last six years [since her appointment] my
life has been under a microscope, right? You make the bid for
entry to the School of Graduate Studies so that you can do
graduate supervision and here it's a bid, you have to go through
a process.[4] You go through the tenure process. You go through
the contract renewal process. You go through the rank change
process, and constantly, you're being assessed in terms of your
worth.

(Hester, associate professor)

In North America, achieving tenure has a crucial role in the academic
career, given that refusal of tenure usually means the loss of a job. A
tenure-track position (i.e. one that carries the possibility of tenure)
is a prize for a beginning academic, given the increasing numbers
of contingent positions[5] and decline in permanent tenured ones
(Glazer-Raymo, 2003; Muzzin and Limoges, 2008; and see Chapter 2
in this volume). It represents academic freedom and potential job
security. Yet critical writers identify flaws in the process of award-
ing tenure, such as ambiguous criteria, differential impacts on different sub-groups, and the perpetuation of haves and have-nots
among faculty. There is particular concern around the timing of the
tenure review process for women who are starting families (Acker
and Armenti, 2004; Ward and Wolf-Wendel, 2004) and about extra
work expected of minority faculty who frequently mentor minority
students without being given formal credit for their efforts (Tierney
and Bensimon, 1996).

Awarded approximately five years after being newly hired as an
assistant professor, tenure is preceded by an earlier probationary or
contract-renewal review. It is accompanied or followed closely by
consideration for promotion to associate professorship. An ongoing
study of tenure practices in Ontario entitled 'Disciplining Academics'
(Acker and Webber, 2006) suggests that tenure review practices vary
considerably in detail from one institution to another and are usually
subject to collective bargaining (the majority of Ontario universities

have unionized faculty associations). As in the earlier research, exemplified in the quotations from Helen and Hester above, tenure is clearly a source of high anxiety for junior academics, becoming more so after the first few years of learning the ropes. To be successful at tenure requires competent or better teaching (as indicated by course evaluations, letters from students and other forms of internal review) and some level of demonstrated research achievement.[6]

A period as a contract researcher is not a prior requirement to taking a position that leads to permanence. Research experience is more likely to be acquired during graduate school although the amount and quality is somewhat haphazard. Some graduates will find postdoctoral positions in which they have another year or two to gain research competence but such positions are relatively rare in the social sciences. The deeper level of growing and developing as a researcher described by Gerlese Åkerlind in Chapter 3 is likely to be acquired only after becoming a tenure track academic. Teaching experience might be gained from a teaching assistantship during graduate studies (helping with undergraduate teaching) or a contingent (temporary) position (see note 5). As Ann Austin shows for the United States in Chapter 2, new academics in Canada will not normally be systematically prepared by their doctoral studies for the competencies they need for academic work, often leading to stress around the tenure process, given its expectations that a certain amount of competence can be demonstrated after a relatively short time on the job.

Interviews from 'Disciplining Academics' suggest that even those junior faculty members who feel reasonably confident about being reviewed for tenure mention a nagging sense of anxiety, a kind of verbal crossing of fingers:

> Certainly, I have other interests in my life and if I didn't get tenure, I simply would have retired and moved on to some other job. Although not getting tenure would have been a horrible failure and I never would have allowed that to happen (laughs)...I honestly didn't think it was gonna be a problem.
>
> *Interviewer*: After you put in the application, was there any sort of sense of relief, apprehension, anything?
>
> The mildest sense of relief and apprehension, just the mildest and of course, with, with spurts of anxiety that maybe I totally misread the situation and they'll throw me out...You never know.
>
> (Davida, assistant professor,
> waiting for results of tenure review)

If there is continuity between doctoral work and the first years of the faculty experience, as the authors of Chapter 6 and others argue, then we should find advanced doctoral students setting their sights on a career as a tenured academic and aware of the need to develop competence in research, teaching and possibly service (administration).[7] We now turn to our study of students in one doctoral program to see how well their concerns matched this expectation, beginning with a description of the study and some background about the department where it took place.

▶ Doctoral students and academic careers

The study and the department

The specific site for this research project is a graduate sociology department in a faculty of education. At the time of data collection, in 2001–2002, there were approximately 190 graduate students,[8] of whom about 80 were doctoral students, and about 16 faculty members. The department is part of a large, research-intensive university located in a metropolitan area known as a magnet for immigrants and for the consequent diversity of its population. The department itself had a highly diverse student population, attracted by its focus on equity studies and the presence of a number of ethnocultural minority faculty, about a third of the faculty complement.[9]

One- to two-hour qualitative interviews were conducted with 31 volunteer doctoral students (80.6 per cent women, 19.3 per cent men) and later transcribed. Black students made up the largest single group of our participants (10), while there were 6 White students and 15 others drawn from a range of other ethnocultural backgrounds, including Aboriginal, East Asian, Latina/o, Middle Eastern, South Asian.[10] The current analysis uses 16 transcripts of students, including 11 who are in advanced stages of the program (those who had already written their comprehensive examination,[11] mostly in year 4, with a few in year 3 or 5 – hereafter called '*candidates*') and 5 who have recently completed their doctorates after 5 to 10 years (hereafter called '*completers*'). Our logic is that these students are those most likely to be aware of and planning for the future (Gardner, 2008).

Our group of 16 completers and candidates includes 4 White students, 6 Black students and 6 students from other ethnocultural backgrounds; 14 women and 2 men.[12] Pseudonyms have been devised that also identify which group participants are in: names from A to E are the completers and F to P the candidates.

To ensure greater openness, all interviews were conducted by Eve, at the time a fellow doctoral student, and herself of South Asian background. She assured students that all identifying data would be removed before Sandra, also a researcher on the project as well as a professor and chair of the department during the research period, could see any of the transcripts.

With regard to student financial support, a 1999 departmental report indicates that there were 2 or 3 entry scholarships and 14 graduate (research) assistantships available for new students (masters and doctoral), awarded competitively.[13] The lack of an undergraduate population associated with the department meant that there were no teaching assistantships.[14] Many of the transcripts contain expressions of bewilderment that so little funding was available, incoming students having assumed optimistically that they would be given support of some kind. Although the department was located in an education faculty, only a minority of its students were actually schoolteachers, although many were 'mature' and had worked (for example, in the community) before beginning a graduate program. Students needed a master's degree to apply for the doctorate, which also increased the average age.[15]

Other characteristics of the department and university are mentioned as appropriate within the analysis. In order to assess the level of connection between the doctoral student orientations and expectations for new faculty, we now turn to participants' ideas about academic careers, teaching and publications.

Looking forward?

Maybe there should be some demystification of what the professoriate[16] is about. We don't know anything about what a professor actually does. We just think OK, we are gonna be academics. It sounds like a good job but we really don't know what it's all about until we actually have to do it.

(Beth)

Most of the students appeared to expect an academic career, although they did not talk extensively about it in the interviews and some did not talk about it at all. Perry was the only student in the 16 explicitly to mention tenure as a feature of academic life, in the context of needing to publish: 'That's the basis of our career getting tenured, it's all based on publication.' Hannah indicated a desire to teach 'in a small college somewhere', making a distinction between that career and 'being a professor' in a university, which she identified as her earlier expect-ation. Her observations of her supervisor and other faculty members 'completely turned me off': 'I see that you're the ass and the carrot [is] in front of you and you're constantly running.' Inez was implicitly critical of her professors: 'I know that when I am a prof and when I eventually am teaching graduate students, I'll do things differently, you know?'

Some students were fairly laconic about moving into academic work: 'I anticipate that I will be able to get a job' (Melanie), while for others it was a source of anxiety:

> Sometimes when I think of it in terms of getting a job, what kind of job? . . . and it is a main issue for all of us, so what will happen after we graduate and, you know, to have access to jobs in our field. So [there are] all these issues, publications and participation in conferences, but now it's so hard to be able to attend conferences and to get access to publications, which means that what might happen to us after we graduate? . . . Other candidates have access to funding, to publications, and conferences and so on. It is a long, huge struggle. We are students of colour and some of us don't have funding and even the emotional support.
>
> (Francine)

Francine's statement brings together a number of themes evident in some of the other interviews: worries about a very vague future and the actions needed to secure it; suspicion that other students have competitive advantages; awareness of belonging to a minority group and concern over its implications.

In considering whether the degree had been worth all the effort, Danielle remarked:

> Anytime I hear anyone doing a PhD I kind of feel [it in] my stomach. I think, oh, my God, do you know what you're getting into? . . . Job possibilities are extremely limited of the things a PhD qualifies you for – mainly academic – the jobs that exist like the kind of jobs that I do are crappy, exploited, you don't get paid any money.

Beth, another completer, also showed trepidation about the future: 'I don't know what lies ahead for me. At least when you are a student you know [what your goal is] . . . It also took so much a big part of your life and was the priority so you could push other things [aside].'

As with other topics, students expressed a desire for greater guidance regarding finding and transitioning into an academic job. Completers, in particular, had ideas about how the situation could be improved, such as postdoctoral positions or temporary arrangements for four or five months after the doctorate where the department was not saying 'Oh, you're finished so we're finished with you' (Carol).

Teaching

Four of the five completers were currently or recently had been teaching in stipend or contract positions in post-secondary institutions. These types of appointments, also called sessional or contingent positions, do not carry job security and may be part-time (see note 5). Two of the eleven candidates also had this type of experience. We can surmise that as students come closer to completing their dissertations, they are more attractive to local institutions for contingent positions; moreover, the students themselves may seek out such placements, possibly for the sake of experience or because they have exhausted the university-based work opportunities or come to the end of external scholarships.

Yet students did not on the whole discuss teaching work as an intentional bridge to academe. While some thought that the experience could help on the job market, for many, the work was seen as a necessary evil in the interests of financial survival, something that interfered with the timely completion of their doctorates as well as with other activities such as publishing. There is an interesting parallel with an American study of a program that prepared graduate students to be teaching assistants (TAs). By stressing the utilitarian needs of the TAs, the program inadvertently reinforced the belief that teaching was a low-level inconvenience while research would be their real work to come (Janke and Colbeck, 2008). The experience of our students and graduates with contingent work might also be conveying generally negative messages about teaching.

For example, Beth talked about how stretched she was with her contract teaching and not enough time to sleep:

> Now you're teaching, you're grading, you're marking, you're doing all the shit work that you don't really want to do and you have no time for your own work...and once you are no longer a student you are supposed to start paying all your debt.

When asked about her interests in publishing, she indicated that she would like to do it, but stated flatly 'I don't have time.' Danielle noted that while working as a teaching assistant was good for her self-esteem – 'you realize you actually know something' – she estimated that subsequent teaching on contract for financial reasons had cost her at least a year on her thesis. Carol described the poor conditions sessional instructors often face, calling it 'the new exploitation' and 'proletarian labour'.

As noted earlier, for our students, no teaching assistant offers accompanied acceptance into the program and any such positions had to be sought out and applied for elsewhere. A very few of the students had managed to acquire some kind of independent teaching responsibility within the university. One of the completers, Elaine, gave a rare discussion of pedagogy *per se*, talking about the challenges involved in teaching a topic where emotions ran high. For most, achieving a publication record was more of an overt concern than teaching. Perhaps they assumed that teaching could be learned on the job. And perhaps their immersion in a research-intensive institution, after all, shaped their imagination around the future.

Publishing

> You get these messages... that you've gotta publish, you've gotta do this, you've gotta do these many conferences ... I do not know how to go and get a job in an institution. I do not know how to make a CV that would look like something. I do not know what the requirements are. I do not know how to go and get my stuff published. I do not know how to prepare for an interview or even create a course...there are so many things that I need to know that I do not know...this should be a part of the process.
>
> (Hannah)

In the abstract, students believed that they should publish while doing doctoral studies. Publication (like sessional teaching) appeared to be implicitly or explicitly a means to an end, getting an academic job. Students did not often mention taking pleasure in the writing process. Rather, for many, publishing was a mystery and source of anxiety. Opal said: 'It wasn't until my third year that someone said "Oh, yeah, by the way, you know that you should have at least three things published before you leave, right?" And then you go, "Huh?" ... It's good information. I wish I had it in my first year.' Grace had published early in her doctoral studies: 'I published a very long big essay which is a part of my comprehensive [examination] as well', adding 'I came in having already had some thought about a project to pursue.' Compared to others, Grace appeared to be moving quickly through the program and already had a publication record. Moreover:

> I have discovered all of those things on my own. I don't think I was even told the difference between submitting a chapter to a book versus publishing in a refereed journal…and I have figured that I need to publish and produce and I think during the time I was doing my coursework…I have also published five pieces…I've done all of it on my own.

The 'on my own' theme was echoed by others and is reminiscent of the 'personal sense of responsibility' or agency discussed in Chapter 6. The remarks may also reflect a separation between professorial research and student research. While students might work as graduate assistants on a faculty member's research project, it could be unrelated to their own interests. Inez commented: 'I was helping someone else with her career and wasn't helping myself.' Later, she phrased it as having been used as 'a commodity'. Austin (2002) points out that both teaching and research assistantships for graduate students often function more for the benefit of the institution than as a learning experience for the student. The authors of Chapter 6 point to similar circumstances and note that agency is often negotiated through interactions with more powerful figures.

Inez was one of the students who thought faculty should incorporate publication opportunities into their courses. Two students reported just such an experience. Leonard explained: 'Part of the goal of the course was to have a published article at the end of it…that was fantastic.' He was encouraged by this professor as well as another one who 'made it possible for me to present papers at various venues'. As a consequence:

> A paper that was developed in [Professor A's] course [was] then presented at the sociology association [conference] and also published…a paper that I wrote in [Professor B's] course was subsequently presented at two conferences and published in a journal.

Sponsorship, encouragement and mentoring (or their absence) were mentioned by many of the students, often with regard to publishing. Kara had an extraordinary level of sponsorship, having co-authored a series of publications with her supervisor. These opportunities accompanied Kara's work on research projects:

> [Professor] asked me to work on the study...I was there to do the data analysis and writing for the report. Then we looked at it collaboratively and developed it into a book...and that overlapped with doing my master's coursework and once we finished that study we started another one...I was on that research team from start to finish.

It is probably no accident that Kara is one of the few students to talk very specifically about preparing for work in academe. She stated:

> For me, doing a PhD is not just getting the letters at the end of my name, but it's about building a career. So many people walk out of here and we all have PhDs when we leave, so what separates you from someone else is the body of work you take with you, what's on your CV.

Kara's situation makes an interesting contrast with Inez's experience of assisting a professor and does suggest that under certain circumstances, faculty can organize their work in such a way that at least some students gain career-enhancing opportunities. Students like Elaine, whose study was in continuity with her supervisor's, tended to be relatively satisfied with their experience: 'My supervisor was my MA supervisor as well, ...so I had a really smooth ride, very, very smooth ride...My project was so very close to my supervisor's work...so there wasn't a lot of conflict.'

Many students have a dream and desire for a high level of attention that amounts to mentoring rather than supervision *per se* (Acker, 2007), a level which would involve much greater provision of information, attention, contacts and opportunities. Some believed that faculty were rationing these opportunities. Their perceptions of the reasons for selective attention were related to what they saw as faculty 'busyness' (usually assumed to be focused on their research) and favouritism. For example, Danielle comments on two aspects of her supervisor's style:

> One is that she is incredibly stressed and overwhelmed and is probably doing too much and [the other is] the way she manages her students. [For some] she's not interested, she's not committed; [for others] she has the odd student that she adores and throws herself [into when researching a] very similar area.

The theme of differentiated opportunities permeated many of the interviews and many such comments pertained to the conditions that would support publishing. Carol explained that there were 'two tiers [of students] in this school.' One tier is 'people that have an OK situation' while the other is those who 'just have endless jobs and are running around like crazy and they're all fighting amongst each other thinking you're getting it a lot better than I am'.

Francine worried about opportunities for students of colour: 'I don't want to have spent all these years doing a PhD and then, you know, just to be [not hired as an academic] because there are other candidates who have access to funding, to publications and conferences and so on.' Opal echoed her point, adding to it the disadvantages faced by older students with children:

> You know it's very much the pet students that information is made easily accessible to, the favourite students…it's those students who work most comfortably with profs…which all students can't do, because if I have to be at home by 3 or 3:30 to pick my kids up, I can't be here evenings, and it's the students who can who are involved in this and that, and you know what? I can't do it…As a Black student, we don't have access to the same networks as some of the White students may have, and your areas of interest don't necessarily match with those of the staff.

Interestingly, despite her analysis of 'pets', Opal had one of the most strategic approaches to gaining what she needed from faculty. She outlined the way in which she would say to a professor:

> Help me to understand what I need to do, what are the little pieces that I have to put in place. So [I am then] able to work with a prof who says, 'Okay, what do you want to get accomplished this year?' And we can sit together and [I] say…[names various objectives] and [then it's] her picking up the phone or sending me an e-mail saying 'Oh, by the way, did you see this?' [Or a conference] is coming up, submit something.

A minority of other students also gave examples of ways in which they had learned to be strategic. It appears to the doctoral students that resources such as sponsorship and information are in short supply and thus a student must be able to function on one's own and/or carefully strategize to access what is needed for success in the program and (sometimes) in the future.

Up to this point, the emphasis has been on student perspectives. In the following section, we reflect on the contextual features which we believe are shaping and at times limiting these perspectives.

The importance of context

Melanie, one of the candidates, told a lengthy story of misunderstanding over the comprehensive examination requirement. Trying to understand her situation, she then generalized the issue, alluding to ambiguities related to lack of structure: 'That's problematic for me in terms of the way the structure works at the school or the lack of clarity or the lack of input from my advisor or something...it seems to me something is missing.'

Is something missing, as Melanie suspected, or are the struggles reported simply part of the necessary rites of passage required of doctoral students? Do students misunderstand the fundamental nature of the graduate student experience (Shulman and Silver, 2003)? Addressing graduate sociology students, Shulman and Silver explicitly state: 'It is not the faculty's job to get you publications. It is their job to help develop sociologists who can generate publishable works. It is your job to get published' (ibid., p. 66). Our students, especially those who believed sponsorship was a form of capital, accessible only by the favoured few, would likely disagree. Right or wrong, such perceptions have important consequences and it is likely that the belief that they are entitled to assistance that they are not receiving is counterproductive both to student satisfaction and to progress.

Our argument is that it would be too simplistic to view the results as a consequence of either confused students or selfish faculty. First, there are counterexamples – students (like Opal) who are proactive, and faculty (like Kara's supervisor and Leonard's instructor) who are generous and imaginative with time and sponsorship. Yet we still need to explain why so many students believe they are inadequately guided or mentored.

Additionally, at least three (and likely more) contextual features have to be taken into account. Differences in contextual features may explain why negative emotions figure more prominently in our research than they appear to in the McAlpine *et al.* study reported in the next chapter. One major impediment to orienting towards a future academic career lies in the low level of financial support available for the participants in our study. Rather like Maslow's well-known (1943) hierarchy of needs, survival and getting through the program became more important to the students than self-actualization or planning for the future.

Recall our earlier discussion of the paucity of Canadian government funding for post-secondary education, especially in the social sciences, and especially in the 1990s. Most students in the candidate group began their studies in 1997 or 1998, just when national funding for social science research was especially sparse. The transcripts were filled with laments over inadequate funding and descriptions of trying for external scholarships and graduate assistantships. To make ends meet, students often worked at several part-time jobs, both on and off campus. At the time of interview, one of Francine's jobs was in a distant suburb. She explained: 'I start at 8 so basically I leave my home around 6:30 to be there at 8:00 because [the bus] takes about an hour and a half. Then I'm paid for three hours.' She added: 'I can't detach myself from my life, the thing of survival, it worries me so much that even when I study I have to think about these things. How am I going to survive?... How am I going to pay my rent [and] eat, and transport is very expensive.'[17]

A second contextual feature concerns the faculty. Faculty 'busyness' could be understood through the many studies that have examined their ever-intensifying workloads (Acker, 2003). It could also be related to the particular context of the research. The 1999 departmental report mentioned earlier shows that around the time many of these students began their programs there was a spike in departmental doctoral admissions, from 14 new PhD students in 1995/96 to 24 in 1998/99, pushing total PhD enrolment from 51 to 84. The report noted that 13 departmental faculty members were full members of the university's School of Graduate Studies (see note 4) and thus allowed to supervise doctoral students. In other words, the department concerned had a very high ratio of doctoral students to faculty. Faculty also supervised master's degree students and served on student thesis committees.[18] Supervision and thesis committee membership were an optional (though expected) part of faculty work, but not officially acknowledged as part of teaching workload, expectations for which were based solely on class teaching. Furthermore, certain specialties and individuals were in more demand than others, so some faculty members became greatly overloaded. There are no norms for the amount of time or energy faculty should spend on supervision – it is an aspect of academic life often learned by doing and has been called a 'deeply uncertain practice' (Grant, 2005, p. 337). It can be argued that supervisors, at least in this case, do not have the time available to sponsor each student. Even if we assume that most faculty members fulfil the implicit contract by guiding students through the dissertation process, they might well ration their 'extra' (sponsorship) efforts in some way, for example, giving more attention to students like Kara or Elaine who appear to share their interests or can help them with their own research and writing.

Grant and Graham (1994, p. 165) remind us that the dissertation 'is likely to be the student's major work focus while it is one small aspect of the supervisor's current workload'. Basically, faculty and students come into the situation from different standpoints and there are many impediments to comprehending the perspective of the other. As Austin (2002) also found, students had only partial understandings of faculty work as a whole – the often time-consuming aspect of institutional service, for example, was probably underestimated and not commented upon. Conversely, the excruciating financial situations some of these students faced were usually unknown to faculty; even if aware, they did not know how to fix the problem. Contrary to some students' assumptions, money for students did not flow through the department, and many faculty did not understand the minutiae of the (ever-changing) financial support systems available at the university.

The third contextual feature is the academic labour market and its connection to doctoral education. Sociologists of education know that not every secondary school student or undergraduate will graduate at the top of their class – it is impossible by definition – and some analysts have seen the schooling system as intentionally stratifying students so that they enter differentiated workplace and labour market hierarchies or continue their education. They also realize that some students have far more economic, social and cultural capital than others (Bourdieu, 1986), and that outcomes are shaped, if not determined, by those conditions. While graduate students are themselves highly successful in the education system, the differentiation is likely to occur again, as there are rarely enough academic positions (especially desirable ones) for all of the doctoral graduates who might want them. Chapter 4 depicts a parallel situation for social anthropologists in the UK, where only a minority find positions in their field, while others end up in related fields, and a big group is consigned to marginal positions doing contract research. Increasing North American reliance on casualized teaching is an analogous situation. If our students look locally, they mostly see the short-term teaching positions that were described so unfavourably by our completers. It is not surprising that some students see the doctoral years as a struggle for the survival of the fittest and suspect that some students are favoured over others.

▶ Conclusion and implications for practice

It is time to return to our original question about continuities or dis-
continuities between doctoral student life and the early-career concerns of academics. We found that while students mostly intended an
academic career, they were hazy about specifics and rarely mentioned
that huge challenge for junior faculty, the tenure review. Publishing
and stipend teaching were generally seen as necessary means to an
end, that end being acquiring the academic job, rather than heralding
one's lifetime work. The lists of tasks that new faculty must master that
we gave near the beginning of this chapter bore little resemblance to
the content of the interviews. To some extent the nature of our study
could be responsible, as we did not ask specifically about students'
knowledge of course planning, teaching portfolios and other such
topics. Our feeling, however, is that the students had too much else
on their plates to anticipate those details. They were strongly focused
on financial survival and getting through their programs. While a few
workshops on getting academic jobs were available in the institution,
there were no extended professional preparation programs such as
the ones described in the US literature. Would they have made a difference? Perhaps. One imagines that students in such programs would
feel sponsored and that itself could make a difference.

While the discontinuity between the specific preoccupations of the
doctoral students and early-career faculty members looms large, there
is another, more cynical, way to look at the question. If the early career
is a period of uncertainty, instability and the need to make sense
of new cultures and hidden requirements, what better preparation
could there be than the very similar challenges of doctoral study? In a
thoughtful analysis of interviews with women of colour graduate students, Margolis and Romero (2001) question many taken-for-granted
assumptions about mentoring and link it to the sometimes unques-
tioned reproduction of the status quo. Resistance to traditional forms
of knowledge were more important to some of the students in their
study than following in the footsteps of the faculty. Our research location appears to differ from theirs in the greater availability of faculty of
colour. Yet both studies raise the question of whether diverse student
populations require new ways of thinking about graduate schooling.

What, then, are the *implications for practice*? We have identified
structural features that appear to play a part in impeding student
progress, especially lack of guaranteed, reliable and sufficient funding
and a faculty labour process that overworks academics and fails to

give credit for mentoring. *There are some obvious policy changes that would likely help* the situation, such as restricting student numbers to match available faculty capacity; keeping better track of students, perhaps through a cohort rather than the individual student model which allows students to fade away without anyone noticing (Lovitts, 2001); and introducing appropriate workload credit for supervisors.

A chronic difficulty is that after the first few years of completing requirements, students become distanced from their departments and often complete their dissertations in isolation from peers and departmental activities. At the point where they may begin to be more interested in systematically preparing for an academic future, they are least able to engage in relevant efforts. Funding typically lasts for fewer years than students in the social sciences need, so we again have the survival phenomenon of students taking jobs like contingent teaching outside the university and becoming increasingly detached while, ironically, their time to completion may increase. *Some supervisors set up monthly thesis groups in which their students meet once a month* to update each other on progress, present draft papers, talk about challenges and so forth, and we suggest this model become more widely adopted and institutionalized (with workload credit for supervisors). As with other mechanisms, provision is currently haphazard – for example, students whose supervisors do not have enough students to form a group typically lose out. It would not be impossible to organize such students into a group by, for example, combining students of several supervisors.

We do have some reservations about provision of workshops for doctoral students as future faculty. First, there is the problem of isolation and remoteness for advanced students described above, which usually means that the students attending such workshops are in their early years of study. Second, although workshops can hardly do any harm, they need to be carefully planned so as not to suggest that only students who can line up tenure-track jobs are worthy of the department's attention. Third, we have noticed that advertised institutional-level workshops rarely attract large numbers; the students in our study, even when advocating such efforts, tended not to have taken advantage of what was available. Finally, with no funding provided, it would be the same overloaded faculty who would be asked to take on the additional responsibilities. *The department we studied now has a required non-credit workshop course called 'Learning to succeed in graduate school'* that orients new doctoral students to the diverse requirements of the program such as writing comprehensive examinations and finding a supervisor. We think that extending this model, so that processes such as constructing CVs, gaining research experience, understanding publication and finding academic jobs would be built into the curriculum rather than introduced haphazardly, would be worth exploring. The reality of contingent positions for many graduates needs to be discussed openly and students encouraged to plan careers that take into account such possibilities.

We also suggest that an arm's length support person be appointed in each faculty (faculty of education, faculty of arts, etc.) *or cluster of departments.* Some universities already have an ombudsperson who has similar functions, but we are thinking of more prominent, accessible positions – possibly located in student services or counselling. This person would be someone who could not only direct students to appropriate services for all academic-related issues, such as funding, job search, writing support, and so on, but could also mediate complex issues between student and supervisor as they arise. Having an independent person to consult would bypass student fears that department chairs (most often called upon in the Canadian academy to deal with problems between student and supervisor) could not be objective in these mediations given their close working relationship with supervisors. As well, this kind of appointment might lessen the workload of faculty members and chairs. We would also like to see greater empathy between the principal actors in this drama, the students and the faculty. As we have said several times, each 'side' seems mired in its own positionality, only partially aware of the constraints the other group experiences. In the interests of empathy as well as anticipatory socialization, perhaps students could shadow a faculty member for a short period as part of something like the 'learning to succeed in graduate school' course.

Here there could also be a role for faculty development – courses or workshops for new faculty and new supervisors could include study of chapters (and books) such as this one or work like that of Lovitts (2001), Austin (2002) and Gardner (2007, 2008). Common in Australia, New Zealand and the UK, training for new supervisors seems rarely found in Canada, so there is room for development efforts in this regard. In the end, we are faced with the dilemma characteristic of much educational reform: how to keep believing that local improvements will make a difference when structural factors remain difficult to change. We do not want to surrender to pessimism. The iceberg remains two-thirds submerged, and is not of our creation, but we can find creative ways around it to get to the safety of the shore.

▶ Notes

1. In 2000, the Government of Canada invested $300 million to establish 2000 research professorships ('chairs') in universities across the country by 2008. This program has been controversial for various reasons, including its relatively low allocation of chairs to social sciences and humanities (compared to natural sciences, engineering and health sciences) and its under-representation of women (Side and Robbins, 2007).
2. By 2005–2006, these numbers had increased to 4200 and 36,700 respectively (Statistics Canada, 2008a, 2008b).
3. Projects drawn upon in this section are on various facets of the academic experience and have taken place from 1994 onwards, funded by the Social Sciences and Humanities Research Council of Canada. They include 'Making a Difference' (Sandra Acker with Carol Baines, Marcia Boyd, Grace Feuerverger and Linda Muzzin); 'Traditions and Transitions in Teacher Education' (Sandra Acker with Jo-Anne Dillabough, Thérèse Hamel, Dianne Miller and Elizabeth Smyth); 'Disciplining Academics' (Sandra Acker with Elizabeth Smyth and Michelle Webber). We thank SSHRC and the (then) graduate students and researchers who have worked on the projects over the years, including Jennifer Ajandi, Juliet Hess, Nicole Sanderson, Barbara Soren, Amy Sullivan, Michelle Webber. Representative publications are Acker and Armenti (2004); Acker and Dillabough (2007); and Acker and Feuerverger (1996).
4. Application for appointment of faculty members to a School or Faculty of Graduate Studies at the university is commonplace in Canada. This school or faculty is a unit that co-ordinates and regulates the governance of all aspects of graduate study, including determining admissions criteria, curricular approval and other related standards. Appointment to this school or faculty is required in order to supervise graduate students and teach graduate courses. However, there are differences in practices across universities surrounding what qualifications are required and at what point in an academic career applications can be approved.
5. The term 'contingent' covers a range of part-time or full-time academic positions, usually teaching-focused, that are temporary in nature and do not usually carry job security and benefits.
6. It should be noted that very few people are actually turned down for tenure, at least in the universities we have studied, and likely in Canada as a whole. Exact figures are difficult to come by, as people

may leave at any point before or during the process if it appears they will be unsuccessful, and there are elaborate appeal processes which also can result in an eventual granting of tenure. The high probability of success does not, we believe, make junior faculty notably less anxious.

7. Although student involvement in departmental life and politics was an important feature of the department under study – the organizational career strand identified in Chapter 6 – given the limited space available we do not discuss it here.

8. We use the terminology 'graduate student' for what is elsewhere called postgraduate student or research student. Graduate students are normally enrolled in a program leading to a master's or doctoral degree. See Chapters 2 and 6 for descriptions of typical requirements in such programs in North America.

9. Generalizations about the institution and the department rely on unpublished documents as well as what might be considered the ethnographic or autoethnographic component of our study, namely our personal experience with the setting.

10. Minority students may have been slightly over-chosen; however, we do not have any official figures to check representation against. We are aware that even this description does not represent identity very well. There is considerable variation within each ethnocultural category. For example, Black students may have immigrated either from the Caribbean or Africa either as adults or as children, or they might have been born in Canada to immigrant or non-immigrant parents. Age, children and other characteristics also cut across any identification by race, ethnicity or gender.

11. A comprehensive exam is typically an examination that must be passed by graduate students in doctoral programs after their coursework is completed. Although the form and general requirements vary across department, discipline and universities, it typically tests the student's knowledge of their subject and related areas. As well, passing the comprehensive exam typically determines the candidate's eligibility to continue on in their program of study. See also Chapter 2.

12. We do not want to identify each student by their demographic characteristics, given promises of anonymity, and instead only use phrases like 'women of colour' when they are contained within a quotation from the student.

13. The amount of financial support offered to incoming graduate students varies across departments, disciplines and universities. At

the time, the number of scholarships and assistantships described would have been considered a low level of support given the number of admissions.

14. There is considerable institutional variation in the availability of research and teaching assistantships for graduate students. Teaching assistants (TAs) provide marking and often teaching assistance to course instructors while research assistants (called graduate assistants – GAs – in the institution under study) provide research assistance to faculty members on their research projects. All graduate students who hold these assistantships are paid a set hourly wage for their work and this payment is counted as part of the funding package awarded to the graduate student. (See also Chapter 2.) In the department we studied, some students might seek out teaching opportunities in the institution's teacher education program or in other departments or other universities; similarly there were other possibilities that enterprising students might discover, such as paid research work (beyond the institutional research assistantships) on a faculty project. Students could also apply for external scholarships.

15. The requirement of a master's degree before beginning a doctorate is common in Canada (Leyton-Brown, 2008).

16. In North America, 'professor' (and in this quotation, 'professoriate') is a generic term for academics.

17. More recently, the university initiated a guaranteed funding package for certain categories of students which has eased some of the distress, although many would still consider it inadequate.

18. Doctoral students needed a supervisor and two additional faculty members on their thesis committees. MA students required a supervisor and second reader, while M Ed students needed only one supervisor.

▶ **References**

Acker, S. (2001) 'The hidden curriculum of dissertation advising', in E. Margolis (ed.) *The Hidden Curriculum in Higher Education*. New York: Routledge.

Acker, S. (2003) 'The concerns of Canadian women academics: Will faculty shortages make things better or worse?', *McGill Journal of Education*, 38(3): 391–405.

Acker, S. (2007) 'Advising and mentoring in graduate education', in B. Bank (ed.) *Gender and Education: An Encyclopedia*. New York: Greenwood Press.

Acker, S. (2008) 'Gender and the chair', in A. Wagner, S. Acker and K. Mayuzumi (eds) *Whose University Is It, Anyway? Power and Privilege on Gendered Terrain*. Toronto: Sumach Press.

Acker, S. and Armenti, C. (2004) 'Sleepless in academia', *Gender and Education*, 16(1): 3–24.

Acker, S. and Dillabough, J. (2007) 'Women "learning to labour" in the "male emporium": Exploring gendered work in teacher education', *Gender and Education*, 19(3): 297–316.

Acker, S. and Feuerverger, G. (1996) 'Doing good and feeling bad: The work of women university teachers', *Cambridge Journal of Education*, 26(3): 401–22.

Acker, S. and Webber, M. (2006) 'Admission to the knowledge community: The role of tenure in university practice', paper presented at the Canadian Society for Studies in Higher Education Conference, Congress of Social Sciences and Humanities, York University.

Archer, L. (2008) 'Younger academics' constructions of "authenticity", "success" and professional identity', *Studies in Higher Education*, 33(4): 385–403.

Austin, A. (2002) 'Preparing the next generation of faculty: Graduate education as socialization to the academic career', *Journal of Higher Education*, 73: 94–122.

Bourdieu, P. (1986) 'The forms of capital', in J.G. Richardson (ed.) *Handbook of Theory and Research for the Sociology of Education*. Westport, CT: Greenwood Press.

Brooks, R. and Heiland, D. (2007) 'Accountability, assessment and doctoral education: recommendations for moving forward', *European Journal of Education*, 42(3): 351–62.

Gardner, S. (2007) ' "I heard it through the grapevine": Doctoral student socialization in chemistry and history', *Higher Education*, 54: 723–40.

Gardner, S. (2008) ' "What's too much and what's too little?" The process of becoming an independent researcher in doctoral education', *Journal of Higher Education*, 79(3): 326–50.

Glazer-Raymo, J. (2003) 'Women faculty and part-time employment: The impact of public policy', in B. Ropers-Huilman (ed.) *Gendered Futures in Higher Education*. Albany, NY: State University of New York Press.

Gluszynski, T. and Peters, V. (2005) *Survey of Earned Doctorates: A Profile of Doctoral Degree Recipients*. Ottawa: Statistics Canada. Cat. 81–595-MIE-No.032.

Golde, C. and Dore, T. (2001) 'At cross-purposes: What the experiences of today's doctoral students reveal about doctoral education', Pew Charitable Trusts, available at: http://www.phd.survey.org.

Grant, B. (2005) 'Fighting for space in supervision: Fantasies, fairytales, fictions and fallacies', *International Journal of Qualitative Studies in Higher Education*, 31(4): 337–54.

Grant, B. and Graham, A. (1994) 'Guidelines for discussion: A tool for managing postgraduate supervision', in O. Zuber-Skerritt and Y. Ryan (eds) *Quality in Postgraduate Education*. London: Kogan Page.

Janke, E. and Colbeck, C. (2008) 'Lost in translation: Learning professional roles through the situated curriculum', *New Directions in Teaching and Learning*, 113: 57–68.

Leyton-Brown, D. (2008) 'Social and legal aspects of doctoral training in Canada: Criteria and consequences of admission', *Higher Education in Europe*, 33(1): 111–23.

Lovitts, B. (2001) *Leaving the Ivory Tower: The Causes and Consequences of Departure from Doctoral Study*. Lanham, MD: Rowman and Littlefield.

Margolis, E. and Romero, M. (2001) ' "In the image and likeness…": How mentoring functions in the hidden curriculum', in E. Margolis (ed.) *The Hidden Curriculum in Higher Education*. New York: Routledge.

Maslow, A.H. (1943) 'A theory of human motivation', *Psychological Review*, 50(4): 370–96.

McAlpine, L. and Norton, J. (2006) 'Reframing our approach to doctoral programs: An integrative framework for action and research', *Higher Education Research and Development*, 25(1): 3–17.

McCormick, C. and Barnes, B. (2008) 'Getting started in academia: A guide for educational psychologists', *Educational Psychology Review*, 20(1): 5–18.

Muzzin, L. and Limoges, J. (2008) ' "A pretty incredible structural injustice": Contingent faculty in Canadian university nursing', in A. Wagner, S. Acker and K. Mayuzumi (eds) *Whose University Is It, Anyway? Power and Privilege on Gendered Terrain*. Toronto: Sumach Press.

Shanahan, T. and Jones, G. (2007) 'Shifting roles and approaches: Government coordination of post-secondary education in Canada, 1995–2006', *Higher Education Research and Development*, 26(1): 31–43.

Shulman, D. and Silver, I. (2003) 'The business of becoming a professional sociologist: Unpacking the informal training of graduate school', *The American Sociologist*, Fall: 56–72.

Side, K. and Robbins, W. (2007) 'Institutionalizing inequalities in Canadian universities: The Canada Research Chairs Program', *NWSA Journal*, 19(3): 163–81.

Solem, M., Foote, K. and Monk, J. (2009) *Aspiring Academics: A Resource Book for Graduate Students and Early Career Faculty*. Upper Saddle River, NJ: Pearson Education.

Statistics Canada (2008a) 'University degrees, diplomas and certificates awarded', *The Daily*, February 7, 2008.

Statistics Canada (2008b) 'University enrolment', *The Daily*, February 7, 2008.

Tierney, W. and Bensimon, E. (1996) *Promotion and Tenure: Community and Socialization in Academe*. Albany, NY: State University of New York Press.

Walker, G.E., Golde, C.M., Jones, L., Bueschel, A.C. and Hutchings, P. (2008) *The Formation of Scholars: Rethinking Doctoral Education for the Twenty-First Century*. San Francisco: Jossey-Bass.

Ward, K. and Wolf-Wendel, L. (2004) 'Academic motherhood: Managing complex roles in research universities', *The Review of Higher Education*, 27(2): 233–57.

Williams, G. (2008) 'Canada', in Nerad, M. and Heggelund, M. (eds) *Towards a Global PhD?* Seattle: University of Washington Press, pp. 249–77.

6 Living and Imagining Academic Identities

Lynn McAlpine, Cheryl Amundsen and Marian Jazvac-Martek

▶ Author perspectives

Lynn's story
Prior to entering academia, I spent twenty years as a professional developer for the Canadian government. This previous experience may explain why I view myself as an academic developer as well as higher education researcher. In doing a master's and then a doctorate during the twenty years, I very much focused on my own inquiry. I had no understanding that the reading and writing related to my thesis and then dissertation were connecting me to a network of individuals past and present and that I could seek out those still alive to engage in conversation – even though I acted as an editorial assistant for a journal. I did not understand writing as something that might ultimately make a contribution to others' thinking; my work was for the eyes of my supervisor and committee. As well, I had little sense of institutional resources and impediments – depending largely on my supervisor for information. This description makes me sound quite uninformed about academic life and that was indeed the case.

I began pre-tenure work at McGill University in Canada when my life circumstances had dramatically changed and I had the opportunity to guide a community-based aboriginal teacher education program. I began to understand more of how institutional resources and constraints were influencing the decisions I made. Also, I was the only one in this field in my institution and I began to see I needed a network of individuals doing similar work beyond the university. And, since I viewed this work as important and under-examined, I began to write about it for a wider audience – learning as I went about peer review and publishing. At the same time, it was lonely work – an outsider from the dominant culture trying to represent a minority culture. So, after some years, I shifted from aboriginal teacher education into educational development and began guiding a teaching and learning unit and researching how academics develop their understanding of teaching.

This shift was not straightforward as the aboriginal teacher education network (virtual, historical, and physical) was not in any way connected to that of educational development; the move meant learning a new litera- ture, a new set of relationships, and a new understanding of what the gaps and questions were. Nevertheless, I was fortunate to have a local network of colleagues who supported my learning. In addition, my research involved a team of students and through working with them I became particularly interested in how they made sense of academic work and how as a more senior academic I might support their learning. This led to my present research interest in early career academic experience. Fortunately, this intellectual shift did not involve developing a whole new network; rather it led to a focus on a sub-set and extension of the network I already knew.

And, this new interest led me eventually to a different institution, the University of Oxford, in a different country, the UK. This pursuit of intellec- tual interests has, of course, led to disruptions in my personal life, and the challenge of maintaining relationships at a distance. As well, despite nearly twenty years of academic work, this re-location has led me to question some of the knowledge I took for granted, e.g., criteria for assessing doc- toral and master's work. These new experiences and interactions are slowly becoming integrated into how I view the world and academic work – and it is this broader perspective which permeates the way I think, act and write.

Cheryl's story

I have always been driven by purpose and a good portion of that pur- pose must be about supporting others. My first graduate degree was in Learning Disabilities, following six years as a public school teacher. When I finished my degree, my thesis supervisor offered me a position teaching at the university and working with her in the development work that was her passion. Our writing was focused on program development and evaluation and this is what I understood scholarship to be. I enjoyed the academic environment and my next step was to pursue a PhD so that I could pursue an academic job.

During my PhD studies, my notion of what constituted scholarship or academic work broadened. Previously, I had consulted the literature because my master's thesis needed a literature review or because the development grants we applied for or the papers we wrote required refer- ences to the literature to defend the projects we wanted to implement. My PhD program was about something different – it was about coming to understand the scholarly field in which I was working. The program was very active in inviting visiting scholars. We spent time with and came to know these people – they became 'real' with all of their scholarly brilliance, personal strengths and flaws. While some of these people clearly had a goal to make a name for themselves, most seemed also to be dedicated to their work as a way to improve education. I came to understand scholarly writing as being less about defending ideas, and more as a way to build useful knowledge in a field and try out ideas that had actual utility. I began to find my purpose as an academic.

My biggest challenge came upon assuming my first academic appointment at McGill University. In my new position I was cross-appointed to the Dept. of Educational and Counselling Psychology and the Centre for University Teaching and Learning where I did individual and project-based work to support professors as teachers. It took me some time to begin to think of the teaching development work and the research requirements together. I found great purpose in the academic development work (working for others) – but the other part of my role seemed to be steeped in the discourse of 'building my CV' and 'playing the tenure and promotion game' (working for myself). It took me a few years, but I began just writing with colleagues about the academic work that we were doing and at first simply trying to figure out the impact of that work on teaching development. Here was something I could believe in and once again I was motivated, having found purpose to continue. I spent 10 years at McGill University and have now spent a little more than that at Simon Fraser University. At both universities, my academic development work has brought me into contact with new academics and I find that my own experience of seeking personal meaning or purpose in academic work is also central for many of them. Many are not motivated by the discourse of 'making a name for yourself', 'building your CV', and 'playing the tenure and promotion game' and may even find this discourse debilitating. So I advise new academics who seem hampered by institutional expectations to find personal meaning in academic work and pursue it. It will then be easy to explain what you have done and why you have done it.

Marian's story

Having only 'just' entered the academic arena with a recently completed PhD degree, I consider myself to have spent a reasonable amount of time engaging in and with the structures of higher education, in diverse roles and exposed to multiple perspectives. While both an MA and PhD student, I took on many independent teaching roles, having taught more than a dozen university course sessions at both the undergraduate and graduate levels. In conjunction with this, I worked in an academic development centre and had the privilege of engaging with many professors in collaborative initiatives to improve teaching and learning at the university, as well as contribute to ventures aimed at ameliorating doctoral student experiences. While both are tangentially related to the 'intellectual' strand of my own research agenda, each venture has facilitated an explicit interweaving of institutional and networking identity strands with the intellectual one. In the research realm, I have benefited from working on several research teams and learning what it means to 'do' research from several highly skilled and expert researchers. Upon reflection, I doubt that my experiences are the norm, as I have had opportunities that are often not typical of most North American graduate student experiences, but it does, however, underscore how doctoral students can indeed share many experiences with pre-tenure academics. Often I have been simultaneously sitting in various chairs: acting as a pseudo-faculty member when I teach or am engaged in academic development, or as a consultant when sitting on various committees or participating in meetings that may impact public university initiatives, or being the vulnerable and struggling doctoral student when I sought increased clarity every time I combed through my mountain of collected qualitative data, or spent hours attempting to find the best way to articulate the ideas and insights that were clear in my mind, but all too elusive for words. These multiple roles and perspectives are augmented by the subject matter I have chosen to study over the years. I have examined conceptions of teaching in higher education while still developing my own teaching style, struggled with better understanding teacher evaluation while learning to cope with evaluations of my own work and my own impacts as a teacher, and most recently, after changing directions and supervisors, trying to better understand others' doctoral student academic identity experiences in my own dissertation work and as part of my own intellectual journey. While I have yet to concretize and define my own academic perspective, I continue my academic pathway in a 'hall of mirrors', as I currently engage in post-doctoral research work which focuses on both the experiences of the doctorate and the experiences of those, like myself, who have earned a degree and are forging their own academic pathways. Each experience has been distinct, and in hindsight each is intricately related to my own growth and the development of an academic identity that is continuously being re-shaped, re-imagined, and eternally questioned.

▶ **Overview of this chapter**

In this chapter, we develop the notion of academic identity as a trajectory through time. (And if you have read our personal perspectives, you will have a sense of our three trajectories.) The academic identity-trajectory begins with years spent as a doctoral student (and perhaps even earlier) through the time as a new academic and on to more established academic status[1] and is interwoven into the fabric of personal experiences and relationships. The trajectory emerges through and is embodied in cumulative day-to-day experiences of varied and complex intentions, actions and interactions with others (including those in the non-academic sphere) that may include setbacks as well as unexpected detours and opportunities. The notion of an academic identity-trajectory underscores the extent to which individuals tend to link past–present–future experiences in some fashion, whether imagining forward or looking back on a journey that is not necessarily, or perhaps rarely, straightforward.

In our research the experiences of early career academics – pre-tenure academics[2] and doctoral students imagining academic careers – appeared similar, despite somewhat different contexts and activities. The common themes in the experiences of both led to the idea of identity-trajectory. After describing the themes, we present a framework of three distinct but interrelated strands to examine identity-trajectory through time – both to look back and reflect on the myriad of complex activities and interactions of an individual's trajectory as well as imagine forward. The framework facilitates a weaving together of apparently disparate experiences, thus making clearer personal future intentions and desired directions, and offers insights for early career academics and those working with them. (While our research has not encompassed research staff – those hired to do others' research as well as post docs, the ideas presented here resonate with research Lynn has done with UK colleagues in a range of social sciences in three universities regarding research staff as well as doctoral students and new lecturers.)

▶ Our research in the Canadian context

Chapter 5 explored whether continuity or disjuncture is to be expected between doctoral studies and pre-tenure work. In that chapter, the students in advanced stages of doctoral study or with recently completed degrees rarely revealed clear planning or understanding of the challenges of working as a pre-tenure academic. The chapter suggests this finding was not surprising, given contextual features that are impediments to long-term career planning. We would agree that understanding the challenges of academic work is not straightforward, and that it is often difficult to know whether contextual features may be impediments to the present and future, or provide serendipitous opportunities.

This chapter draws on the varied studies that our Canadian research team has undertaken over the past four years with both pre-tenure academics and doctoral students who intended to remain in the academic arena. The research took place in two Faculties of Education in two provinces in Canada (both different provinces from those described in Chapter 5). More than 40 doctoral students and 20 pre-tenure professors participated in the studies, which took place from 2006–2009, somewhat later than in the previous chapter (2000–2001). The two faculties represented here incorporate a range of graduate programs. In one, there are programs ranging from curriculum to educational psychology to information sciences; in the other, there is a similar variation of programs from instructional technology to subject-specific programs (e.g., math education) and also a professional doctoral degree (EdD) in Educational Leadership. However, only PhD students were included in the research.

The body of work of the research team[3] informs our understanding of early career academic experience; however, this chapter draws particularly on studies in which, (1) doctoral students completed electronic logs once a month over two years about their activities during the previous week or month, and were then interviewed by doctoral students on the research team; and (2) pre-tenure academics provided electronic descriptions of their pre-tenure experiences and were interviewed by faculty members from the research team about being a new supervisor within the context of their pre-tenure work.

While there are differences in the roughly 50 higher education institutions in Canada, these are not perhaps as dramatic in type and status as in other countries (e.g., in the UK, 'post-92' universities represent institutions which prior to 1992 offered technical-vocational preparation). One university in the study belongs to the G13, a grouping which represents Canadian research-intensive universities (similar to the G8 in Australia or the Russell Group in the UK); these groups graduate the greatest proportion of doctoral students and PhD graduates in their respective countries. The other university, like many in Canada, is called a comprehensive university; these do not have all of the professional schools (e.g., medicine and law) of research-intensive universities, and thus do not contribute as substantially to the number of doctoral graduates.

In Canada, as in the US, there is an oral defence (called a viva in the UK) of the dissertation (called a thesis in the UK and Australia) that is mostly semi-public (in contrast to the UK where it is largely private, and Australia where there is only rarely an oral defence of the dissertation). The oral defence committee varies from university to university, but generally includes something along the following lines: an examiner external to the dissertation/thesis committee but internal to the university, an examiner external to the university, a neutral chair from outside the home faculty, the supervisor and one or more of the dissertation committee. Other distinct features of Canadian, and more generally North American doctorates, are course work which can extend up to two to three years, comprehensive exams (which take various forms but are intended for the student to demonstrate depth and/or breadth in the field and may or may not include an oral defence before a committee). This is followed by an oral defence of the dissertation proposal (a specific description of the studies to be completed) to the dissertation committee, and finally the oral defence of the dissertation. The students in our research represented individuals in mid to later stages of required course work (i.e. before comprehensive exams) or those engaged in independent research towards their dissertation (i.e. after coursework and exams). Students located in the research-intensive university were predominantly full-time students, and wished to pursue academic careers post completion; those at the comprehensive university were a mix of both full-time students and part-time students fully employed in other jobs, and although also wishing academic careers, more often expressed reservations about the academic pathway.

For pre-tenure academics in Canada, universities have different policies and practices. In general, individuals are hired for a three-year term and during that time are expected to develop their research, teaching and service – including institutional, disciplinary and community service. The proportion of time allocated to these three areas is roughly 40/40/20, or 50/40/10, though in the first three years individuals may not be expected to teach as many courses as normal. Near the end of the second year, individuals seek renewal for a further three years by submitting a dossier demonstrating their efforts in the three areas. If renewed, they will submit a tenure dossier at the end of the fifth year arguing for having demonstrated excellence in at least two of the three areas of academic work. Pre-tenure professors are often expected, in addition to a publication record and good teaching evaluations, to have funded research and a number of doctoral students with some finished or nearing completion. As regards supervision specifically, there may or may not be clear guidelines as to when and how pre-tenure academics can supervise doctoral students (as well as what the expectations are regarding teaching and research). In the two universities represented here, regulations concerning who can supervise are not as strict as in some other universities, so pre-tenure professors in both universities often find themselves being doctoral supervisors with minimal support or preparation. The experience of the pre-tenure academics in our research ranged from one to six years as an academic. One participant had supervised a PhD student to completion, another an EdD student to completion, yet most had not supervised either a master's or doctoral student to completion at the time of the research.

▷ Themes common to early career academics: doctoral students and pre-tenure professors

Four themes common in both roles led to the idea of identity-trajectory: (1) opaque expectations; (2) personal intention and emotion; (3) academic and personal connection; and (4) past–present–future perspective. However, there were instances where the contexts – not the perceptions – for doctoral students and pre-tenure academics[4] appeared distinct, so these are also referred to explicitly.

Opaque expectations create challenges

> [There is] much that is not clear – that surprised me – you are valued so intensely, yet the criteria are vague.
>
> (Kate, pre-tenure professor)

> I think…the biggest challenge was trying to find out…the expectations…put on doctoral students…that [weren't] explicit, and so the challenge was figuring out what the expectations were for myself as well as what expectations there were from [academics] here.
>
> (Charles, doctoral student)

A consistent thread running through the accounts of making sense of daily experiences was the opaqueness of expectations. This finding was not surprising given reports elsewhere in studies of doctoral students (Austin, 2002) and pre-tenure academics (Schrodt *et al.*, 2003) as well as in Chapters 3 and 4 about research staff. Nevertheless, this opaqueness is a constant presence running through the three remaining themes.

Personal intentions negotiated with others are sometimes more powerful, and varied emotions are evoked

I don't mind trying to learn the culture [of the department]...but you understand that it is all connected to the so-called criteria for your employment...if you question [more senior others] when you are new, you get into that whole thing of politics around issues. So...I'm trying to navigate [and] be respectful of that. But, I'm also trying to develop an integrity – a kind of professional integrity where I have to make my decisions on my own.

(Karen, pre-tenure)

Do something you feel very passionate about...and [still be]...willing to kind of strip yourself naked...be vulnerable in front of your peers as well [as]...people that – are probably in some hierarchy relationship with you – and...[be] willing to...take things that you kind of took for granted about yourself and re-order and re-learn and, you know, re-shape them.

(Corinne, doctoral student)

Karen's and Corinne's comments represent perceptions expressed by others in the research. Individuals often expressed personal intentions which they cared deeply about (e.g., for Karen, authenticity, for Corinne, passion), yet also the need to be open to challenges emerging from relationships and practices with those more senior. Opening personal ideas and work to others' critiques involves risk. Nevertheless, individuals in both roles described being purposeful and reported their achievements, or at least movement toward their goals, through different actions and interactions. Overall, they appeared to assume that desires and intentions could be achieved.

Doctoral students often described the importance of an academic network of relationships beyond the supervisor; they negotiated with, for instance, their student peers and more senior academics (within and beyond their faculty and department) to achieve personal goals. The same was true of pre-tenure academics. They had relationships elsewhere, sometimes established earlier, which provided them with support. These external relationships are important in thinking about power. Student interactions with supervisors could confirm their institutional role as students (not-yet-academics), whereas conference conversations with more senior academics were viewed as more egalitarian. A comparable type of relationship was often experienced by pre-tenure academics in their departments when they approached more senior colleagues and were affirmed in their 'not-quite-colleague' status, while in their interactions with colleagues elsewhere this difference in status appeared not to be the case.

This range of interactions was often linked to emotion. For doctoral students, it was the thrill of contributing to the knowledge in the field, the difficulty of studying and also needing to have salaried work. For pre-tenure professors, it was the rewards of stimulating discussions with colleagues and the new and daunting responsibility for the potential careers of doctoral students (Amundsen and McAlpine, 2009). Neumann (2006) has described this emotional investment in academic work as 'passionate thought'. Based on her research with experienced academics, she describes moments of peak positive emotion – of concentration, absorption, deep involvement, joy, a sense of accomplishment – which are intrinsically motivating. However, such moments were infrequent and fleeting and the academics in her study also noted periods of tension, doubt, and disappointment. Our research suggests such varied emotions are equally true of doctoral students and new appointees.

The academic inter-woven with the personal

We pretend that the academic work that we do is out there, and that we are in here, but it is so tied up with who we are and our personal values, right? And so when someone said, 'Oh yeah, [your work is] really interesting' not only did that give me value as an academic, but personally as Holly: 'Oh, that's something that is interesting and worthwhile.'

(Holly)

Who is Holly? It matters not whether she is a doctoral student or a pre-tenure academic since she is expressing an idea that was common across our participants regardless of their role. Our identities are learned through and embodied in our intentions, thinking, actions and interactions with others over time. Such actions and interactions are directed to being recognized and feeling recognized as *the kind of person each is seeking to be(come)*. Holly's statement emphasizes how the vocational aspects of academic work led her to integrate the academic kind of person she was seeking to be within her broader sense of who she was becoming. This theme is essential to the understanding of identity as a trajectory. Personal lives may be rarely referred to in research on academic work (e.g., in this research, individuals downplayed references to illness and family responsibilities), yet personal values, needs and responsibilities influence how and why individuals engage in such work.

Thus, integral to these stories of intention and emotion was situating academic work within life beyond the academy (Acker and Armenti, 2004). Our research made very evident the importance of relationships and activities elsewhere. For instance, a doctoral student described doing her degree while working in a salaried position and raising three children as a single mother; another noted how her partner took over child care so she could continue her writing. As for the pre-tenure professors, child care responsibilities meant that one had chosen to limit her job search to local universities only. Another wished for her students to see that 'Life comes first…you don't have to be half a person when you do this.' Thus, she considered it a 'failure' that two of her master's students have told her that while they had originally imagined doing a PhD, they have changed their minds since seeing the nature of her work. The students' decision reflects that of the academic in Chapter 4 who ultimately resigned from her position because of quality of life concerns.

Learning and reflection link past–present–future

Learn as you go and try and reflect on what works well and didn't work well…I must say, a lot of reflection.

(Jeanette, pre-tenure)

I approach this [dissertation] as a very self-reflective learner…[because] I need to do the work and to show progress.

(Melissa, doctoral student)

What was intriguing and is seen in Jeanette's and Melissa's comments was the unsolicited references to both what and how individuals were learning from daily experiences across a multitude of complex contexts and interactions while dealing with opaque expectations. This awareness of learning highlighted the often overlooked importance of daily activities and interactions which cumulatively link past–present–future and influence the ways in which individuals construct, embody and negotiate intentions and respond emotionally to interactions with others.

Further, in addition to noting learning in the present, individuals referred to past experience as the basis for present decisions or actions, as well as imagining how they would use the present to inform their imagined futures. In linking past to present, the past was sometimes characterized as similar to the present, so forming the basis for current action. The past was also described as different from or not compatible with the present. Here Valerie described how she both drew on and acted against what she had experienced in the supervisory relationship in the past:

> Right now, I do it the way that I was myself supervised…most of what I know is what I've picked up myself as a grad student…I don't think I'm exactly like my supervisor because I've learned from his mistakes too.
>
> (Valerie, pre-tenure)

It was also apparent that what you think you have learned and know will change in relation to new experiences as in Nancy's comment in relation to her comprehensive exams:

> [There is] a tension…between what you know and what you've learned and the sort of need to know…And I guess your feeling about what sort of dominates depends on where you are or what kind of work you are doing. So in writing [the exams]…and getting ready to submit you have sort of the feeling, 'Okay, this is what I know.' But then you go to your comps defense…the [questions] were all questions that [were]…pushing you already…in the direction of where you need to go next and then you start that sort of, 'Okay, so now we need to do more.'
>
> (Nancy, doctoral student)

While individuals in both roles were integrating past and present towards the future, there was some variation in that 'future'. Students were establishing a direction for their intellectual contributions and developing their disciplinary networks, but their institutional context post-PhD was still only imagined. (Students appeared to assume that getting an academic position was possible.) In contrast, for pre-tenure professors, while their intellectual contributions and networks were likely more advanced than those of doctoral students, their institutional contexts were a new reality to integrate into their own trajectories.

A feature of this learning was its being directed towards the self – how individuals learned from reflecting on past efforts to set personal goals, and then negotiated achievement with others. There was a strong sense of personal responsibility for dealing with difficulties and making sense of opaque expectations. It was rare for individuals to reflect in a critical way. Thus, while they might question and occasionally challenge individuals more powerful than themselves, they rarely named or explored why things were the way they were, that is, challenged the constraints as well as affordances of the institutional contexts in which they were embedded. We return to this point near the end of the chapter.

Overall, these four themes foreground early career academic experience as a dynamic biographical process grounded in history and memory (Walker, 2001). Pre-existing personal understandings influence how individuals interpret the present and the future, and there continue to be new experiences often with opaque expectations that individuals can learn from. While the specifics of the argument will vary with context, given similar patterns emerging in Lynn's UK research, the notion of academic identity-trajectory appears useful for doctoral students and pre-tenure academics in a range of other institutional contexts to the two described here. It is this potential we explore next.

▶ The potential of identity-trajectory: be(com)ing the person we imagine be(com)ing

What insights might the notion of trajectory provide for doctoral students and pre-tenure academics and those working with them? These individuals are constructing a past–present–future trajectory with the possibility of some intentional navigation in the complexity of the academic world, situated within their lives beyond the academy. Yet the participants in our research reported setbacks and detours in negotiating their own intentions with others' sometimes competing desires – individuals who in some cases were more powerful and also important in providing direction and affirmation. Thus, the experiences and perceptions reported in our research here affirmed that negotiating with others to achieve personal intentions is critical (McAlpine and Amundsen, 2009). Clearly, in participating in academic work, individuals encounter certain freedoms that may engender a sense of agency (e.g., relative flexibility in choosing and organizing work) as well as constraints which may reduce a sense of agency (e.g., demand to publish, insufficient time to meet all expectations in ways each might like). This variation is a reminder of the tension between the intrinsic drivers of an academic vocation, what draws individuals and is a motivator for staying, and the extrinsic drivers in the complex conditions under which academic work is done that may challenge or discourage (e.g., availability of positions and resources). This tension between external and intrinsic was also reported by the both doctoral students and new appointees in Chapter 2 while those in Chapter 5 were more focused on the extrinsic drivers.

Individuals' efforts to negotiate their intentions within these disparate events, actions and interactions evoked a range of emotions, from anger, to frustration through to excitement and exhilaration. Emotion is important as it speaks to personal values as an academic; intellectual challenge and inquiry are not dispassionate and neutral. They are, as Graue (2006, p. 38) notes, 'flashpoints for emotion because [they are] bound up with who we are and what we know'. Karen's reflection on a previous relationship emphasizes the importance of the personal within the academic:

> I had a mentor [not my supervisor]…He invested in me as a person – invested in me, nurtured me as a thoughtful person and it made the whole difference…What he was trying to honor in me and in my work was not understood by my senior supervisor. So what I noticed was that if you don't have a person who sees you, you cannot do the work. So I vowed to work to the ethic of my mentor.
>
> (Karen, pre-tenure)

Given the unpredictable and shifting ways in which individuals live and embody academic work, the experience of positive over negative emotion may be vital in sustaining individual motivation and commitment rather than disillusionment and alienation. Charles, a student, sums this up well:

> No matter what people may say about 'the system' being unsupportive, or plagued with biases and power differentials, I honestly believe that each [of us] needs to acknowledge these barriers and move ahead with things as best as possible. This means focusing energy and getting things done, which is ultimately an individual effort.
>
> (Charles, doctoral student)

These individuals were prepared to take risks to learn, remained committed to academic work, and continued to have a sense that they could enact their intentions through working with others.

▶ Trajectory strands: weaving together varied experiences through time

> If the early career [pre-tenure] is a period of uncertainty, instability and the need to make sense of new cultures and hidden require-ments, what better preparation could there be than the very similar challenges of doctoral study? (Chapter 5)

Identity-trajectory emphasizes the desire to enact personal inten-tions and hopes over time; to maintain a momentum in constructing identity despite challenges and detours; and to imagine possible futures. When analysed through time, identity-trajectories can be characterized as encompassing three distinct strands of experi-ence – intellectual, networking, institutional. Each strand develops asynchronously through time and space,[5] yet is integrated into and influences the other strands of the trajectory. For clarity, each of these strands is described separately; at the same time, examples are provided that demonstrate their integration and how tensions may emerge within and across them. For simplicity of representation, life beyond the academic is not directly addressed; readers will hopefully draw on earlier references to how the two are coupled in people's experiences.

Intellectual strand
The intellectual strand represents the contribution an individual has made and is making to a chosen intellectual field through scholar-ship. This strand leaves a trail of artifacts, e.g., papers, publications, citations, invitations to speak, and also, though often less recognized: course, curriculum and program designs. These artifacts represent an individual's thinking which exists independently of and long after the individual is no longer present. The trail will vary individually in length, size, and impact, and will change over time.

How an individual's intellectual strand is seen and the efforts an individual makes to develop this strand are situated in trends such as recent funding council expectations of social impact, strategic grant calls, and expectations of collaboration resulting in increas-ing co-authorship internationally (Gingras, 2002). Technologies have also altered how academics are expected to remain current, and how manuscripts and other intellectual contributions are cre-ated and communicated (Starke-Meyerring, 2005). Our research suggests awareness of such trends is influencing doctoral student efforts to be published before graduation (McAlpine *et al.*, 2008), and pre-tenure academic decisions to co-author with students in order to advance their own intellectual strand while advancing their students' simultaneously (Amundsen and McAlpine, 2009). Such demands, external drivers, can create tensions and concerns which go to the heart of an individual's sense of identity. Barbara, a doctoral student, noted:

> Some times you wonder: what you are doing? You wonder if it is important enough, you wonder if you will be taken seriously – all of these things. Like when you are trying to publish and get rejected.
>
> (Barbara, doctoral student)

This perception of the import of others' academic judgements on individual sense of identity hinges on what has been called a 'rejection environment' (Baruch and Hall, 2004) in academia. Still, individuals in both roles also reported many occasions when they received emotionally rewarding affirmations for their accomplishments.

Individuals described their intellectual strands through time. Here, Regina describes developing her intellectual contribution and representing this growth in her comprehensive exams, for her the first and to date largest form of risk-taking she had engaged in, and what that meant for her future intellectual strand:

> I really invested my ideas and what I would like to do with my dissertation, which is the stepping stone to ideas that I would have for the rest of my academic career…so it's big and it's vulnerable,…and I am a little nervous because it was very independent.
>
> (Regina, doctoral student)

And, Howard, pre-tenure, looks back to describe the development of his intellectual strand:

> Because I've had my worldview changed by research and information, it seems to me that it could be something just as powerful for other[s]…So that's [what]…I find fascinating and interesting…the whole idea of research to practice…to policy, so how we can use research to actually make change.
>
> (Howard, pre-tenure)

Networking strand

The networking strand represents the range of local, national and international networks an individual has been and is connected with. These networks include: (1) academic colleagues (doctoral students, research staff, academic appointees) wherever located; (2) practising professionals, especially for those in professional schools and faculties; (3) membership of journal review boards, and grant proposal review committees; (4) those cited as contributing to an individual's thinking; (5) the journals one prefers reading and publishing in; and (6) research collaborations and co-publications with other scholars, graduate students and professionals.[6] The networking strand also varies individually in length, size, and impact, over time.

How an individual's networking strand is seen and the efforts an individual makes to develop it are situated in, for instance, technologies that enable more contact with greater numbers of spatially separate individuals (Menzies and Newsome, 2007), and access to more publications. Our research suggests that students (as well as pre-tenure professors) are intentional in developing and drawing on a range of relationships beyond the department and university which may be aided by such technologies. Individuals referred to virtual as well as face-to-face interactions; there were also historical instances, e.g., reading an author who helped further intellectual thinking.

Importantly, positive emotion was often invoked in these interactions which stimulated engagement, connection and the co-construction of ideas. For instance, June, pre-tenure, described working with a student at 4pm on a Saturday afternoon:

> Like one day last month she said, 'Let me ask you this question and [we started and]' – she left and then she came back with her husband and he is a science teacher and a math teacher so he could understand and translate some of the stuff for her too. And we were just mapping it all out on the board and it was so fun to...have that kind of connection.

June's comment is a reminder that doctoral students are often an academic's closest colleagues (McAlpine and Weiss, 2000). Regina, a student, describes her response to an 'academic' discussion that seems to capture what makes this trajectory strand so motivating:

> Part of what I see being a professional and an academic...is networking, knowing what people are doing, collaborating, sharing

resources and it's that stimulating conversation that you get once in a while – that really is why I'm here...The nature of the interaction is engaging – I don't know if it is high level questions, or questions that are unique, it's being open and sharing ideas that really have a basis in something and with people who know things that you don't know about.

As is likely evident in Regina's comment, the intellectual and networking strands, which represent an individual's scholarly interest, are reciprocal. In fact, based on our research, developing the networking strand is essential in establishing the intellectual location for personal contributions. As such, the networking strand could be associated with daunting intellectual challenge. Nancy described being 'pushed' during her comprehensive exam: being 'pushed' affirmed that she would be able to answer the difficult questions at some point in the future:

[The committee was] challenging and pushing [me] to go further than I had done when writing and thinking...These challenges of 'How are you going to go from here?' and 'How do you see this?' got me thinking and forced me to think about issues beyond what I had written...So if a question is addressed to you, you can't just say, 'Oh, that's interesting' and then not say anything. You have to respond even if it is 'I don't know' – which, of course, we don't want to say ... [This] was pushing my limits a bit...They are real questions and you are actually seen as somebody who might or might not at this moment, but eventually, will be able to answer these questions or think about these questions.

The networking strand likely begins earlier than the intellectual strand; at the master's level, and even before that individuals are beginning to develop networks of intellectual colleagues through reading and choice of field. Second, the intellectual and networking strands generate their own tasks and standards of conduct. For many academics, these strands may represent the intrinsic source of their desire for and enactment of agency and more positive perceptions of emotion, and form the basis for their values and academic allegiance.

Institutional strand

The intellectual and networking strands do not, however, provide two essential features of work – income and resources. These are provided through the development of an institutional strand which varies individually over time and represents each person's relationships, responsibilities and resources wherever they are physically located. Responsibilities include roles such as teacher, supervisor, teaching assistant, research assistant, committee member, and administrative roles such as head of department or program director. Institutional resources and responsibilities can support or constrain an individual's networking and intellectual strands. Thus, how an individual's institutional strand is viewed and the efforts an individual makes to develop this strand are situated in, for instance, availability or lack of lab space, access or not to research funding and assistantships, good or poor library/electronic support and high or low expectations of committee work, the loss of support staff and subsequent increase in 'self-administration' for all, and expectation of shorter times to completion for doctoral students. It is also evident in calls for public accountability where external organizations set criteria by which institutions and therefore the individuals in them are judged.

Once in an institution, both doctoral students and pre-tenure academics can, through scholarly productivity (e.g., peer-reviewed publications and research funding) and teaching quality (e.g., positive course evaluations), enhance both income and resources. Thus, the purposes of the intellectual and networking strands contrast with the institutional one. An individual's intellectual and networking strands are related to the expectations of and contributions to a scholarly field, whereas the organizational system has stakeholders beyond the academic world, e.g., students, donors, auditors, whose expectations may be divergent from personal academic aspirations.

Institutional resources can support or constrain an individual's networking and intellectual strands. Evidence from our research supporting this view was pre-tenure academics' reports of tension in their desire to advance their own intellectual efforts to publish while also complying with departmental expectations to take on more supervision (Amundsen and McAlpine, 2009). As for doctoral students, some are very aware of the (negative) influence of the institutional strand on their experiences, e.g., pressure to finish within three to four years regardless of discipline (McAlpine et al., 2008). Yet, despite this strand often being overlooked as a feature of doctoral experience, chances to provide institutional leadership are reported as extremely positive (McAlpine and Asghar, in press).

A vital feature of the institutional strand may be the 'rites of passage' marking an individual's changing status and thus potential to access more resources both institutionally and beyond. The rites differ for doctoral students (e.g., defence) and pre-tenure academics (e.g., tenure and promotion). Yet, in both roles individuals were cognizant of how the judgements of others could both help them move forward in achieving their desires (and be emotionally affirming) as well as be potentially devastating in limiting their development. These rites were described as sites where different strands combined. For instance, Howard describes how student graduation links institutional, intellectual and networking strands for the pre-tenure academic; he will be known within his network by the quality of his student's work:

> When [students] get their degree that is our way of saying that we as an institution think that they are independent researchers...and can engage in the broader scholarly community. So I want to make sure that if my name is on the dissertation that I feel comfortable in them going forward as an independent researcher.

As well, the institutional strand was often where tensions emerged. Here Kate expressed concern not only about institutional expectations for tenure, but also the extent to which there didn't appear to be equity – a level playing field – for all pre-tenure academics:

> The thing about PhD supervising...again, there are no standards...[There is a] lack of consistency in workload, and yet, my [tenure] application will be considered at the same time as the others and I'm not sure that [difference] is taken into account.

And, Jeanette described the experience of 'inheriting a student':

> Another element of frustration for me is that I didn't want to work with this student from the beginning. She ended up with me because no one else in the program wanted to work with her.

Students reported similar kinds of tensions. Regina described the tension between doing the independent thinking inherent in PhD level work, while simultaneously respecting the hierarchy of power when working as a paid researcher for a professor:

> It is not outrageous for a professor to feel like they have authority over a student...I know that I have to tame my ego, or my need for independence, and that I am a paid employee and that I do actually

have to do what the people tell me to do. So, it's a balancing act, and it is difficult because I am given so much freedom [in my own dissertation work].

And Nellie, a seasoned instructor of a particular graduate level seminar in her field of expertise, experienced tension in her dual position as a PhD student and an instructor (a part-time teaching position). While her expertise had been recognized in continuous opportunities to teach, she was still reminded by students and full-time academics that she was not 'a normal professor'.

> There are tensions in the way I'm perceived, my classroom students see me very much as a PhD student (and not a normal professor), so I find the tensions are tough when I take on a more authoritative role as the instructor...and when push comes to shove and there is an incident, ... I'm made keenly aware [from the department] that I'm just an instructor, just a PhD student and not full-time faculty.

Tensions could also exist between the institutional strand and the networking-intellectual strands. Maria wanted to continue interacting with colleagues from her doctoral program and found her departmental colleagues unsupportive:

> I'm the only faculty that goes regularly [to a research group meeting at another university]...My colleagues could come if they wanted to...And it has been said 'Why would you go over [there]?'....But when they say things like [that]...I just don't listen and I don't respond. They [have] no business telling me that. It's my decision...And I'm connecting with a whole community of scholars that I would otherwise not be linked to...Well it makes me cross, actually...if I want to do it, then it's my business.

While others reported tensions and struggles with peers, acting in defiance of peers as Maria did was rare in our research.

Yet, the institutional strand was also a source of learning for the future: Valerie, pre-tenure, noted the ways in which she learnt from participating in program meetings:

> I pick up tips that help me advise my students better and also it's...*good ... for learning about potential pitfalls* like what

happens if a student...doesn't get things done ... *And so it's kind of learning by watching other people.*

And Annie, a student, described what she had learned from participating in a Faculty committee with a mandate to better support doctoral students:

So, *I can see myself later in my career in the university trying to do things like that,* to improve a little bit the quality of life of the students, to improve the sense of belonging.

Integrating the strands in identity-trajectories

These strands offer a framework for analysing and reflecting on individual identity-trajectories: what each individual has done, is doing and learning, and may be doing or plan to do in the future. This framework provides a personal view on identity development – attending to the whole person, embodied practice. Thus, it provides a counterpoint to, for instance, the discourse of training researchers. Further, it highlights the tensions between individual and institutional purposes.

So, for instance, the framework acts as a prompt to attend to the networking and institutional strands and not to focus principally on the intellectual strand as is often the case. It is also a reminder to attend to the inter-play among the three strands, particularly how the institutional strand, which is often experienced as a source of accountability, may also be a source of some resources, e.g., space for research activities, funding for conferences.

As an example, the experience and development of doctoral students' institutional strand may be ignored or overlooked since students are not usually salaried, are not seen as individuals who will be present and influence the institution for any length of time, and do not easily gain access to resources, yet, McAlpine and Amundsen (2009) suggest that opportunities to develop an institutional strand can be important in learning about agency, collective effort and leadership. Similarly, when thinking about the networking strand, McAlpine and Jazvac-Martek (2008) report important connections made by doctoral students with individuals other than the supervisor, yet, these relationships have not traditionally been emphasized as important in doctoral education.

Still, the intellectual strand is a challenging new demand for doctoral students and requires support in its development. While previous academic work has been largely course-based, doctoral students are expected to project forward where and how they might make an intel-lectual contribution with few earlier traces to guide this strand of the trajectory. Similarly, while pre-tenure academics are also growing their intellectual and networking strands, they are now dealing with a new strand – their institutional one. Not only will it be different from their previous 'home', it may be particularly challenging if they have not earlier had the occasion to engage in work related to it. They are trying to fit in, tread carefully, while learning what the new responsibilities and resources are (Amundsen and McAlpine, 2009).

As the strands of an individual's trajectory develop and are reflected on, individuals may make choices about the weighting and effort each wishes to invest in the respective strands of their individual trajec-tories. For instance, some may downplay the intellectual strand and privilege the institutional; others will do the reverse. Whatever the choice, it is likely best done intentionally.

▶ So what might identity-trajectory mean for practice?

Identity-trajectory offers a perspective from which early career academics as well as those mandated to provide support for them may view their experiences as connected through time and as consisting of three distinct but interrelated strands. This framework can be used to reflect on actions and interactions, which may sometimes appear as disparate, as detours and serendipity, and through this process assess how the identity-trajectory is developing in relation to personal intentions. Given this information, new directions and intentions may emerge.

However, while we propose identity-trajectory as a useful framework, at the same time, it should not be used uniquely to analyse experience since it does not attend to more distant and de-contextualized influ-ences on daily intentions, actions and interactions. In other words, the identity-trajectories were largely focused in the close-to-home context and rarely in the more distant but powerful contexts influencing indi-viduals' lives. There was not in these identity-trajectories an acknow-ledgement that academic lives are lived against dominant definitions of 'normality' (Walker, 2001), including socially conditioned understand-ings of, for instance, power and gender. Roth (2004) has suggested that individuals may internalize what are inherent structural contradictions and attribute to themselves the problems; for instance, an inability to reconcile competing demands may be seen as a failure of personal organization rather than a structural aspect of the environment.

It is not easy as either a doctoral student or pre-tenure academic to recognize influences beyond the local that influence the day-to-day, and often taken-for-granted, practices within a department or program. Even more so, it was difficult for such individuals in our research, having less power, to challenge taken-for-granted practices. These two factors may explain why individuals did not refer to the complex and shifting landscapes of academia referred to in Chapter 1 or the possibility of challenging the increasing demands, though there was some questioning and occasionally challenging of local expectations, relationships and practices. The implications of silence about these issues by more established academics are considered after first describing the implications of identity-trajectory for early career academics.

Implications for early career academics

The idea of identity-trajectory can serve as a reminder of the incredible individual variation that exists in experiences and perceptions of academic work within the broader life project; individuals all construct and are constructed by their identities in different ways, so comparison of a personal trajectory with others' trajectories needs to be done carefully.

Identity-trajectory prompts recognizing the impact of daily activities for learning and the value of seeking time to review and reflect on them in order to more meaningfully connect past–present–future. Such reflection can enable an analysis of the respective strands – the degree to which each has been developed or overlooked, and the extent to which the three weave together in a way that is personally meaningful.

Further, within each individual trajectory, issues of emotion and power (both within and outside academia) are natural features of daily experience. Both doctoral students and pre-tenure academics desire affirmation and direction from academics around them, including those more senior. Nonetheless, both also receive affirmation and direction from individuals beyond the local and from within the academy which were reported in our research as just as compelling. Affirmation and direction are necessary since individuals often cannot know how well they are doing without feedback from those with whom they interact (evaluating personal development and achievement on the basis of how others are evaluating these two). Yet, within the institutional strand of an individual's trajectory, the desire for affirmation and direction from others coincides with the possibility of tensions with these same individuals.

From our perspective, identity-trajectory makes visible the link between intentions and the emotional ups and downs of involvement in academic work. It affirms that while individuals may experience and perceive these from a unique and solitary perspective (unless named to others) they are very much a common feature of academia. Individuals are constantly negotiating their own intentions and purposes with others who may have different desires and more power – power that can be affirming and supportive but also sometimes constraining and distressing. Yet, in most cases there are sufficient moments of passionate thought to remain intrinsically motivated. Watching for such emotions, valuing and remembering them would seem important in maintaining equilibrium and resilience given the many dips and turns that occur. What is essential in this environment is developing endurance and resilience, the capacity to adapt positively and successfully to, and to bounce back from, adverse circumstances by negotiating personal intentions, and sustaining socially positive relationships (Day, 2008).

Lastly, though there may be institutional distinctions made between being a student and being a new academic, in fact, the learning and the identity-trajectory are not necessarily experienced or perceived as that distinct. And, for individuals thinking about the development of the respective strands (intellectual, networking and institutional) finding a personally comfortable balance among the three would seem significant. While avoiding too much attention to one strand may be a useful strategy, individuals will, and need to, make personal choices as to which strands they wish to invest. Lastly, as Maria commented, attending to outside joys – family, friends – is essential; individuals can both be an academic and 'have a life'!

Implications for more established academics generally

Since early career academics may not recognize structural impediments or may internalize structural contradictions as a personal failure, the presence of such impediments and contradictions needs to be raised by more established individuals (e.g., educational developers, department chairs, directors of graduate studies) and explored in relatively low-risk contexts. The goal is to ensure that early career academics have a clearer sense of the opaque but shifting complexity of the academic world beyond what they are presently experiencing. More experienced academics can model as well as make explicit the need to challenge some of the historically (as well as socially) generated taken-for-granted policies and practices that influence academic work; for instance, holding meetings at the end of the day that conflict with family responsibilities, or tacit tenure criteria that privilege certain kinds of activities over others. Taking a more critical stance to contradictions requires a broadening of reflection from an evaluation of each individual's own efforts – which remains important – to collective reflection that takes a questioning perspective on taken-for-granted practices.

Implications for educational/ academic developers

The educational development implications of 'identity-trajectory' are compelling as they raise issues about the usual form of provision offered by institutions, for instance, often distinguishing the roles of doctoral student and pre-tenure academics by offering different supports for each. In other words, one of the difficulties of the present common arrangement for development may be the segregation of early career academics by role, experience, and activity when individuals in both roles may benefit from understanding more of the commonalities of experiences.

Here are some questions that might be posed: To what extent do educational developers help doctoral students and new academics examine their past trajectories and the ways in which the three strands of their individual trajectories are developing and becoming integrated (or not)? How might the three strands of identity-trajectory inform academic development plans and initiatives? To what extent do academic developers take advantage of knowing that there is much informal learning occurring in the day-to-day experience of academic work? To what extent do they attend to the varied emotional reactions, the ups and downs, which influence the academics they are supporting? Lastly, developers also have an important role in raising these questions with more senior academics and administrators (e.g., Jeanette Macdonald in her commentary on this chapter).

Implications for department chairs and directors of graduate programs

Similarly, for department chairs and directors of graduate programs, the notion of identity-trajectory can meaningfully inform policies and practices beyond the questions asked in the previous paragraph. What is opaque for students and new academics that needn't be opaque? What activities and structures might make more explicit an examination and development of the three strands of early career academic trajectories? While not suggesting that everything can be or should be transparent, there are expectations that can be articulated, if not in policies, then in practices. For instance, doctoral students could be encouraged to develop their networking strand by seeking opportunities for disciplinary service, using new technologies to contact those they are citing, and acting as editorial assistants, etc. Such strategies could lead them to think about and develop networks with those who are their intellectual inspirations. Additionally, they can be made aware of the ways in which they are engaged principally in informal learning in all three strands, not just the intellectual.

As regards the institutional strand, there is a need to encourage pre-tenure professors and doctoral students to consider the resources (including key people) and responsibilities as well as benefits of institutional roles. Further, it is important for them to explore the potentials and constraints of their institutional location as regards the other two strands. Finally, are there safe opportunities for students and pre-tenure academics to explore opaque expectations and experiences, to share concerns and challenges, to learn more about negotiating agency?

Implications for disciplinary organizations

Lastly, the notion of identity-trajectory raises a question about the role of disciplinary organizations in supporting the development of early career academics. For instance, since conferences are authentic workplaces in which academics with a range of experiences come together, how might disciplinary organizations facilitate occasions for academics with diverse experiences to collectively and explicitly explore career trajectories?

We have over the past two years, piloted such activities in which doctoral students, research staff, professors of all ranks from a range of universities, yet sharing a common intellectual specialism, spend a day together (McAlpine and Hopwood, 2009). During the day, they collectively explore the shifting nature of academic work and the influence of the different strands of their respective trajectories, and what these two perspectives mean in terms of learning and developing an academic identity-trajectory. These events, which participants have evaluated very positively, represent a rare opportunity to discuss what it is to do academic work, to become aware of resources, and most importantly how to reconcile the demands with the pleasures.

We hope that the idea of academic identity-trajectory proves useful as a personal tool for reflection and analysis as well as a heuristic for developers and more senior academics in positions to mentor early career academics so that they may be confident and resilient in their work for decades to come.

▶ Acknowledgements

This research has been partly supported by the Social Sciences and Humanities Research Council of Canada.

▶ Notes

1. Jon Driver in a commentary on this chapter emphasizes this point:

    > that one's entire career as an academic is a continuum, and that one is constantly engaged by challenges similar to those that doctoral students and untenured faculty experience. I have experienced 'learning curves' in every administrative role to which I have been appointed, and also during times when my research has shifted to different parts of the world and different cultures.

    And Frances Helyar, in another commentary makes the point that it is possible to hold roles as a doctoral student and pre-tenure academic at once.
2. Pre-tenure academics are in their first 5–6-year appointment with the title assistant professor; during this time they apply for tenure and if they receive it are generally promoted to associate professor.
3. These have captured: (1) students' on-going experiences over time; (2) their perceptions of the influence of new technologies on academic writing; (3) the learning that emerges from service work; (4) the ways in which dissertation writing is negotiated between student and supervisor; (5) variation in oral defense policies and practices in Canadian universities; and (6) pre-tenure academics' experiences of establishing themselves as supervisors in the broader context of academic work.
4. We do not address here the case of those who hold both roles at the same time as is often the case in Australia, the UK or Europe.
5. This view draws on but has substantially modified work by Laudel and Glaser (2008) in which they proposed career strands as mechanisms to explain their view that the early career phase of academic work contains a status passage from the apprentice to the colleague state. We draw on the notion of career strands but not on their assumption of status passage.

6. Equally important for more experienced academics are the students who go on to academic careers and students who bring scholarly influence to their own professional practice through the influence of our mentorship.

▶ References

Acker, S. and Armenti, C. (2004) 'Sleepless in academia', *Gender and Education*, 16(1): 3–24.

Amundsen, C. and McAlpine, L. (2009) ' "Learning supervision": Trial by fire?', *Innovations in Education and Teaching International*, 46(3): 331–42.

Austin, A. (2002) 'Preparing the next generation of faculty: Graduate school as socialization to the academic career', *Journal of Higher Education*, 73(1): 94–122.

Baruch, Y. and Hall, D. (2004) 'The academic career: A model for future careers in other sectors?' *Journal of Vocational Behavior*, 64: 241–62.

Day, C. (2008) 'Committed for life? Variation in teachers' work, lives and effectiveness', *Journal of Educational Change*, 9: 243–60.

Gingras, Y. (2002) 'Les formes spécifique de l'internationalité du champs sciéntifique', *Actes de la recherché en sciences sociales*, 1415: 31–45.

Graue, B. (2006) 'The transformative power of reviewing', *Educational Researcher*, 35: 36–41.

Laudel, G. and Glaser, J. (2008) 'From apprentice to colleague: The metamorphosis of early career researchers', *Higher Education*, 55: 387–406.

McAlpine, L. and Amundsen, C. (2009) 'Identity and agency: Pleasures and collegiality among the challenges of the doctoral journey', *Studies in Continuing Education*, 31(2): 107–23.

McAlpine, L. and Asghar, A. (in press) 'Doctoral students: Peer learning to collectively develop "academic identity"', *International Journal for Academic Development*.

McAlpine, L. and Hopwood, N. (2009) ' "Third spaces": A useful developmental lens?' *International Journal for Academic Development*, 14(2): 159–62.

McAlpine, L. and Jazvac, M. (2008) *What Weekly Logs Tell Us About the Nature of Doctoral Students' Experience: Implications for Faculty Development*. New York: AERA.

McAlpine, L., Paré, A. and Starke-Meyerring, D. (2008) 'Disciplinary voices: A shifting landscape for English Doctoral Education in the 21st century', in Boud, D. and Lee, A. (eds) *Changing Practices in Doctoral Education*. London: Routledge, pp. 42–53.

McAlpine, L. and Weiss, J. (2000) 'Mostly true confessions: Joint meaning-making about the thesis journey', *Canadian Journal of Higher Education*, 30(1): 1–26.

Menzies, H. and Newsome, J. (2007) 'No time to think', *Time and Society*, 16(1): 83–98.

Neumann, A. (2006) 'Professing passion: Emotion in the scholarship of professors at research universities', *American Educational Research Journal*, 43(3): 381–424.

Roth, W. (2004) 'Activity theory and education: An introduction', *Mind, Culture and Activity*, 11(1): 1–8.

Schrodt, P., Cawyer, C. and Sanders, R. (2003) 'An examination of academic mentoring behaviours and new faculty members' satisfaction with socialization and tenure and promotion processes', *Communication Education*, 52(1): 17–29.

Starke-Meyerring, D. (2005) 'Meeting the challenges of globalization: A framework for global literacies in professional communication programs', *Journal of Business and Technical Communication*, 19: 468–99.

Walker, M. (2001) 'Engineering identities', *British Journal of Sociology of Education*, 22(1): 75–89.

7 Rethinking Preparation for Academic Careers

Gerlese S. Åkerlind and Lynn McAlpine

The starting point for this book was the need to reconsider the nature of academic careers and how developing academics prepare for them, given the rapidly shifting landscape of higher education described in Chapter 1. We set out to provide a research-informed picture of early career academics' experiences of academic practice, with the aim of drawing out implications for better supporting their ongoing development.

One of our promises in Chapter 1 was that this book would address the following questions:

- What do PhDs, post-docs and new academics think it means to have a career in academia? Is 'career' a meaningful term nowadays?
- What are their perceptions of academic practice, and how do these perceptions relate to their intentions and hopes?
- What are the challenges they face in preparing for, participating in and influencing academic work?
- How do their perceptions relate to their sense of academic purpose and identity...their engagement in and contribution to an academic community?

In this final chapter, we summarize what the book as a whole has had to say about each of these questions. In doing this, we highlight what we see as privileged and neglected aspects of academic practice and preparation for academia, ending the chapter with some practical implications for the key audiences for this book.

▶ Rethinking preparation for academic careers: key questions

Turning now to the questions that we posed at the start of this book, we address each in turn.

What do PhDs, post-docs and new academics think it means to have a career in academia? Is 'career' a meaningful term nowadays?

The term 'career' typically has two connotations: long-term employment and professional progress, usually associated with some growing status such as promotion. It is clear that this traditional expectation is no longer available for many, and may even be actively misleading as a guide for early career academics' expectations and planning. The preceding chapters highlight three ways in which current academic careers can conflict with traditional expectations: with respect to being long-term, following a clear path and involving growing status. This creates a need to reframe definitions of an academic career to suit current conditions.

For some, their academic careers will be short-term, ending with their PhD, post-doc, or first appointment. Others may find themselves in academia long-term, but through holding a succession of contracts rather than a permanent appointment, and where contract renewal or next appointment does not necessarily involve a progression in status. Nevertheless, because of the personal value they placed on academic work, a number of early career academics in previous chapters were clear about being willing to stay in academia for as long as possible, even though they did not expect a long-term career or growing status as a consequence (see Chapter 3 for example). However, others felt distressed that they had invested so much time and energy in academic work when a permanent position was unlikely to eventuate (see, for example, Chapter 5).

This situation is aggravated by the lack of a clear path through academia, making career outcomes somewhat unpredictable. Current routes to academic careers are diverse. Recent literature reports people moving in and out of academia, sometimes in counterintuitive ways, before finding a long-term 'home'. For instance, those who achieve a short-term academic appointment immediately following their PhD or post-doc may fail to find a long-term position, while others who initially take an appointment outside of academia may end up returning (e.g., UK Vitae, 2009).

Given current uncertainties and diversities in academic careers, it is important to find a way to acknowledge that people in early career roles can make valuable academic and social contributions, even if they are not in academia long-term. That traditional academic careers are still held up by many senior academics as the default expectation may be experienced as demoralizing by early career academics who don't move immediately into academic positions (Åkerlind, 2005a). This stance may also unnecessarily limit ways of thinking about academic careers.

Building ways of publicly and personally accepting and valuing short-term careers in academia is one approach to this issue. For instance, more senior academics, be they developers, administrators or supervisors, can acknowledge and affirm that individuals in these early career roles make valuable academic and social contributions, even if they are not in academia long-term.

We also suggest that public expectations of a career can be reframed to evoke a more personal face. For example, 'career' could be reframed in relation to personal progress and contribution rather than in relation to a particular position or institutional status. In other words, long-term professional progression could be conceived as following a personal intellectual agenda over time, which could focus on personal growth and social and intellectual contributions, rather than permanence and status.

This more personal definition of a career is one reason that we have been using the term 'academic practice' rather than 'academic career' in this book. For us, 'practice' represents more than a job, appointment or title that academics hold. We see practice as incorporating the totality of personal experiences; it brings into play the underlying, sometimes implicit, purpose(s) and values that motivate us to be academics and through which it is possible to integrate an array of multi-faceted duties, responsibilities, skills and knowledge into a coherent sense of academic identity, regardless of the nature of one's appointments.

What are early career academic perceptions of academic practice? What are the challenges they face? In what ways are these perceptions and challenges influencing their intentions and hopes for a career in academia?

These questions obviously relate to the previous ones, though taking a different perspective. And again, we find in the chapters of this book both variation as well as commonalities in the perceptions of early career academics. Some expressed strong personal enjoyment, enthusiasm and passion about academic practice (for example, Chapters 2 and 6). Others were drawn to intrinsic academic values, such as the relative autonomy and freedom of academic work (for example, Chapters 2 and 4). Some were consumed by concerns with the uncertain nature of academic employment (for example, Chapter 5). And others turned away from academia, questioning academic expectations and values in relation to personal values and desires. This was particularly notable in Chapter 4, in which individuals described trying to reconcile their sense of purpose and vocation with the lived experiences of academic work. Most poignant was Terezinha's decision to give up her permanent job because her valuing of family and personal life could not be reconciled with the demands of academic work.

For those still invested in academia, uncertainty about what is required to ensure a long-term career was often combined with an awareness that any envisaged future depended on making sense of the present 'rules' or expectations of academic practice, many of which seemed implicit or even hidden. Often, those early in their career felt it was their responsibility to figure these implicit expectations out, partly due to their own commitment to academia, but also due to a sense that they were expected to know, and could be seen as 'wanting' by those more senior if they indicated that they didn't know or understand. Thus, it is not surprising that some of the early career academics described in the chapters were focused on simply meeting the next requirement rather than reflecting on the nature of their practice as academics (for example, Chapter 5). The challenge for those supporting new and intending academics is balancing a responsibility for making explicit some of these unknowns, opening up 'spaces' for discussions, yet not codifying these unwritten expectations in policies that could reduce the potential for individuality, freedom and personal passion that is critical to the development of academic identity.

Another challenge for early career academics is the increasing variability in types of academic positions and the appointment conditions that new academics can expect to hold, aggravating uncertainty about how best to achieve a long-term academic career. For instance, several of those represented in the chapters described taking short-term casual teaching appointments in higher education, thinking that this would increase their chances of an academic career, to find out only later that these positions did not offer the opportunities for research and publication that were essential for traditional advancement.

We suggest that the diversity of titles, responsibilities and tasks within academia (as illustrated for postdoctoral researchers in Chapter 3) may not even be well understood by more senior academics. At the same time, one cannot assume that the role(s) an individual holds (the public face of academic practice) tells much about that individual's past accomplishments, present intentions and future hopes (the personal face of academic practice). Policy and developmental support for early career academics needs to reflect the personal aspects of academic work as much as the public. Explicit discussion and counselling about personal hopes and purposes in relation to career choices is necessary.

How do early career academic perceptions relate to their sense of academic purpose and identity... their engagement in and contribution to an academic community?

While this question is inevitably related to the others, it tends to be more neglected in discussions of academic practice. Yet, we feel that it is the most important of the questions originally posed. This is not to deny the significance of the others, but as they are raised far more frequently, there is no need to argue for their importance in the way there is for this final question.

We saw substantial variation across chapters in the extent to which early career academics' developing sense of academic purpose and identity emerged as a significant issue, or even as something that they thought about at all. We would argue that this is a consequence of both the priority given to the public aspects as opposed to the personal aspects of academic practice, and the often stressful contexts in which early career academics find themselves. Nowhere in the book is this stress more vividly illustrated than in Chapter 5, where students' concerns with completing their doctorates and positioning themselves as well as possible for future academic employment dominated. It is no accident, we believe, that this stress and focus on the extrinsic requirements of an academic career came through most strongly in this chapter, set as it is in a context in which financial strain and concerns with 'survival' were most evident.

The authors of that chapter, Sandra and Eve, suggest these perceptions may be explained in terms of Maslow's hierarchy – that higher-order needs (e.g., self-actualization) can only be focused on when basic survival needs have been satisfied. While we agree with this argument (see Åkerlind 2005b), it is also important to note that there is no guarantee that higher-order attention to meaning and purpose will then spontaneously emerge once the doctorate has been awarded, the academic position found, tenure achieved... The well-documented workload pressures being faced by most academics today often mean that we are in a permanent state of worrying about our survival.

A contrast is found in Chapter 2, where Ann describes research on new academics as showing that 'they are excited by the intrinsic aspects of academic work ... they are eager to engage in "meaningful work"...they want to have an impact on their fields, their institutions and the broader community, and have a sense of idealism about what they can accomplish'. Yet, there were reports here too about tensions and challenges. This same balancing of positive and negative was apparent in Chapter 6, where there were emotional highs along with the struggles as individuals interacted with those more powerful than themselves. In Chapter 4, David suggested that a valuing of intellectual autonomy might explain the commitment to staying in academia despite the personal challenges. And, in Chapter 6, Lynn, Cheryl and Marian note that it might be the relative proportion of positive to negative emotion that leads to a commitment to stay; the relative sense of belonging versus alienation.

All this suggests that the personal 'why' underlying ongoing commitment to academic work is critical in relation to the public demands made on what academics are expected to do and the kinds of knowledge that are publicly valued. In other words, the reality of the individual lived experience of academic practice includes a diverse range of shifting emotions, values and motivations. It is obvious that academics may be motivated by a sense of contribution to others as well as by self-interest and self-promotion. While one motivation may predominate, clearly these motivations can and often do co-exist. We suggest it is rarely an either–or scenario, and while concerns with survival may override other concerns, it is not inevitable that they do (Åkerlind, 2005b).

At the same time, as was noted in Chapter 6, while many early career academics express intentionality and personal responsibility for achieving their goals despite the frustrations, challenges to the public expectations of academia were rare. While individuals were very aware of the many warts which made academic life at times not so attractive, efforts to openly challenge or change these conditions were not invoked (perhaps due to an awareness of the power of others). Yet, we note that senior academics also tend not to challenge the public requirements of academia, but rather to find ways to accommodate or bypass them when they are experienced as being in conflict with their personal academic values. In other words, more experienced academics rarely model the possibility of public challenge. Yet, as the pressures associated with academia continue to grow, this raises the question of why (and for how long) early career academics will stay; what will be sufficiently engaging that they remain prepared to invest in developing their careers and identities in academia, despite the unattractive features? We contend that it is only through cultivation of personal meaning and purpose in academic practice that an answer to such questions can be found.

▶ Privileged and neglected aspects of academic practice

Throughout our response to the questions above, we draw a recurring distinction between more public versus more personal aspects of academic practice. The *'public' aspects* focus on what is perceived as common across academics, such as academic classifications and hierarchies, government or institutional policies and regulations, as well as expectations and requirements. In contrast, the *'personal' aspects* focus on individuals and their feelings, intentions and experiences – highlighting variation in practice with respect to academic identity, values and purpose.

Given its widespread representation in policies, reports and the media, the public face is relatively visible: seen, heard, read and recognized by others. We see it as representing the more extrinsically and activity-driven aspects of academic practice, represented by words such as performance, production, recognition, achievements, accountability, measurement, promotions, reward. In contrast, the personal face represents more intrinsically and purpose-driven aspects, linked to words such as learning, identity, embodied, emotion, meaning, purpose, intentions, past experience, future hope. However, because it varies between individuals, the personal face may be relatively invisible to others.

The personal and the public aspects exist in a reciprocal (though somewhat uneven) relationship in which each influences the other. However, the greater visibility of the public face allows it to dominate current perceptions of academic practice, academic preparation programs, and even the research questions asked when investigating the nature of academia. Yet the personal face is at least as significant, if not more so, as this is what motivates individuals to engage in academic work...or to turn away. It is also what guides individual decisions, for instance, to prioritize status aspects of academic work (a focus on recognition and reward) or to emphasize academic citizenry and the social good (a focus on contribution and service) or to seek a balance between the two.

The personal face directs attention away from the positions that an individual holds and more towards the varied and situated ways in which individuals develop a sense of who they are and what they want to become. Such variation is rooted in unique past experiences, day-to-day activities and interactions, emotional responses to present opportunities and challenges, as well as past, present and future hopes and intentions. This is what most contributes to a sense of academic purpose, meaning and identity. In other words, the personal face of academic practice is what motivates individuals to engage in academic work and contributes to their developing personal understanding of academic practice over time.

The personal face can also play an integrative role. It can facilitate a sense of coherence across the varying routes and detours that are taken within academia and also between the often competing activities, demands and pressures individuals face as academics. Further, a focus on personal meaning and coherence highlights how early career academics can be their own agents of learning and change as they engage in and prepare for their futures.

We contend that the current dominance of public descriptions of academic practice in the preparation of early career academics over-privileges this aspect of academic work, and thus needs to be counterbalanced by a greater focus on the relatively neglected personal aspects of being an academic. We do *not* aim to replace the current priority placed on the public with a priority on the personal, but rather we wish to rebalance the emphases so that they are more equally weighted in the minds of all – early career academics considering their future directions; senior academics advising their students and junior colleagues; academic developers designing academic preparation programs; senior administrators setting policies that impact on academic preparation and academic practice in their institution; and educational researchers investigating the nature of academic practice. For this reason, we explore more fully below how the personal face – identity, meaning and purpose – contributes to an understanding of academic work.

▷ Developing the personal: finding meaning and purpose in academic work

Sensitizing intending academics to the personal face of academic practice involves highlighting individual meaning, purpose and identity as an academic. Our identities are dynamic, grounded in our previous experiences – in effect, a developing biographical history (Walker, 2001). Whether taking on the role of doctoral student, postdoctoral researcher or newly appointed academic, individuals have pre-existing personal understandings and motivations that influence how they interpret the present, reflect on the past and imagine the future (Billett, 2006). While they may know little from personal experience about the nature of what people do in the new context, individuals still bring a wealth of knowledge, personal values and intentions that can contribute to either successful or unsuccessful interactions. And through their active participation they hope to develop knowledge and capabilities – to learn in order to eventually contribute in ways that will be valued by others.

Central to an identity perspective is individual variation in intentions. In other words, identity and meaning are evoked and shaped in the kinds of actions and interactions individuals engage in and respond to as they endeavour to contribute to the dynamics of academic life in ways that they hope are distinct, yet also collectively valued by their academic community – that help develop a feeling of belonging. Their personal values, motivations, perceptions of rewards and challenges are all present (implicitly or explicitly) in how they evaluate their past and present and create hopes and desires for the future. Equally important and varied are underlying values and emotions, both positive and negative, which influence how academic work is experienced (Neumann, 2006).

One way in which individuals learn as they engage in day-to-day interactions and activities is through reflecting on what they are experiencing, and learning informally from interactions with others. In the process of reflection, early career academics can create personal meaning and make sense of their experiences, weaving together disparate experiences as they create a personal perspective on what being an academic means to them, and what their own hopes and intentions might be. Such a personal perspective may also facilitate a more integrative view of activities that public policy and institutional structures may separate, for instance, research, teaching, supervision and administration. However, from time to time, reflection may also lead individuals to challenge taken-for-granted practices. Through participation in and reflection on academic work, individuals are learning; they are constructing personal knowledge and meaning that enable them to negotiate their way in sometimes difficult situations.

Overall, a key feature of highlighting the personal in academic practice is that it reinforces the notion that academic work is embodied in individual intentions, feelings and values. Hopefully, it broadens the focus from the public face of academic practice (e.g., national imperatives to compete internationally, institutional pressures to complete degrees promptly) to the fact that academic practice is situated in the personal (e.g. lived experiences of individuals), and it is here that there is potential for individuals and groups to initiate change that may impact on the public face of academia. We explore this further below, drawing out implications for each of the key audiences for this book.

▶ Implications for development of early career academics: publicly valuing the personal

We now draw out some more practical implications for redressing the current imbalance between the public and personal faces of academic practice. Here, we explore ways in which the suggestions outlined above could be acted on by the intended audiences of this book: academic developers, early career supervisors and mentors, senior administrators and early career academics themselves. Included in these suggestions are strategies that encourage and enable early career academics to be their own agents of development and change.

Reframing 'career' in terms that include the personal

When asking those early in their career to envisage the future, it is common to ask questions such as where they would like to be in five years time. However, this question is often posed and considered primarily in terms of the public face of a career. We suggest at least equal consideration of where they would like to be intellectually and emotionally. Hopefully, this would encourage a focus on both the internal motivations that attract them to academic work and makes that work satisfying and rewarding for them, and to think in terms of work that provides these opportunities more broadly, not necessarily restricted to academia.

Another common approach to help early career academics envisage their futures is to bring together panels of more senior academics to discuss their own career history, thus providing illustrative examples of variation in career paths. We would suggest that it is equally as important to encourage such panels to discuss the 'why' underlying their career choices, activities and outcomes, as much as the 'what' and 'how'. A useful tool for encouraging panel members to address both the personal and public face may be to explicitly distinguish between the extrinsic and intrinsic rewards of their work, including the extrinsic and intrinsic benefit of career development activities such as conference attendance and networking. Given the growing prevalence of individuals moving in and out of academia, we would also suggest that career panels should include representatives from non-traditional academic career paths.

It may sound as if these ideas are primarily relevant to careers advisors or academic developers, but Heads of Departments or Directors of Graduate Studies could organize similar events, and individual supervisors or mentors of junior academics could aim to address such topics in their own one-to-one conversations. In addition, disciplinary organizations could be encouraged to organize sessions for early career academics – perhaps in response to the suggestions of senior academics with influence in the organization. For instance, they could arrange 'fireside chats', where more senior academics talk to junior academics in a more personal way. Or create space for early career academics to mix informally with senior academics, for instance, by organizing 'lunch with a professor' sessions, as at a recent conference we attended. At the conference, volunteering professors were asked to set aside one lunchtime to chat with early career academics, who signed up for the sessions using sheets posted on the conference notice board.

Another idea is disciplinary-based 'academic practice days', such as those co-hosted by the Higher Education Academy subject centres and a university in the UK. In these events, individuals with a range of academic experiences, roles and responsibilities within a disciplinary or specialist cluster meet for a day to discuss the nature of academic practice, how it is changing, and what this means for the personal experience of learning and doing academic work (McAlpine and Hopwood, 2009). Individuals come from a range of different institutions so that they can see not just how academic practice is changing through time but also how it changes across institutions. Such events could also be organized by development units in coordination with disciplinary areas, ideally involving a number of universities where they are not too geographically dispersed.

To help spread these ideas and strategies among doctoral and postdoctoral supervisors, advisers and managers, we suggest they be raised for discussion in induction programs for new supervisors and managers, or update sessions for experienced supervisors. Of course, not all universities provide such sessions, especially for more experienced supervisors, but it is important to acknowledge that the situation facing early career academics is changing, and those who entered academia in earlier times may not be fully sensitive to the extent or implications of the changes that are occurring.

This has policy implications with respect to expectations of supervisors and managers. As government and social expectations of the outcomes of research education and training change, so do expectations of the roles of supervisors/managers. For example, in the UK, the Research Councils' Joint Statement of Skills Training Requirements for Research Postgraduates (Research Councils UK, 2001) has led to expectations that supervisors/managers take responsibility for ensuring personal and professional skills development in doctoral students and postdoctoral researchers, in addition to the traditional research skills. Supervisory Codes of Practice, sometimes including expectations of ongoing professional development as a supervisor, have become common in Australia and the UK, and provide one source of institutional change in preparation of early career academics. Policies on mentoring of intending academics provide another source.

Explicitly valuing short-term contributions to academia

To appropriately value those who may only be in academia short-term requires supervisors, administrators and developers to be clear in their own minds about the contribution that doctoral students, postdoctoral researchers and academics on short-term appointments make to universities, society and the creation of knowledge. The growing numbers of doctoral and postdoctoral researchers make a major contribution to research output, especially in the laboratory-based sciences, where programs of research are dependent upon layers of research students and post-docs, coordinated through a senior academic to explore related aspects of a central topic. Such programs of research could not progress without the input of students and post-docs. Similarly, current financial constraints, combined with rising undergraduate numbers and student–staff ratios, have ensured the need for casual and short-term teachers. The increasing casualization of the academic work force shows the rising dependence of modern universities on short-term academic appointments. Again, universities would have difficulty functioning without the flexibility and financial safety net that they provide.

The magnitude and range of input to the functioning of the higher education system made by postdoctoral researchers, for instance, are illustrated in Åkerlind (2005a), where 50 per cent of the post-docs surveyed reported being involved in formal supervision of research students, almost 40 per cent in lecturing, and a quarter in tutoring/demonstrating and in conference organization. Other duties included administration, committee work, staff supervision, reviewing journal papers, examining theses, applying for grants, undertaking consultancies and clinical duties. Explicit acknowledgement of the breadth of input into academic collegiality, management and peer review, as well as the depth of contribution to research, teaching and supervision, would go a long way towards reducing any potential sense of waste or failure associated with not seeking or finding a long-term home in academia.

Integrating different aspects of academic work

It has become increasingly common to treat teaching and research as independent aspects of academic work. For public universities, there are commonly separate government funding streams for teaching and research. Many universities now have the separation of these roles reinforced at the institutional level by having separate senior executive portfolios overseeing teaching and research at the Deputy Vice-Chancellor, President or Provost levels. Similarly, at the faculty or school level, the creation of separate Associate Dean Education and Research management roles is growing. Academic staff development units typically focus on professional development in teaching in isolation from other aspects of academic work. Promotions criteria commonly separate teaching and research; universities may be research-intensive or education-intensive, and so on.

One of the explicit distortions resulting from this separation is that research education and research supervision often have to be publicly positioned as primarily belonging to academic research or academic teaching portfolios, rather than belonging to both. A less explicit, but no less significant, distortion is that academics are encouraged to artificially separate these activities in their performance reviews, tenure and promotion applications, and in giving and receiving career advice and mentoring. Similarly, approaches to developing as a teacher are considered in isolation from development as a researcher, through separation of educational development units and research offices, reducing any potential for synergy between the two. This potential personal synergy has been a particular focus of research for Gerlese, whose studies indicate that teaching and research are integrated through the personal aspects of academic work, that is, what academics are trying to achieve through their practice (Åkerlind, 2005b, 2008). This is an area where ignoring the personal aspects of academic practice has a particular impact, as a sense of integration between teaching and research commonly occurs through a focus on common or overlapping academic purposes, whereas when looked at solely as an academic *activity*, it is not unusual for academics to report teaching and research as competing in workload terms.

Creating more opportunities for academic work to be positioned in a holistic and integrated way is a clear area with potential for structural and policy change. One starting point would be to integrate teaching and research and other aspects of academic work (e.g., leadership, project management) within the roles of academic development units; another would be to allow for (or even encourage) a holistic presentation of academic work in performance reviews, promotion and tenure applications – in terms of purpose and achievements *across* teaching, research, and even service and administration. Even without structural change, education development units can raise for discussion relationships between teaching and research, within the limits of their mission. Plus, individual supervisors and mentors can make this an explicit part of their discussions with students and junior colleagues.

Highlighting the personal meanings and intentions underlying academic work

In addition to considering career paths and career development activities in more personal ways, the personal aspect of academic activities and responsibilities also deserves to be better highlighted. For instance, workshops addressing teaching and research development could include opportunities to discuss how these duties are being interpreted, what early career (and/or more senior) academics see as the purpose of these activities and how they can be personally integrated into one's experience of academic work (McAlpine *et al.*, 2009). They should also aim to highlight individual variation in interpretation, thus challenging any myth of uniform academic practice. However, we would like to emphasise that it is not our intention to have such discussions *replace* skills development, but rather *accompany* it, so that skills are not presented in isolation from purpose.

Similarly, supervisors and managers could create opportunities to acknowledge the significance of personal goals when they advise early career academics or potential research students. Asking potential students and intending academics 'why' they are interested in a PhD or an academic career, and being willing to model the role of the personal in one's own academic life illustrate some steps that could be taken. Constantly leaving such questions unasked is not a neutral activity, but can send implicit messages that the reasons can be assumed, because everyone (or at least all 'good' academics) has the same reasons for doing a PhD or moving into academia. An alternative interpretation of silence on questions of intentions and motivations is that they must not be important to success in doctoral work or academia. Motivations and purposes may thus be unintentionally positioned as either not important, or not varying.

This raises the question (which is also worthy of discussion with intending academics) of what defines success. Personal and public success may not coincide, but each is valuable in its own terms. For instance, academics who put a lot of time and energy into contributing to society through community service, or to student development through teaching, may sometimes become disillusioned when they experience these activities as not being rewarded in public career terms. Similarly, some academics who choose or have been advised to reduce the effort they spend on teaching to spend more time on research, can subsequently find their teaching unrewarding in personal terms because they do not put a satisfying level of creativity into it. Acknowledging and discussing the importance of both personal and public 'success' has the potential to lead to more conscious decision-making on such issues, and thus less disillusionment over time.

▶ References

Åkerlind, G.S. (2005a) 'Postdoctoral researchers: Roles, functions and career prospects', *Higher Education Research and Development*, 24: 21–40.

Åkerlind, G.S. (2005b) 'Academic growth and development: How do university academics experience it?', *Higher Education*, 50: 1–32.

Åkerlind, G.S. (2008b) 'Growing and developing as a university researcher', *Higher Education*, 55: 241–54.

Billett, S. (2006) 'Relational interdependence between social and individual agency in work and working life', *Mind, Culture and Activity*, 13(1): 53–69.

McAlpine, L., Amundsen, C., Clement, M. and Light, G. (2009) 'Academic development: Rethinking our underlying assumptions about what we do and why we do it', *Studies in Continuing Education*, 31(3): 261–80.

McAlpine, L. and Hopwood, N. (2009) ' "Third spaces": A useful developmental lens?' *International Journal for Academic Development*, 14(2): 159–62.

Neumann, A. (2006) 'Professing passion: Emotion in the scholarship of professors at research universities', *American Educational Research Journal*, 43(3): 381–424.

Research Councils UK (2001) *Joint Statement of Skills Training Requirements of Research Postgraduates*. Available at: http://www.grad.ac.uk/cms/ShowPage/Home_page/Policy/National_policy/Research_Councils_training_requirements/p!eaLXeFl.

UK Vitae (2009) *What Do PhDs Do?: First Destinations for PhD Graduates*. Cambridge: UK Vitae Programme.

Walker, M. (2001) Engineering identities. *British Journal of Sociology of Education*, 22(1): 75–89.

Commentaries from Early Career Academics, Developers and Administrators

Individuals representing different academic roles and audiences for the book were invited to read a chapter and provide a commentary. The aim was to discover the relevance of the chapters to different audiences, the extent to which chapter conclusions 'rang true', and any further issues and implications that were important to address. The commentaries (three per chapter) are grouped together, with a brief preface summarizing key ideas from the respective chapter.

▶ Responses to Chapter 2: Expectations and Experiences of Aspiring and Early Career Academics
Ann E. Austin

The preparation of future academics is one of the major responsibilities for doctoral education. This chapter presents findings from research conducted over the past 15 years in the United States concerning the experiences of early career academics and doctoral students (called aspiring faculty members), and the implications of these experiences for career preparation for the professoriate and support for early career faculty. The chapter contributes to the dynamic discussion regarding the role of doctoral education in effective career preparation of future academics.

Melissa McDaniels
Project Director,
Advancing Diversity through the Alignment of Policies and
Practices and NSF ADVANCE program,
Michigan State University, USA

I am a member of the fixed-term research faculty at Michigan State University (MSU, United States). I direct a National Science Foundation program that seeks to help MSU do a better job recruiting, retaining, and promoting female faculty in the STEM fields. Having this role allows me to utilize my research expertise to impact institutional and national higher education policy.

I have been asked, as a former doctoral student of Dr. Ann Austin, to write this commentary and respond to the question of the extent to which this chapter reflects my experience and provides insights that I can use in my career in the academy. I am in an interesting position to write this commentary as I have published with Dr. Austin, and engaged in my own empirical research projects, on the doctoral experience. Thus the fundamental question for me is, given my immersion in the doctoral education literature, what novel insights about my own experience as a doctoral student might this writing task generate?

Dr. Austin mentioned three behaviors that she found her study participants displayed that served to propel them through their doctoral work. Those three recommendations include: (1) be proactive; (2) make connections; and (3) engage in self-reflection. As a doctoral student I was proactive, I did make connections and engage in self-reflection. However, I also observed other doctoral students not engaging in these behaviors, despite knowing intellectually that these were things that they could do to help themselves negotiate the terrain of doctoral education. What might account for this inconsistency? What are the precursors to being able to successfully take the initiative, build professional networks, and discern one's own strengths and weaknesses? How do we support all students in building the cognitive-emotional foundation necessary for life-long learning?

As a Caucasian, middle class woman who grew up with parents and grandparents who were scholars, the culture of the academy was not foreign to me. I was privileged to have been given the emotional, financial, and interpersonal resources throughout my life that would allow me to 'just know' how to maximize my chances for success in all organizational arenas. I believed that I had something to offer and was worthy of getting my needs met. Various mentors had instilled this belief in me over the course of my lifetime. This is a foundational belief that all professionals need in order to take the advice that Dr. Austin offered in her chapter. I understood how to balance advocating for myself, while being open to learning from others. I was able to understand the short- vs. long-term value of engaging in the behaviors Dr. Austin suggests. Much of the literature about how to improve doctoral education focuses on how *institutions* can improve the doctoral experience for all. Reading this chapter forced me to make explicit my assumptions about *doctoral student agency* – how to build and cultivate it, and how to empower students to engage in these behaviors that Dr. Austin clearly articulates in her chapter. Reading this chapter was an important reminder for me as I move forward with my own supervision of doctoral students, and engage in further research about doctoral education.

Laura L. B. Border
Director, Graduate Teacher Program,
University of Colorado at Boulder, USA
Having directed the Graduate Teacher Program (a Graduate School initiative to prepare graduate students for their current teaching roles at the University of Colorado at Boulder and for their future careers as faculty in postsecondary institutions) for 25 years, I find Dr. Austin's research essential. Underscoring the need for development programs at the graduate and beginning faculty levels, her three themes (unclear expectations for sufficient progress, concerns about balancing academic and personal roles and needs, and a desire to become part of a scholarly and supportive community) resonate with my experience. Her first theme suggests workshops such as those we offer on academic goal setting, our certificate in college teaching, and the kinds of portfolio development support we provide. Our preparing future faculty program offers workshops on college teaching and site visits to explore academic life in various academic cultures, thus paralleling her second theme. And, third, our centralized and departmental workshops provide an environment in which academics who yearn for collegial discourse can share their ideas. Additionally, our Lead Graduate Teacher Network involves 50 graduate students from seven schools and colleges in leadership activities, academic management, peer consultation, and the opportunity to work on a cross-disciplinary team.

Dr. Austin and I agree that we need to study further questions such as: (1) what are the parallels between the needs of graduate students and beginning faculty?; (2) what kinds of teaching and professional support should the institution as a whole provide to graduate students and faculty?; (3) how can academic or graduate and professional student development programs provide support to the departments and the faculty who employ and educate graduate teaching assistants and to the graduate students themselves?; (4) in an increasingly complex technological age, how can institutions better support their teaching staff to provide excellence in undergraduate teaching?; and, finally, (5) how can we encourage all academics to seek out and embrace opportunities for continued professional development? Over my career, I have seen similar ideas and programming taking hold in more departments and in more disciplinary associations. However, it is difficult for academic programming to stay ahead of societal needs. As Dr. Austin points out, few academics have a spouse at home who can take care of daily life while they concentrate on students, research, and academic services. These stresses need to be addressed by society in general and by academe specifically, for example, on-campus child care for graduate students and faculty would reduce not only financial and emotional stress, but create more time for academic work.

Regarding the implications for novel approaches to and priorities for the development of early career academics, Dr. Austin's research points to a need to clarify a logical continuum in the education and preparation of young academics that is carefully targeted to parallel progressive responsibilities for teaching, research, and service; to define potential career track options; and to assure the retention and success of academics as they move through careers that are not only personally meaningful and productive, but also indispensable to society.

Janet Bokemeier

Professor and Department Chair, Sociology,
Michigan State University, USA
I am currently in the twilight of my academic career with 31 years as a tenure-track faculty member in research-intensive land grant universities. After working my way through the academic credentialing and tenure granting stages, I discovered I was well suited for administrative work. As an academic administrator I have served in several roles including department chair in three different settings, once involving the merger of four units into one department. Ann Austin's research has been of great interest to me as a scholar and administrator. For over 15 years it has informed my perspectives on faculty relationships, development and evaluation. As I reflect on her insights in this chapter, I will follow her three questions as an organizing tool for my comments.

First, relative to changes in faculty employment and academic work, I am struck by how the rate of change and knowledge accumulation has exploded. When I was an assistant professor we did not have high performing computers, or even reasonably performing desktops, and the

American Sociological Association only had about a third the number of sections (i.e., areas of specialization). Intellectual life was less convoluted. How does this impact doctoral students and new faculty? For new faculty, they may not find anyone in their department who is reading the same literature as they are or is interested in their methodology or analytical approaches. This I think is the most intellectually isolating factor among faculty in my department and it is definitely a detriment to collegiality. New faculty members find themselves in ever wider professional and intellectual networks that reach far beyond their campuses.

Another change that has profound impacts for academic work is the globalization of academic life. Scholars around the world contribute to our specialized knowledge and more US departments are recruiting international faculty members. Just as women and minorities find they confront unique issues in academe, international faculty are challenged in the classroom, their departments, and disciplines. In public universities, students resent and rebel at their accents rather than welcoming their diverse contributions to learning. International faculty face challenges to their credentials and must prove themselves as they adjust to a foreign culture.

I whole heartedly agree that the expectations and standards for tenure are changing. At my university, the dean instructs new faculty that to be awarded tenure they must enrich and enhance the quality of scholarship in their departments. They must improve on the accomplishments of their predecessors. Emphasis on multidisciplinary scholarship with collaborative and multi-authored publications has emerged. Universities now expect to find evidence of externally-sponsored research activity in the dossiers of faculty-seeking promotion and tenure. This pressure to be grant-active and entrepreneurial will lead to profound changes in academic careers. On the other hand, some things have not changed. The lack of clear guidelines or minimum standards has been an issue for decades, as has the struggle to balance work and life demands.

Research on young professionals find this struggle typical among new entrants. I would like to know if the experience of new faculty is changing in ways that experiences of new lawyers or ministers find their first job changing – longer hours of work, more difficulty work – life balance, rising bar for promotion.

Given all these challenges, how should we prepare graduate students for academic careers? My department is currently debating whether to continue a required course on professional development. Some faculty believe that major professors can provide the necessary mentoring.

This has led to examination of the expectations of dissertation advisors as mentors. In particular, I question whether dissertation advisors will devote adequate time to professional development related to teaching, service and outreach.

My department has adopted several practices to address concerns of academic development. In our department graduate students are admitted only if two faculty will serve as their advisors. Faculty are awarded additional merit for co-authoring with their graduate students. We have a mentor program for new faculty involving a yearly assessment by the chair, regular joint meetings of all mentors and mentees, and additional merit for serving as a mentor.

▶ Responses to Chapter 3: Developing as an Academic Researcher Post-PhD
Gerlese S. Åkerlind

This chapter explores key issues in postdoctoral researchers' preparation for academic careers. In part one, the postdoctoral research terrain is mapped out, highlighting the substantial variability in types and duties of contract research positions, what postdocs hope to gain from these positions and the developmental opportunities available to them. Then, in part two, variation in what it means to develop as a researcher in academia is explored. The aim here is to foreground unacknowledged variation in researcher intentions, motivations and experiences of development.

Kezia Scales
Research Associate, University of Nottingham, UK
I hold a 12-month contract as a Research Associate in the School of Sociology and Social Policy at the University of Nottingham. I completed my postgraduate study in the Department of Social Policy and Social Work at the University of Oxford.

I followed a circuitous route into academic research, having worked in the voluntary sector for several years before embarking on postgraduate study. As an activist, I resisted returning to the (perceived) insularity of academia. However, as soon as I took up my degree, I knew I'd made the right choice, and set about doing all the things that academics do – finding a research post, reviewing articles, presenting at conferences, pursuing publication – in order to secure a credible foothold in my new career.

Åkerlind's chapter challenged me to step back from this focus on the *what* of developing academic professional development, which I have understood in binary contrast to the *what* of non-academic development, to consider the *why* and *how*. Fortunately, my current post offers good opportunities to explore these issues. Although occupying the 'pair of hands' category that Åkerlind identifies – ultimately accountable to the project lead regarding major issues including the project timetable, methodology, and output – I enjoy sufficient independence to feel like a 'project manager' in my daily work. Furthermore, unlike a substantial proportion of Åkerlind's respondents, I am rarely distracted from my objectives by non-research responsibilities. I also benefit from a clear and well-defined relationship with my supervisor, who demonstrates pro-active commitment to supporting my professional development as well as my current research. Reading about the 'ad hoc and unstructured' nature of postdoctoral supervision has encouraged me not to take this support for granted.

At this 'apprentice' stage, I am focusing on three of the aspects of professional development that Åkerlind outlines. Building *confidence* is my primary objective, as I make the transition from hopeful but inexperienced student to competent academic. Increased external *output* reflects this growing internal confidence although, taking the point about quantity versus quality, I place equal emphasis on enhancing the *sophistication* of my output. In fact, I was surprised to read that many academics believe their research development ends with a PhD; if I thought that was the case myself, I'd stop now. Perhaps naïvely, I am drawn to an academic career precisely for the ongoing opportunity to build my skills, widen my perspective, and deepen my understanding.

The fourth aspect, *recognition*, currently has less salience. As a contract researcher, I occupy the periphery of my department: my office is located in a distant wing and I have very little collegial contact. Lack of recognition within my immediate setting limits my expectations of broader external recognition; this is exacerbated by the fact that I work on someone else's project and, as part of a collaborative team, find few opportunities to distinguish my individual contribution. Although I don't mind this lack of external recognition, I worry that it may compromise my ability to secure the next contract.

Åkerlind has reminded me to consider each development opportunity in light of my personal goals, rather than uncritically trying to 'catch up' with my academic colleagues. As well as grounds for reflection, she provides substantial practical guidance: namely, to consider 'what am I trying to achieve?' with each activity in order to maximize the benefits derived, to take an 'activity focus' in pursuing defined goals, and to ask colleagues why *they* do what they do. All this will, I hope, help me better assess the myriad academic paths available and forge the best one for myself.

Jo McKenzie
Associate Professor and Director,
Institute for Interactive Media and Learning,
University of Technology Sydney, Australia

I have worked in academic development units for 20 years, beginning as a research assistant and casual tutor, progressing to contract academic positions, then gaining a continuing Associate Lecturer (tutor) position in 1993 before starting my PhD. I am now Associate Professor and Director of an academic development unit. I co-ordinated our Graduate Certificate in Higher Education for over 10 years, including a subject on Reflective Academic Practice. My research has focused on academics' experiences of professional learning and change over time and I have been involved in projects that focused on learning and teaching development, casual academics and research supervision.

Åkerlind's chapter invites academic developers and others to consider the variation in postdocs' research positions, academic activities and aspirations. It encourages us to provide opportunities for postdocs, and early career academics in general, to explore the meanings that research and research development have for them and how these meanings vary among their colleagues. As such, the chapter resonated with and discomforted me. It resonated because I strongly agree with its emphasis on considering the varying meanings that academic work has for academics and their varying intentions for growth and development. It was discomforting because academic development in Australia, and I suspect elsewhere, has placed little emphasis on the development of postdocs.

A search of the *International Journal for Academic Development* reveals no articles with 'postdoctoral', 'post-doctoral', 'postdoc' or similar in their titles, keywords or abstracts. While there is increasing emphasis on preparing early career academics for their teaching roles, postdocs are typically perceived as research-only and, as the chapter points out, development opportunities are often ad hoc or absent.

Because of their research focus and diverse roles, postdoctoral researchers are often betwixt and between the opportunities we provide for new academics and the increasing range of opportunities that are available for doctoral students. They may participate in development activities that focus on parts of their work, such as research supervision, applying for grants or casual teaching. A few participate in components of foundations programs or graduate courses for early career academics, but often in their own time and not necessarily with the support of their supervisors.

By contrast, some academic development programs for early career academics have expanded their focus to include but go well beyond the focus on teaching strategies and reflective practice that began several decades ago. In the Graduate Certificate in Higher Education in which I teach, participants are encouraged to experience variation in ways of experiencing teaching and learning, in ways similar to those described by Åkerlind (2008c). They reflect on their own experiences of change in teaching and of growing and developing as a teacher and researcher and compare these with patterns of variation found through research (e.g., Åkerlind, 2005b; McKenzie, 2003). In the broader context they compare the range and focus of their academic work with the Boyer (1990) scholarships of discovery, application, integration and teaching, offering a different range of variation as those in different disciplines compare the reasons behind the different emphases of their fields and their differing personal interests.

It can be reassuring for new academics to explore stage theories of development (delineating qualitative shifts between novice and expert practice) that validate current uncertainties and help academics to see what they might do next. Yet, I agree with Åkerlind that stage theories can hide the very different foci taken by different academics and therefore their different possibilities for future development. One aim of exploring variation in understandings and intentions from multiple perspectives is to enable new academics, including postdocs, to see that they have options in the ways that they develop their careers. However, for some, the awareness of this variation creates the additional challenge of expanding their personal expectations in institutional environments that might value some intentions more highly than others. Academic developers need to be careful in the ways in which we assist new academics to consider their priorities for development in relation to their contexts.

Mandy Thomas
Pro-Vice Chancellor – Research,
Australian National University, Australia
The present environment for higher education around the globe presents multiple imperatives and opportunities for universities to

transform and innovate. This chapter makes an important contribution to policy that will support the necessary innovation required in universities by proposing an evidence-based model of postdoctoral training and development. This model focuses not on a top-down approach but on the perspectives of early career researchers themselves.

By exploring the experience of postdoctoral work from the perspective of those undertaking it, the chapter brings a fresh approach to our understanding of the difficult issues researchers confront in developing their careers – from the mixed messages they receive about the nature of the work through to the lack of clear guidance on how to proceed up the academic ladder. Postdoctoral researchers are one of the most important groups of researchers for the future because the academic workforce is ageing and we need early career researchers not just to replace those retiring but also to provide training, skills and the capacity to innovate within the contemporary knowledge economy. In spite of the very high value universities place on early career academics, much of their training has been unstructured, does not take account of each individual's motivations for undertaking postdoctoral work and is often undertaken within an environment characterized by unclear roles and responsibilities of supervisors and postdoctoral fellows.

The material collected for the study reveals the very diverse understandings that academics have about the nature of their work and their different motivations for undertaking it at the time they are starting out on their careers. The chapter identifies that the foundation for successful researchers' career development involves the integration of the following elements: confidence in one's professional abilities, recognition as a researcher, sophistication in scholarly practice, and academic productivity.

The study highlights that early career academics can benefit from being cognizant of these elements in their development and can learn to prioritize activity to support these. At the university level, the policy implications for this approach are that it provides us with the tools to engage with and support postdoctoral researchers in a way that will benefit not only the individual researchers in being able to evaluate and integrate development opportunities but has wider implications for our support for the next generation of researchers in order that they too might contribute at higher levels. By exploring the preoccupations and career aspirations of individual postdoctoral researchers and clarifying their duties and obligations, we might be able to provide more effective opportunities for them to gain confidence and recognition that are more tailored to individual needs.

Ultimately if the effective development of postdoctoral researchers is embraced and incorporated across the university, this leaves a legacy of great consequence as many of society's future leaders are among the group of postdoctoral researchers who are today setting out on their careers.

▶ Responses to Chapter 4: Employment Patterns In and Beyond One's Discipline
David Mills

This chapter uses the discipline of anthropology to illustrate the changing shape of the social sciences in the UK, and the academic employment possibilities and pressures that result. It shows how the 'big-picture' UK statistical trends are made meaningful by individual academics in their working lives, professional commitments and scholarly vocations. The findings are used to reflect on the relationship between disciplinary and institutional location as a doctoral student and subsequent academic career trajectory – particularly in terms of the stratification that exists within and between disciplines.

Alis Oancea
Research Fellow at the Department of Education,
joint fellowship with the Oxford Institute of Ageing,
University of Oxford, and Jr Research Fellow of St Hilda's College, UK
I have been an academic for over ten years, having built two different careers (albeit in the same 'discipline') in two different countries. I'd held a tenured academic position for a few years when I decided to move to Oxford University, do a second PhD there, and stay on as research fellow in research policy and governance. I am also Chair of the Research Staff Forum in my department, and have a scholarly interest in issues related to the preparation of beginning researchers and career trajectories in the social sciences. Mine is a rather unusual trajectory, which also involved three disciplines – education, philosophy, and demography. Drawing on this background, what struck me most in David's chapter were issues around disciplinary hierarchies. I'll expand on these issues in this brief response.

As David helpfully points out, Anthropology is one of the fields with the 'highest status' among the social sciences. Academic employment of its traditionally 'white, middle-class' graduates can mean vastly more opportunities than those confined to anthropology departments. Although some of David's respondents, who had 'migrated' to other departments, reported a perception of disciplinary 'compromise', they were still able to retain a (admittedly challenged) sense of identity rooted in their initial preparation as anthropologists.

This observation made me wonder about graduates of the 'lesser' disciplines – Education included. These disciplines are larger in size, thus in theory providing more employment opportunities, but of contested status. In comparing themselves to other social disciplines, education researchers are often very critical of the quality of, and capacity for, research in their own field. They see the gap between their 'discipline' (often called simply 'field') and other social sciences as a deficit (e.g., of skills) rather than as difference. A traditional strategy in coping with such contestation was to patch the gap by importing researchers from other fields. To this day, education departments are a melee of psychologists, anthropologists, economists, sociologists who in time develop a common ground but never seem to fully acknowledge this fact. (Philosophers also used to be 'imported' for added academic weight, but they are thin on the ground nowadays, presumably as a reflection of the fact that education departments are now clearly oriented towards the social sciences, rather than the humanities, as their ideal 'disciplinary matrices'.)

A potential consequence of this is that early career researchers/ academics in education may find that their postgraduate education degree does not necessarily have the same currency in the academic labour market as those from other social science disciplines (although they may be at an advantage in other segments of employment). In their (attempted) cross-disciplinary migrations, they find themselves having, not just to 'compromise', but to deny their initial identities. They have to develop chameleonic (or should I say Protean?) qualities that make them change discourse and attitude with the different contexts in which they find themselves. They are practitioners when they speak to teachers; sociologists, when speaking to educationists; educationists, when speaking to sociologists. I do not have comprehensive, up-to-date data to verify my informed guesses (the most recent publicly available review is Mills *et al.*, 2006), but I imagine that the issue is not one of contested individual academic 'authority', but, rather, one of confusion about academic territories and knowledge standards. In this sense, Education, too, makes an interesting case-study.

Jonathan Wyatt
Head of Professional Development, Oxford Learning Institute,
University of Oxford, UK

I am Head of Professional Development at the Oxford Learning Institute. Together with colleagues across the University, and among other activities that we undertake in the Institute, we provide career and professional development opportunities for research staff. There are around 3000 research staff in all, and within the Social Sciences, 318.

My close colleague, Rebecca Nestor, currently leads our work on research staff and she has also read David Mills' chapter. There were two main elements that struck both of us.

First, David writes about the prevalence, and accompanying low status, of fixed-term research and teaching contracts, whose holders, in David's words, survive 'on the disciplinary margins'. This situation is familiar to both Rebecca and me, with the issue arising regularly in events that we run. On such occasions, researchers in the sciences sometimes use the demeaning term 'lab fodder' to describe themselves; and one social scientist, who was in his late thirties, spoke to me about how, in his view, he did all the work of an established academic and received none of the recognition that accompanies that role. He taught Master's courses, supervised doctoral theses, undertook research, published, did his share of 'service', and all the while was employed on a fixed-term contract that had been serially renewed.

There is some work that we are involved in at University policy level that is genuinely attempting to address such problems, and there has been definite progress. Also, last year we held a two-day conference for researchers, with talks, group discussion, one-to-one support (and a conference dinner) that provided participants with an intense, focused opportunity to look at themselves and their careers. Our intention was to support people in being as active as they can in their career choices so that they can avoid becoming stuck. We're running a similar conference again this year.

Second, the complexity introduced in David's conclusion resonated strongly with both Rebecca and me. It introduces useful, interesting, new material. David writes about academic idealism and vocationalism and how these link with long hours and the gender/family issues articulated earlier in the chapter. This reminds us of a speaker whom we invited to talk to a group of research staff at the end of a term's leadership course that we ran a year ago. He was a warm and passionate research group leader within the sciences and he set out uncompromisingly his vision for what he expected of his researchers – long hours, no holiday, full dedication. In the audience there was a group of twenty participants and four tutors, but none of us challenged his vision at the time. We wondered why – especially when some participants, both men and women, objected to it privately afterwards. On reflection, we now think that we were probably hampered by our sense of how important academic work is, and we could not find a way of challenging or engaging with the speaker's approach that would not have felt like a betrayal of that sense. The way that David expresses the contradiction provides a framework that could enable a thoughtful discussion. We can see this being useful for a range of our programmes – not only our research staff events but, for example, Springboard (a programme for women staff that has within each cohort some research and academic staff), and events for heads of research groups and new heads of department.

Matthew Smart
Administrator, University of Oxford, UK
I am an administrator at the University of Oxford, based for the past three years in the Social Sciences division, including a year's secondment to the Higher Education Funding Council for England for RAE2008 (the UK's 'Research Assessment Exercise'). Since 1998, I have worked in medical and social sciences on research programmes and in departmental and central university administration. My current role includes research strategy and funding, research staff support and management policy, and teaching policy. This chapter is the type of document which I read to inform my administrative work.

At my university we are keen to continue to support research staff following a period of expansion and a demographic shift to a higher proportion of research staff in the social sciences. This focus is of considerable current relevance given conflicting external drivers which need to be considered and planned for: an economic downturn, with potential reductions in grant and other funding to support university activities, and sector-wide aims to improve employment stability for research staff through increased use of open-ended contracts. Like climate change, we could later find ourselves in a position of saying that we should have recognized the signs, and managed the situation, before it became problematic. With research staff issues we are all, in higher education at least, responsible and affected.

Dr Mills' 2006 *Demographic Review of the UK Social Sciences* remains a key document. This chapter updates our knowledge of what Dr Mills terms those big picture statistical trends, which are highly beneficial in devising effective, long-term institutional staff management policies. This chapter also takes the useful standpoint that the default model of an academic career path is unrepresentative. Career paths outside academia comprise conscious choices, and relate to national funding debates on public and policy impact of universities. Acknowledging practitioner, industrial and charitable elements of career paths could help redress the governmental stance of thinking of higher education as discrete and isolated when considering its funding and societal contribution.

The chapter begins to explore qualitative, philosophical aspects which, more than is usually the case, should inform policy-making. For example, low representation of demographic groups in the workforce tends to be used to demonstrate lack of opportunity. Biographical evidence might show that the policy-makers' goal of 'opportunity to secure full-time work', aimed to increase national productivity and income tax, may not be a goal shared by the population. A converse goal of 'opportunity to be a full-time parent' would yield alternative goal-based policies. Dr Mills' exploration of individuals' sense of purpose, vocation, desires for mobility, researcher solidarity, and the career limitations of teaching posts, are policy-relevant issues which contextualize the statistics. The section on gender and family life in particular covers a range of issues and experiences both broad and deep, giving new life to these long-standing aspects of staff management.

The value of Dr Mills' chapter is that it complements the multitude of high-level documents through well-reasoned statistics, and on-the-ground realism. It should be useful both to academic policy leaders, and to forewarn, advise and encourage those planning a research-based career.

▶ Responses to Chapter 5: Doctoral Students and a Future in Academe?
Sandra Acker and Eve Haque

This chapter considers whether continuity or disjuncture is to be expected between doctoral studies and new faculty work. The primary focus is an analysis of academic career expectations based on interviews with doctoral students in advanced stages of doctoral study or having recently completed their degrees. Few accounts revealed clear planning and understanding of the challenges of working as a faculty member – perhaps not surprising, given contextual features that work as impediments to long-term career planning.

Bathseba Opini
PhD Graduate, University of Toronto, Canada

Some of the commonest questions I hear graduate students, myself included, ask are 'What are we gonna do?', 'Where are the jobs?', and 'What does the future hold for us?' I recently received my PhD from one of the universities in Ontario and am currently working as an instructor (also referred to as contingent/stipend faculty in the chapter) at two universities in the city of Toronto. My long-term goal is to secure a faculty position in a higher education institution. The chief concern is how to get there.

In their straightforward and stimulating chapter, Acker and Haque point to ways graduate life experiences inform the lives and career of those starting out as professional academics. The chapter could not have come at a better time than when Canadian universities are experiencing hiring freezes, because of the economic downturn. The organization of the chapter, starting with the authors' subject locations, meshes well with some of the challenges I have dealt with as a graduate student and now as an aspiring academic. While it is not easy to delve extensively into all the emerging issues in the narratives presented in this single chapter, the authors did an excellent job uncovering the challenges of funding, mentoring, faculty workloads and the limited awareness among graduate students of possibilities for transitioning from student life to becoming academics. This is, however, changing slowly as the department under study puts in place mechanisms, including courses and thesis support groups, to assist graduate students. In my graduate school life, I found these thesis group meetings extremely useful when I was analyzing my data and writing my dissertation. The groups helped me connect with other students and exchange ideas throughout the entire process.

The authors' analysis in this chapter of the challenge of funding in particular, stood out for me. It reminded me of when I started my doctoral degree in 2004 as a non-funded student, and survived in this status until my fourth year. Those three years were rough and it was all about 'survival of the fittest'. I had to become assertive in looking for jobs, seeking opportunities to present at conferences and working on research projects, and try to publish so as to be competitive with other students who were funded. Although I was fortunate to have great mentors, the whole process required initiative, good time management and ability to balance my own work and faculty research. I did work as a teaching assistant and later as a sessional instructor, but mainly for purposes of 'paying my bills' not as a preparation to work in the academy. Reading Acker and Haque's chapter made me realize that these experiences are important especially when it comes to creating networks. Very few graduate students are cognizant of this fact.

This exemplary chapter demonstrates the need for universities to develop strategies to help graduate students fully comprehend the realities of graduate life. The authors reveal that there is more to becoming an academic aside from publishing. There is some degree of continuity from graduate school to being an academic but there is also a lot of learning and re-learning to do. The chapter demystifies graduate life and the process of becoming an academic and also offers useful insights into how institutions and faculty can enhance this transition. Most valuable in their analysis is the realization that a doctoral degree does not necessarily mean that one is destined to be in the academy, but that there are other possibilities out there. Acker and Haque offer an important framework, stating that graduate students need to determine where the end of the graduate school journey might take them. The chapter is relevant to Canadian and international higher education institutions. I will definitely recommend it, most of all to graduate students and beginning faculty.

Joy Mighty
Director, Centre for Teaching and Learning,
Queen's University, Canada

I often describe myself as a 'professor turned administrator', as I am currently the director of a centre for teaching and learning at a mid-sized research-intensive Canadian university, where I provide leadership in educational development while being cross-appointed as a tenured full professor in a professional school. My work is grounded in a strong academic background with degrees in several disciplines including English, Education and Business, and more than 35 years of professional and practical experience in a combination of teaching, researching, managing and consulting roles. I have directed the research of 31 graduate students and I have provided leadership in enhancing the quality of education at regional, national and international levels.

In my various roles, I have encountered many of the issues raised in the chapter. My colleagues and I in the Centre for Teaching and Learning have adopted the approach that graduate students are our junior colleagues. We are explicitly committed to supporting the professional development needs of all teachers at my institution across the spectrum of their careers, from their time as graduate student teaching assistants through to their senior years. We have therefore developed a systematic approach that provides support at each stage of a teacher's development. Our staged developmental approach begins with our graduate students, to whom we offer, among other things, a credit course on 'teaching and learning in higher education' that is intended primarily for PhD students who have completed their comprehensive examinations and are interested in an academic career. This course is usually filled each time it is offered and graduates report anecdotally the positive impact it has had on them personally and professionally. The success of this course has been followed by a similar one designed exclusively for law graduates, the first of its kind in Canada, another for PhD students in Business, and Master's level courses in Anatomy. We recognize that many of these students will work elsewhere upon graduation, but our hope is that they will take to other institutions the teaching competencies developed in these programs. Even if they do not become academics, we believe that teaching competence is transferable to other contexts, a point to which I will return later.

Another initiative of note for graduate students is our 'Program for University Teaching and Learning' in which students may earn three certificates. The first focuses on 'Professional Development' and is meant to promote good practice through attendance at a series of workshops on various teaching issues. To receive the second certificate, called 'Practical Experience', the individual must teach in a variety of settings and then write a reflection on this experience. The third certificate, 'Teaching Scholarship', requires participants to make teaching public by creating resources or conducting research on some aspect of university teaching and learning, and sharing results with their colleagues in the form of a research paper. Clearly, these programs are not designed merely to meet the utilitarian needs of Teaching Assistants, a concern expressed by Acker and Haque. For that purpose, we offer a daylong conference to orient students to their role as TAs, since all graduate students are guaranteed teaching assistantships upon acceptance into their programs.

Let me return to the issue of the transferability of teaching competence to other contexts. The chapter points out that many PhD graduates do not take up academic careers. While this may be true, universities have apparently not been doing a very good job of developing in graduate students a set of professional skills that would facilitate their success in other (non-academic) fields. In July 2007, I was invited to coordinate and co-facilitate a think-tank of approximately 50 individuals representing a wide range of stakeholders in graduate education, including graduate students, researchers, educational developers, deans of graduate schools, industry and governments. The event was sponsored by the three major federal granting agencies (the Natural Sciences and Engineering Research Council – NSERC, the Social Sciences and Humanities Research Council – SSHRC, and the Canadian Institute of Health Research – CIHR) and the Canadian Association for Graduate Studies (CAGS), in collaboration with the Society for Teaching and Learning in Higher education (STLHE). Its aim was to identify the most important professional skills as learning outcomes for graduate programs in Canada. The catalyst for the event was a growing concern that many graduate students often lack an array of generic skills that are essential if they are to use their technical, discipline-specific research skills effectively in professional practice. This collaboration has had several implications for the development of graduate curricula and is a significant step toward enhancing the quality of graduate education in universities across Canada.

One outcome at my institution has been an attempt to coordinate opportunities for developing in graduate students generic or professional skills beyond the disciplinary competencies acquired in their specific programs. Thus, the School of Graduate Studies and Research has collaborated with a host of other units across the university to offer the 'Expanding Horizons Workshop Series' that provides a set of professional skills that were not offered to some of the students in the Acker and Haque study. These include skills relating to publishing, teaching, writing a curriculum vitae, time management, project management, leadership, team building, navigating the various processes for advancement in the workplace, and so forth. In addition, at least one of the federal granting agencies has established a new grant that encourages faculty to incorporate training in such professional skills for their graduate students. Unfortunately, consistent with the concerns expressed by Acker and Haque, the social sciences and humanities still lack such a program.

As these developments suggest, more attention is being given to preparing graduate students for successful careers in the workplace of their choice, including the academy. Attention is also being given to developing faculty members' ability to supervise students successfully. For example, at my institution, the Centre for Teaching and Learning offers, in collaboration with the School of Graduate Studies and Research, a certificate program called 'Focus on Graduate Supervision' for faculty who supervise graduate students. Topics covered include: Expectations and Standards, Mentoring Graduate Students, Supporting the Thesis Writing Process, and Supervising to Completion.

Carolyn Watters
Dean of Graduate Studies, Dalhousie University, Canada
In this chapter the authors highlight a very important transition in the career path of doctoral students. The effectiveness of the transition from success as a student to success in a subsequent career is not based solely on academic preparation but is also dependent on development complementary, sometimes called professional, skills. At least a third of PhD graduates find career opportunities not in academic institutions but in government and non-governmental organizations, and in the private sector. In all cases, the academic discipline is core, yet it is the complementary skills that may become the differentiators in a knowledge economy.

While the arguments and reflections presented in this chapter reflect the social science and educational disciplinary background of the authors and the transition to the academic career trajectory, the arguments have resonance beyond these domains and to other career paths. Consequently it is useful to examine the difficulties and opportunities presented in this chapter for a wider applicability.

The authors speak from personal experience, a review of the literature, and a study based on the analysis of interviews with doctoral students related to their career expectations as academics. The authors examine factors known to be problematic in doctoral programs and that have been shown to contribute to both non-completion of degree programs and long times to completion. They highlight three critical factors in ameliorating these factors: effective mentoring, adequate funding, and the building of community.

The authors then present broad principles for building up competencies during doctoral studies to better prepare students as they transition from student to new academic. While grounded in the academic context, these principles are applicable to a wide range of career contexts, in academic and non-academic (government, non-governmental, and private) sectors. The practical issue of how these skills can be developed is very difficult in a context where the demands on a doctoral student are already high. The authors make several interesting and practical suggestions on how current programmatic activities can be reframed to provide these opportunities for graduate students to build relevant experiences that complement their disciplinary learning.

This chapter highlights the growing awareness in Canada and around the world that universities need to provide learning opportunities in doctoral programs that will support the successful transition from doctoral studies to the workforce, whether that path lies inside or outside of the academy.

▶ Responses to Chapter 6: Living and Imagining Academic Identities
Lynn McAlpine, Cheryl Amundsen and Marian Jazvac-Martek

This chapter draws on research in Canada to develop the idea of individual identity-trajectories integrating academic and personal experiences through time. Identity-trajectory is characterized as encompassing three distinct but closely related strands (intellectual, networking and institutional). It is suggested that despite distinct institutional roles of student and pre-tenure academic, for the individual the perceptions and experiences are similar and cumulative over time.

Frances Helyar
Assistant Professor, Lakehead University, Canada
Since participating in the study on which this chapter is based, I have secured a tenure track position in my field, and completed a year of full-time teaching at the undergraduate level. I am, however, still finishing my thesis. This means that my identity is in extended transition: I'm a student, but I'm also a pre-tenure academic.

I do have a sense of my current situation as logically connected to the sum of my experiences. The authors present the notion of identity-as-trajectory 'beginning with years spent as a doctoral student through the time as a new academic and on to more established academic status'. I would suggest that the fact that I was a student in a Faculty of Education adds another element to the trajectory, one which begins before entry into graduate school. I was a teacher long before I started my Master's or PhD, and while this part of my identity may have been dormant during the early part of my graduate studies, it eventually resurfaced and is fully present in my current work. The person I imagined becoming was based, in part, on my previous teaching experience, and my success so far is based, in part, on my deep knowledge of the difficulty of beginning a teaching career. I didn't need to imagine the challenge of teaching a course for the first time; I'd already experienced it years earlier.

I identify with issues of agency, emotion and powerful others, particularly as I straddle my two identities as student and pre-tenure academic. I find in my job that the expectations are clearly laid out by my collective agreement, but I also have the agency, in the form of academic freedom, to work within the university policies to develop course outlines that reflect my theoretical and philosophical stances. I also feel very much engaged in a community of professionals; I spend a significant amount of time in discussion with my colleagues about research and teaching practices. In contrast, as a student, I feel far more isolated, and weighed down by the pressure of university regulations and supervisory expectations. I feel the power of powerful others much more strongly as a student than I do as an academic. Completing a doctoral dissertation feels like a larger hurdle than establishing a research agenda and a record of teaching.

Most of the time I feel far too overwhelmed to reflect on my experiences, whether as a student or an academic, but I think the research makes it clear how important is the process of self-reflection. My doctoral institution requires an annual progress report but it is highly perfunctory. The institution that employs me requires it in the form of an annual report, and also provides me the opportunity to meet with other early-career academics in my Faculty in an organized, recognized safe space where reflection is encouraged. Outside of these externally created opportunities, why do I not require reflection of myself?

Jeanette McDonald
Manager: Educational Development, Teaching Support Services,
Wilfrid Laurier University, Canada

I am an educational developer (professional staff versus faculty member) with more than 10 years experience at two different institutions – one comprehensive and one primarily undergraduate. My scope of practice includes teaching, service, and scholarship in a variety of forms and contexts, and my approach or orientation to development work is varied. I am also a part-time doctoral student in higher education nearing the end of my graduate journey. My commentary below reflects my collective and most recent experiences as an educational developer and a graduate student in academia.

Not surprisingly the issues raised by the participant excerpts and the chapter authors themselves resonate with me personally and professionally. I liken the notion of 'identity-as-trajectory', for example, to that of a 'journey' in my doctoral and pathways research used to conceptualize the process of becoming an educational developer – an occupation that lacks a prescribed pathway or specific 'academic structures' to guide entry to and advancement within the field. On a professional level, the issue of 'opaqueness' and the example of graduate supervision are contextually salient given the recent and ongoing expansion of the number and diversity (i.e., niche) of graduate programs at my home institution (primarily undergraduate) and the recognized need and expressed desire for graduate student supervision support (e.g., mentoring, networking, certificate programs, institutional policy).

Less so would I say my reading of this chapter brings to light new issues *per se* (at least for me), rather it reinforces and reaffirms (and yes, makes me pause to reflect) what and how we (or should I say 'I') approach, for example, program design and delivery and my interactions with early academics and indeed all academic staff and faculty. In one-on-one consultations, for instance, I am reminded to be cognizant of the type of questions and probes I ask to prompt reflection in and on their (i.e., early academics) academic experiences and to help them identify positive anchors to situate and make sense of their journey in light of experienced tensions, charged emotions, and lived side trips experienced as they move through their career paths (student/professional). Likewise, when interacting and engaging (e.g., project collaborations, chance conversations, institutional committees) with those who have influence over or contact with early academics (e.g., chairs, graduate supervisors), I can see strategic value in approaching these opportunities to 'plant a seed', as a colleague of mine is so fond of saying, to identify and respond to areas of opaqueness and to consider how they can, for example, weave the three strands (intellectual, networking, institutional) described by the chapter authors into their daily interactions, visioning processes, and policy directions to name but a few. Overall, as briefly noted above, this chapter has instilled in me an ongoing need and recognition to pause and reflect upon my developer role and approach to the benefit of the various client and organizational groups I support (translation = make time for).

Jon Driver
Vice-President Academic, Simon Fraser University, Canada
I am a recently appointed Vice-President Academic, with previous experience as dean of graduate studies (eight years), department chair

(three years), and faculty association president. My research discipline (30+ years) is archaeology.

Given the restriction on the length of contributions, I will challenge a few points rather than discussing the areas where I largely agree with the authors.

First, let me suggest that one's entire career as an academic is a continuum, and that one is constantly engaged by challenges similar to those that doctoral students and untenured faculty experience. I have experienced 'learning curves' in every administrative role to which I have been appointed, and also during times when my research has shifted to different parts of the world and different cultures. In Table C.1), I list some early-career challenges identified in this

Table C.1 Early career challenges	
Identified challenge for doctoral and pre-tenure	Examples of equivalent later career anxieties
Complex context; opaque expectations	Taking on administrative position (chair, dean, etc.); PI of multi-institution grant; organizing international conference
Negotiate with more powerful people	Chair negotiates with dean; dealing with major publisher; working with government; promotion to full professor
Need for affirmation	Election to prestigious organization; getting grants; appointment to editorial board; teaching award; salary review; citation indices
Struggles with peers	Allocation of department resources; reaching consensus on committees; ethical issues; maintaining standards;
Opportunities to learn	Dealing with HR issues; creating new curriculum; service roles in institution and discipline; adopting new research tools; using high tech teaching aids; understanding new generations of students; international development
Need to network	Interdisciplinary and international ; administrative peers; senior research peers

chapter, and present examples that would characterize later stages of a career.

There is a constant process of learning as one takes on new responsibilities in teaching, research and administration, and at every stage of one's career there is a need to establish legitimacy with one's peers and to create a mutually supportive network of colleagues. Sometimes this is accomplished through formal processes, such as workshops for new chairs or grant-writing seminars or instructional development programs. I would hope that mentoring programs for doctoral students and pre-tenure faculty would emphasize this facet of academic life.

Second, this chapter rightly suggests that mentoring programs could include discussion of career trajectories. Although the authors do not suggest that a trajectory is planned or smooth, I think the use of 'trajectory' might imply this, and we should be wary of suggesting that successful careers lack randomness. My career as a scholar and an administrator has been influenced far more by unexpected opportunities than by careful planning, and I think it is important to let junior colleagues reflect on this and to reassure them that careers that look planned in retrospect are anything but that as lived experiences.

My final thought concerns a very practical issue. Although I agree that there is much continuity between a doctoral student completing comps and dissertation and an assistant professor working to get published and tenured, I see this as part of a career-long continuum of experiences. In spite of the success of such programs described by the authors, I would be wary of any mentoring process that brought doctoral students and pre-tenure assistant professors together as equals. There is a significant change in status and role that occurs with the completion of a PhD, and while it would be useful for assistant professors to reflect on the pre- to post-PhD continuum, I think most would prefer to do this away from doctoral students. On the other hand, asking an assistant professor to help with a workshop for doctoral students would allow her to retain her new status while sharing her reflections on the continuum.

Glossary

International variations in meaning of terms

ABD   This is an acronym used in North America that stands for 'all but dissertation' and is used to refer to individuals who have completed required coursework and comprehensive examinations and had their research proposals accepted, but have still not completed the research for their PhD despite some years having passed.

Academic   In the UK and Australia, this is the generic term for academic staff, e.g., an academic; academics (also see lecturer for Australia and the UK, and Professor or Faculty for North America). As in North America, the term is also used as an adjective to describe activities by academics, e.g., an academic program.

Advisor   This term is the one usually used in the US to denote the supervisor of the dissertation/ thesis. In Canada, it has a different meaning; the advisor may be the program advisor or the person whom students work with until they have identified their area of study and appropriate supervisor. In Australia, where supervisory panels are common, an advisor is a member of the panel but plays a less significant role than supervisors.

Assistant professor   See pre-tenure.

Associate professor   See pre-tenure for North America, and lecturer for Australia and UK .

College   In the US, this term has a range of references; it can refer to an aggregation of departments, e.g., a School of Education, or community colleges which tend to offer two-year associate degrees or liberal arts colleges which focus principally on four-year undergraduate programs. In Australia, this term is not commonly used; groupings of departments are usually referred to as schools or faculties. In the UK, it refers to residential institutions within a university that house students but also provide teaching (such as the colleges associated with Oxford and Cambridge); there may be many different disciplines taught within such a college. The term in Canada usually refers to institutions that offer non-degree certification of different kinds.

Comprehensive exam(s)   In North America, these are completed by doctoral students some time after their required course work, and are designed for the student to demonstrate depth and/or breadth in the field. They can take various forms from short papers written during an 'exam' to extended papers written over the period of a term. In the latter case, there is usually also an oral defence before a committee. The questions themselves may relate generally to the field or to some extent be directed towards the student's inquiry. In the UK and Australia, required coursework, and thus exams, are less common.

Contingent   This term refers to positions that are temporary and lack security and associated benefits.

Continuing   See tenure.

Contract researcher   See research staff.

Course   In the UK, this term is equivalent to what is called a program in North America. In Australia, the term 'course' is used variably, both to refer to a subject taught within a suite of courses (i.e., program) and to the suite itself, with the former becoming more common.

Dissertation   In North America, this is the written report of the doctoral research project; in the UK and Australia, it is more commonly called a thesis.

Dissertation committee   This is a term used in North America where there is traditionally a committee structure, rather than one supervisor, to support a doctoral student. The supervisor (also called advisor in the USA) still retains principal responsibility for student progress.

Faculty   In Australia, the UK and North America, this is an institutional disciplinary unit; in North America it can also refer to academics as a group and be used as an adjective equivalent in meaning to academic, i.e. faculty member/academic staff, faculty development/ academic development.

Faculty member   See faculty.

Graduate/Postgraduate student   In the UK, those doing post-bachelor level study are usually termed 'postgraduates', whereas in North America they are referred to as 'graduates'. In Australia, both terms are common but are primarily used to refer to students in coursework programs only. Those engaged in Doctoral studies or Master's by research are typically referred to as research students.

Instructor   In the UK and Australia, this term is used only as a generic descriptor; a synonym for teacher. It does not represent a type of appointment as it does in North America – see 'sessional'.

Lecturer   In the UK and Australia, this is the generic term for academic staff (as 'professor' is in North America). It also designates a certain position in terms of academic promotion with a range of terms used to designate movement towards full professorship (e.g., Lecturer, Senior Lecturer, Associate Professor/Reader, Professor). In North America, it often refers to teaching staff with (or without) a PhD.

Open-ended   See tenure.

Non-tenure   See pre-tenure.

Postdoctoral fellow   See research staff.

Pre-tenure   This is a term used in North America to identify individuals who are in their first 5–6 years of appointment in positions that are designated as potentially permanent. They hold the title of Assistant Professor. During this period they may apply for tenure (permanence). If awarded, they are generally promoted simultaneously to the rank of Associate Professor. If not awarded, they typically lose their employment. Individuals in these positions may be referred to as on a 'tenure track'. The contrast is 'non-tenure', 'non-tenure track' positions. Also see probation and sessional.

Pre-tenure track   See pre-tenure.

Probation   In the UK and Australia, permanent positions involve a period of 'probation', often 3–5 years, to assess performance before confirmation of permanency/tenure. However, this does not represent the dramatic hurdle that application for tenure does in North America. Few fail to pass probation. See pre-tenure.

Professor   In North America, this is a generic term that describes any academic staff member (also see lecturer); elsewhere it is a term reserved to designate what in North America is called 'full professor'.

Professoriate   This is a term used in North America to refer to academics generally.

Program(me)   In North America and Australia, this refers to a course of study - involving coursework and/or research; as regards a doctoral program, in North America, there are often many more formal requirements than in programs elsewhere, e.g., see comprehensive exams.

Qualifying exam   See comprehensive exam.

Research assistant   In North America, this refers to a position paid by an academic out of his/her research grant in which graduate students, rather than research officers, provide research support, e.g., data collection and analysis, under the guidance of the researcher. It is seen as an important source of understanding about the research process and also provides for many graduate students an important source of income. In Australia and the UK, research assistants are more likely to be independent appointments without associated graduate study, and may include postdoctoral appointments.

Research staff   In the UK, sometimes called 'contract research staff', this term designates individuals hired to conduct already funded research (in contrast with 'postdoctoral fellow', where the individual him/herself has been awarded funding); positions are temporary and can vary in length from a few months to several years. In North America, the most frequently used equivalent time would be research fellow or researcher. In Australia, postdoctoral fellow is the generic term for those in short-term research positions following a PhD, irrespective of the source of funding.

Research student   In Australia and the UK, this term is used to distinguish students undertaking Doctoral or Master's by research studies, in contrast to (post)graduate coursework studies (i.e., Graduate Certificates, Graduate Diplomas and Master's by Coursework). See Postgraduate/ Graduate student. In North America the equivalent term is graduate student, sometimes abbreviated to grad student.

Sessional   In North America and Australia, this denotes employment on a term or semester basis to teach courses; generally there is no requirement that the individual have a PhD. As in Australia, this form of employment could be described as a 'casual' position.

Staff   This is a term used in Australia and the UK that may refer to academics (i.e., academic staff) as well as non-academic employees (general or administrative staff). This is not the case in North America where the term 'staff' refers only to non-academic employees.

Supervisor   In Australia, the UK and Canada, this is the term used to denote the individual who has principal responsibility for guiding doctoral students to completion. See advisor for USA.

Supervisory panel   Somewhat equivalent to Dissertation Committee in North America. Also see advisor.

Teaching assistant   In North America, this refers to a position paid by the university (sometimes unionized) in which doctoral students provide different kinds of teaching support, e.g., marking assignments, giving tutorials, under the guidance of the instructor responsible for a course. For many doctoral students, this can be an important source of income (similar to research assistant positions). Participation in some kind of training may be required to hold such a position.

Tenure   In North America, this refers to a permanent post. A similar meaning is implied in the term 'continuing' in Australia and 'open-ended' in the UK (though tenure is also used in the UK), in that both terms imply permanence. While several years of probation would be expected before confirmation in continuing and open-end appointments, there is not the same dramatic hurdle that tenure represents in North America. In Australia and the UK, permanence is disassociated from academic status, so that associate professor and full professor status may not include permanence (3–5-year fixed-term or contract positions are common), while more junior appointments may include permanence.

Thesis   See dissertation.

Type of institution   In the US, there is greater variation in institutional type than in Canada, the UK or Australia. In the US, there is a ranking system of universities and colleges developed by the Carnegie Commission on Higher Education to support its program of research and policy analysis; it is widely used in the US to distinguish variation in higher education institutions, for instance, the extent to which research is viewed as central (see earlier reference to 'colleges'). In Canada, the university groupings are 'Primarily Undergraduate', with relatively few graduate programs; 'Comprehensive' with significant research activity and a wide range of programs at the undergraduate and graduate levels; and 'Medical Doctoral' with the broadest range of PhD programs and research. In Australia and the UK, all higher education institutions are universities, engaged in both teaching and research, and offering the full range of disciplines and degrees, from Bachelor to PhD. However, some institutions are more research intensive (and thus more prestigious) than others. For instance, reference may be made to post-92 institutions in the UK – former Polytechnics that became universities– or ex-CAEs in Australia – former Colleges of Advanced Education. Australia also has a post-secondary vocational education sector that offers two-year diplomas or associate diplomas, but this is regarded as 'tertiary' education, rather than 'higher' education.

Index

Note: Page numbers in *italics* denote a table